Modern Language Ass I0393071

Approaches to Teaching
World Literature

Joseph Gibaldi, Series Editor

29. Richard K. Emmerson, ed. *Approaches to Teaching Medieval English Drama*. 1990.
30. Kathleen Blake, ed. *Approaches to Teaching Eliot's* Middlemarch. 1990.
31. María Elena de Valdés and Mario J. Valdés, eds. *Approaches to Teaching García Márquez's* One Hundred Years of Solitude. 1990.
32. Donald D. Kummings, ed. *Approaches to Teaching Whitman's* Leaves of Grass. 1990.
33. Stephen C. Behrendt, ed. *Approaches to Teaching Shelley's* Frankenstein. 1990.
34. June Schlueter and Enoch Brater, eds. *Approaches to Teaching Beckett's* Waiting for Godot. 1991.
35. Walter H. Evert and Jack W. Rhodes, eds. *Approaches to Teaching Keats's Poetry*. 1991
36. Frederick W. Shilstone, ed. *Approaches to Teaching Byron's Poetry*. 1991.

Approaches to Teaching
Teaching
Sir Gawain and the Green Knight

Edited by

Miriam Youngerman Miller

and

Jane Chance

The Modern Language Association of America
New York   1986

© 1986 by The Modern Language Association of America

Library of Congress Cataloging-in-Publication Data

Main entry under title:

Approaches to teaching Sir Gawain and the Green Knight.

(Approaches to teaching masterpieces of world literature ; 9)
Bibliography: p.
Includes index.
1. Gawain and the Grene Knight—Addresses, essays, lectures. 2. Gawain—Romances—Study and teaching—Addresses, essays, lectures. 3. English literature—Middle English, 1100–1500—Study and teaching—Addresses, essays, lectures. 4. Literature, Medieval—Study and teaching—Addresses, essays, lectures. I. Miller, Miriam Youngerman, 1944–   II. Chance, Jane, 1945–   . III. Series.
PR2065.G31A6   1986   821′.1   85–21548
ISBN 0–87352–491–8
ISBN 0–87352–492–6 (pbk.)

Cover illustration of the paperback edition: Pentangle by David Cloyce Smith. Border from *Guiron le Courtois*, Douce ms. 383 (c. 1480–1500), Oxford; rpt. as illus. 354 in Roger Sherman Loomis and Laura Hibbard Loomis, *Arthurian Legends in Medieval Art* (London: Oxford UP; New York: MLA, 1938).

Third printing 1991

Published by The Modern Language Association of America
10 Astor Place, New York, New York 10003

CONTENTS

PREFACE TO THE SERIES

In *The Art of Teaching* Gilbert Highet wrote, "Bad teaching wastes a great deal of effort, and spoils many lives which might have been full of energy and happiness." All too many teachers have failed in their work, Highet argued, simply "because they have not thought about it." We hope that the Approaches to Teaching Masterpieces of World Literature series, sponsored by the Modern Language Association's Committee on Teaching and Related Professional Activities, will not only improve the craft—as well as the art— of teaching but also encourage serious and continuing discussion of the aims and methods of teaching literature.

The principal objective of the series is to collect within each volume different points of view on teaching a specific literary work, a literary tradition, or a writer widely taught at the undergraduate level. The preparation of each volume begins with a wide-ranging survey of instructors, thus enabling us to include in the volume the philosophies and approaches, thoughts and methods of scores of experienced teachers. The result is a sourcebook of material, information, and ideas on teaching the subject of the volume to undergraduates.

The series is intended to serve nonspecialists as well as specialists, inexperienced as well as experienced teachers, graduate students who wish to learn effective ways of teaching as well as senior professors who wish to compare their own approaches with the approaches of colleagues in other schools. Of course, no volume in the series can ever substitute for erudition, intelligence, creativity, and sensitivity in teaching. We hope merely that each book will point readers in useful directions; at most each will offer only a first step in the long journey to successful teaching. We may perhaps adopt as keynote for the series Alfred North Whitehead's observation in "The Aims of Education" that a liberal education "proceeds by imparting a knowledge of the masterpieces of thought, of imaginative literature, and of art."

Joseph Gibaldi
Series Editor

PREFACE TO THE VOLUME

Sir Gawain and the Green Knight exists as one of only four poems contained in the unique Cotton Nero A.x. manuscript. One reason for its singularity in manuscript form may well be its dialect, the obscure and crabbed Northwest Midlands form derived from the Northumbrian dialect of Old English. (Modern English is derived from Southeast Midlands, "Chaucerian" Middle English.) Yet the poem has survived to this day and retained its audience, many of whom are young people, many of whom are our students. As a masterpiece of English literature it is still included in introductory courses and sophomore surveys at every kind of university and college in the nation, although it is rarely taught in the original language at this level. It continues to appeal to us because of its depth, its many-layered (polysemous) form, and its jewellike artistry.

Nevertheless, it poses peculiar problems to the generalist, the beginning teacher, the fresh medievalist, and even the more experienced scholar. How to explain its alliteration and its strange stanzaic form? Why does the poet begin with the fall of Troy (and exactly what connection does Arthur have with Aeneas—and who was Aeneas, and who Brutus)? On what tradition concerning Arthurian legend is the poet drawing? Where does he find his character Gawain? Is this treatment of the character English? What form is the poem—romance? Where did the romance originate? What should students make of the long catalogs of costume, food, hunting, dressing the animals, castles, and so forth? How is one to understand the religious and liturgical aspects of the poem in our somewhat areligious twentieth century? What exactly is the poet doing with the figure of the Green Knight? Is the lady's behavior conventional in the Middle Ages? Why does Arthur's court laugh at the end—is the poem a comedy? How do we read it in the twentieth century, or should we? How important is reading the Middle English? What is lost in translation, and how can we make up for it (at least partially)? Answers to such questions, even with the best of critical and background help, require a certain amount of time and energy.

To explore current practice in meeting these pedagogical challenges, the Modern Language Association distributed questionnaires concerning the teaching of *Gawain* to all members of its Division on Middle English Language and Literature, excluding Chaucer, and to other interested individuals. The ninety responses, received from all types of postsecondary institutions and from all regions of the United States (as well as Canada, Japan, and Spain), provide, we think, a reasonable cross section of approaches and techniques for teaching this medieval masterpiece.

The present volume depends heavily on these responses for its shape and form and for the general and specific teaching materials and approaches included. For example, only one of the essays relates *Gawain* to modern forms of literary theory and criticism: John M. Ganim's description of his course on literary criticism offers a survey of such approaches as the psychoanalytic, Marxist, structural, and semiotic. We feel this balance (or imbalance) appropriate for the volume, however, because the questionnaires—submitted by instructors who use many different methods in many different schools—did not reflect such interests. Accordingly, we offer no critical analysis or guide to critical issues surrounding *Gawain*—indeed, much of this material is already available in various paperback collections of criticism (e.g., Blanch, Sir Gawain *and* Pearl; and Howard and Zacher.)

The volume is divided into two major sections. Part 1, "Materials," contains information necessary for teaching the poem: editions; specific bibliographic material concerning the medieval background of the poem, its sources and analogues, its interpretations; and other aids to teaching. Part 2, "Approaches," begins with a survey of the teaching of *Gawain* and continues with background essays that relate the traditions of romance, chivalry, courtly love, religion and law, and medieval aesthetics to teaching the poems. The other essays in this part present individual approaches to the poem in highly varied courses ranging from the introductory to the graduate, with the work taught in translation as well as in the original.

With regard to the form of the essays and the overall volume, the following editorial guidelines were established. All contributors were invited to append syllabi or bibliographies to their essays, within the space limits allowed, or to incorporate this information into the text through analysis and paraphrase; depending on the type of essay, one approach might have been more appropriate than the other. Thomas L. Wright's courtly-love bibliography is clearly more helpful to the reader as a neat list set apart from the text; in contrast, Richard Hamilton Green's discussion of various influential medieval texts seems an intrinsic and necessary part of his essay. Some treatments of courses similarly required a separate syllabus because of the complexity of the materials, as in Penelope Doob's course Ricardian Poetry; others of a more general nature (such as Julian N. Wasserman's description of a survey) could do without the syllabus because the discussion centered on the approach to the poem rather than on a description of the survey.

Approaches in these essays also varied widely. At least one contributor to the backgrounds section (e.g., Louis Brewer Hall on chivalry) chose a course description as a way of anchoring an approach to teaching a background, whereas others in the sections describing particular approaches (e.g., Jeffrey F. Huntsman on Celtic influences) found it more useful to explain the scholarly justification for such a course than to describe the course in detail. We chose to respect the individual contributor's approach to the work, preferring variety and effectiveness to slavish consistency in approach and format.

The volume also includes a list of survey participants, a list of works cited, and an index. All bibliographic references in the text are keyed to full citations in the list of works cited.

Several essays in *Approaches to Teaching* Sir Gawain and the Green Knight have been delivered as papers at various conferences: at the Eighth International Conference on Patristic, Medieval, and Renaissance Studies (Villanova Univ., Villanova, PA), in September 1983, Maureen Fries and Robert J. Blanch presented portions of their background essays; in two sessions sponsored by the Medieval Academy's CARA Subcommittee on the Teaching of Medieval Studies at the 1984 International Conference on Medieval Studies (Medieval Inst., Western Michigan Univ., Kalamazoo, MI), Rosemary Ascherl, Robert J. Blanch, Judith N. Bronfman, Louis Brewer Hall, Julia Bolton Holloway, and Jeffrey Huntsman delivered essays based on those in this volume; and at the 1985 MLA Convention (Chicago, IL), Jane Chance surveyed some of the material from the questionnaires (portions of the present introduction to part 2), and Penelope B R. Doob, John M. Ganim, and Patricia A. Moody provided versions of their "Approaches" essays in a session devoted to the volume.

In preparing this book we have, of course, received help from many sources, for which we are most grateful. Thanks are due to the many colleagues who graciously completed our voluminous questionnaires (their names are listed at the end of the volume), to our contributors, to the Modern Language Association and the members of its Committee on Teaching and Related Professional Activities for sponsoring the series of which this volume is a part, and to Joseph Gibaldi, general editor of the series. We are also indebted to the helpful suggestions offered at various stages of revision by readers of all or part of the manuscript, including Robert Kindrick (Emporia State Univ.), Lois Roney (Univ. of Texas, Dallas), Julian Wasserman (Loyola Univ. in New Orleans), and Joan Markey (Univ. of St. Thomas). Finally, we are especially grateful to Neil Beshers for the excellence of his copyediting.

We would also like to acknowledge gratefully the support provided by many members of the University of New Orleans community, particularly Richard D. Olson, Dean of the Graduate School, for arranging various clerical services; Donna T. Myers and Juanita Boudreaux for expertly providing these services; Edward M. Socola, Dean of the College of Liberal Arts, and the Advisory Committee on Research Fund Allocation for help in defraying some costs of preparing this volume; and the staff of the Earl K. Long Library (particularly Robert Heriard, Johnny C. Powers, Stephen Alleman, and Evelyn Chandler) for many services in the compilation of the "Materials" section and in verifying bibliographic data.

Finally, we would like to thank Rice University, Alan Grob, chairman of the English department, and Allen Matusow, Dean of the School of Humanities, for providing generous financial assistance for typing and other clerical matters; for the rechecking, compiling, and retyping of the bibliography; for the indexing of this volume; and for many other kinds of support. We are especially grateful to Nancy Dahlberg, Nancy Bosworth, Robert Ford, Elizabeth Jo MacDaniel, and Madeline Fleming for performing many of these tasks.

MYM
JC

Part One

MATERIALS

Miriam Youngerman Miller

Editions and Translations

The instructor who wishes to include *Sir Gawain and the Green Knight* in a syllabus must choose, of course, between a Middle English text and a translation. While the choice is hotly debated by those who teach Chaucer, rather surprisingly there is virtually no difference of opinion when it comes to *Gawain*: according to our survey, instructors overwhelmingly choose a translation for undergraduates, even those in upper-division specialized courses, and a Middle English text for graduate students and, in a few cases, advanced undergraduates. Virginia E. Leland (Bowling Green State Univ.) expressed the general attitude on this issue:

> Everyone knows that *Gawain* presents difficulties of vocabulary, spelling, and form not encountered in reading Chaucer. I am delighted to have students actually read and enjoy *Gawain* without troubling them with the language. Yet I would argue, in contrast, that they had not read Chaucer at all if they read Chaucer modernized.

Middle English Editions

Among the relatively few who teach *Gawain* in the original, whether to PhD candidates or, more rarely, to MA candidates and undergraduate English majors, the J. R. R. Tolkien–E. V. Gordon edition as revised by Norman Davis is considered definitive, both for scholarship and for classroom use, instructors generally citing its "excellent conservative text and glossary." Although available in a conveniently small paperback edition, the Tolkien-Gordon-Davis text does have extensive textual endnotes and glossary. Instructors and students alike will find the appendix on phonology, morphology, lexicon, and meter essential in coping with the difficult dialect of the *Gawain* poet. Some instructors criticize the introduction, which, while briefly describing the manuscript and conjecturing about time and place of composition, concentrates primarily on sources and analogues at the expense of literary questions.

A few instructors use the Early English Text Society (EETS) edition prepared initially by Israel Gollancz and completed by Mabel Day, which also contains extensive endnotes and full glossary; moreover, it features brief marginal summaries of the plot action that may, perhaps, aid students bewildered by the difficulties of the dialect. Those who use this edition call attention to Mabel Day's introductory essay, which concentrates on sources and analogues, and to Mary S. Serjeantson's extensive remarks on dialect; those who do not use it tend to regard it as "old-fashioned."

3

R. A. Waldron's edition of *Gawain* is apparently struggling for acceptance in the face of instructors' long familiarity with Tolkien and Gordon; instructors remark that "Waldron is probably preferable" or "I really ought to use Waldron next time" while nonetheless continuing to specify Tolkien and Gordon on their book orders. The partially modernized spelling of Waldron's text (i.e., the obsolete characters are removed) detracts from it in the eyes of those who admire the conservative editing of Tolkien and Gordon or, conversely, may be a point in its favor when students have limited knowledge of Middle English (as is usually the case). Waldron provides both textual and informational footnotes and a glossary. Unlike Tolkien and Gordon's and Day and Serjeantson's, Waldron's introduction will orient students to romance tradition, chivalry, style, structure, ambiguity, and other background and literary topics. There is a brief discussion of language and meter and a selected bibliography. Those who have used Tolkien and Gordon exclusively may find Waldron a desirable option, particularly if they prefer an introduction that emphasizes literary criticism.

Another option that has so far been little exercised is J. A. Burrow's edition, perhaps because it has only been available in the United States since 1982. This slender book with its three-page introduction on matters of language may be most suitable for undergraduates and master's-level students. Burrow has gone further than Waldron in modernizing spelling, and hence the text looks much less formidable than, say, Tolkien and Gordon. Burrow's apparatus includes the most basic of bibliographies, reasonably full notes, and a glossary. This text lessens the burden of unfamiliarity with the dialect for the student, but it places the responsibility for all orientation to background squarely on the instructor.

Given the language problems inherent in the Middle English text, instructors might want to consider W. R. J. Barron's edition, with its facing-page literal prose translation. The introduction contains a plot summary and some remarks on the romance. Textual footnotes, explanatory endnotes, and a bibliography complete the apparatus. Because no teaching edition of *Gawain* incorporates a poetic translation, Barron's translation will probably serve generally as an aid for students who are primarily responsible for the original. Conversely, this edition would probably have little appeal for instructors who want to work mainly with a translation but who would like to be able to refer periodically and conveniently to the exact wording of the original.

Theodore Silverstein's *Sir Gawain and the Green Knight: A New Critical Edition* appeared in 1984. In addition to the text, this edition includes an introduction to sources, literary conventions and poetic form, the manuscript, authorship, meter, diction and style, and language and dialect. The copious notes stress lengthy discussions of key lexical items and the poet's use of rhetorical ornaments and topoi. Silverstein argues in favor of including *Gawain* in a Senecan-Ciceronian tradition and of reading the poem as a comedy of manners. A substantial analyzed bibliography and a glossary with line references conclude the volume.

Gawain is of course sometimes taught in company with the other poems of Cotton Nero A.x., most commonly with *Pearl*, and several editions of the entire manuscript are used occasionally in the classroom. Perhaps most frequently used is A. C. Cawley and J. J. Anderson's Everyman edition, which supercedes Cawley's edition of *Pearl* and *Gawain*. This edition, with slightly normalized spelling, provides brief introductions (largely plot summary) to each poem, short appendixes on dialect and meter, and a basic bibliography. Instead of a collective glossary, each poem has marginal glosses and—a unique feature—there are extensive running translations of thorny passages at the bottoms of the pages. Most instructors who used Cawley and Anderson disliked this arrangement. They reported that students tended to ignore the text in favor of the translations and that the translations were not well done.

Almost as common in the classroom is *The Poems of the Pearl Manuscript*, edited by Malcolm Andrew and Ronald Waldron. This old-spelling edition has extensive textual and explanatory footnotes, a full collective glossary with line references, and a sizable bibliography. There is a brief treatment of the language and alliterative meters of the four Cotton Nero A x. poems. An unusual feature is the inclusion of the Latin Vulgate sources for *Pearl*, *Cleanness*, and *Patience*. (There are, of course, no biblical sources for *Gawain*.) Each poem has an introduction focusing on key critical issues: the introduction for *Gawain*, for example, deals with such matters as thematically significant words like *cortaysye*, *trawþe*, and *clannes*; style; narrative technique; and ambiguity. A well-designed book with comfortably large type and wide margins, Andrew and Waldron will appeal to those who find the format of Cawley and Anderson unattractive those who dislike the glossing and translation system in Cawley and Anderson will doubtless be more at home with Andrew and Waldron's more conventional and exceptionally complete apparatus.

A third collective edition of ms. Cotton Nero A.x. is that of Charles Moorman. Although intended in part for use by graduate students, it seems more suitable for scholarship than for teaching, and indeed few report using it in the classroom. One possible reason for its infrequent pedagogical use is that it is unpunctuated. The poems are presented in what Moorman offers as chronological order—*Patience, Purity, Pearl, Gawain*—rather than in the manuscript order favored by Andrew and Waldron and by Cawley and Anderson. In contrast to the full glossary of Andrew and Waldron and the marginal glosses and running translations of Cawley and Anderson, Moorman glosses difficult words the first few times they appear in each poem and provides a very basic word list at the back of the book. In keeping with his almost aggressively conservative editorial principles, Moorman eschews the type of literary introduction found in, say, Waldron's edition, instead preferring to cover only such matters as the manuscript; the alliterative revival; authorship, date, and place of composition; sources and analogues; general themes; and language. The segment on literary art discusses theological implications and structure and briefly reviews some critical interpretations of *Gawain*. There are a fairly full bibliography, extensive textual and explanatory footnotes, and, pleasantly, several plates of illuminations from ms. Cotton Nero A.x.

The most recent collective edition is William Vantuono's *The* Pearl *Poems: An Omnibus Edition*, two volumes containing Middle English texts, facing-page Modern English verse translations, textual footnotes, plates of the manuscript illuminations, and extensive variorum commentary. The introduction contains the following sections: "The History of the Manuscript," "Possible Dates and Order of the Poems," "The Poet and His Audience," "Thematic Unity of the Poems," and "Structure." Other apparatus includes a scholarly bibliography through 1980 and appendixes covering such matters as common authorship, verse forms, dialect, and sources and analogues. While the bulk of this edition and its substantial cost probably preclude its use in a survey, it would appear to be a useful, perhaps indispensable, work for specialized courses, reference, independent study, and research.

Finally, for a context that stresses manuscript studies and the editing of Middle English texts, there is the facsimile of ms. Cotton Nero A.x. with an introduction by Israel Gollancz, published by the EETS. The facsimile, of course, makes an excellent visual aid for classroom use in company with any other text or translation.

Translations

Because of the obvious difficulty of dialect and the shortage of time, most instructors use a translation of *Gawain* in the classroom, hoping that acquaintance with a Modern English version will "whet students' appetites for the real poem," as one survey respondent put it. Most find that a translation provides a good introduction to this particular poem; indeed, only one felt *Gawain* to be "untranslatable!" By a margin of about three to one, however, instructors do introduce some elements of the original Middle English into their courses. One instructor schedules informal meetings weekly to help students learn Middle English grammar, but more commonly instructors read aloud from the text or play a recording, hand out some sample passages, refer back to the original when the translation does not catch some nice subtlety or ambiguity, pass around a Middle English text (commonly the EETS facsimile or Tolkien and Gordon), or explain the alliterative meter by scanning sample lines. A substantial number structure their literature courses to do double duty as informal introductions to the history of the English language, lecturing briefly on the language of each reading from *Beowulf* to Malory (or, in one unusual case, from Malory to *Beowulf*), requiring students to compare the *Gawain* poet's dialect to that of Chaucer and introducing students to the use of the *OED* and *MED*.

Poetic Translations of *Gawain*

When it comes to selecting a translation of *Gawain*, the choice is overwhelmingly Marie Borroff's. More than three quarters of all respondents mention Borroff, and when those who teach *Gawain* only in the original are removed from the tally, the percentage is even more impressive. Calling it "brilliant," "both scholarly and poetic," instructors like this translation because it manages to be accurate, "relatively literal," and still preserves the verse form, reproducing both alliterative lines and the bob and wheel. Borroff has included a note on meter and a substantial introduction that comments on theme, structure, and style.

The only other freestanding poetic translation used with any frequency is Brian Stone's Penguin edition. Like Borroff, Stone preserves the stanzaic form and alliteration of the original text. Instructors should be advised that the first edition of Stone's translation, still readily available in libraries and on personal bookshelves, is substantially different from the second edition currently in print, both in the text itself and in the relatively elaborate apparatus. The first edition contains an introduction dealing with basic critical issues (including sources, structure—particularly of the alternating hunting and bedroom scenes—and themes); occasional footnotes; a series of appendixes dealing with the manuscript, the identity of the *Gawain* poet, the character of Gawain as it appears throughout romance tradition, King Arthur, Camelot, the pentangle, Morgan the Fay, and Merlin; and several excerpts from the Middle English. In addition to a reworked translation, the second edition has a revised introduction; endnotes in place of footnotes; a section called "Notes on Arthurian Matters," which consolidates the material previously contained in several appendixes; a bibliography; and three critical essays by Stone: "The Common Enemy of Man" (on the Green Knight), "Gawain's Eternal Jewel," and "The Poem as a Play." Comments from the relatively few instructors who have used this translation lack consensus. One remarks that the translation is "most readable and accurate," while another claims that "students can't read it." One regards the introduction and notes as "balanced," another as "misleading."

A few instructors use James L. Rosenberg's translation, which also preserves the verse form of the original. This edition contains an elaborate introductory essay of some seventy pages prepared by James R. Kreuzer. Kreuzer divides his remarks on the poem into sections on plot, commentary, and evaluation, and also provides an orientation to literary setting, the romance, and courtly love. There are also a brief bibliography and translator's note, but no notes to the text itself.

The final single-work poetic translation that received mention is Burton Raffel's. Like his possibly better-known translations from Old English, Raffel's *Gawain* has an appeal as modern poetry in its own right. It is fluent, avoids the archaic, and is reasonably faithful to the original (with, however, a few notable lapses). Instructors might consider assigning this translation to upper-division undergraduate English majors who are steeped in contemporary poetry and who might therefore find it a more comfortable entrée to the original poem than they find other translations whose style is "older." The instructor should be aware that Raffel's introductory review of scholarship and bibliographical annotations differ substantially in point of view from the scholarly consensus. Neil Isaac's afterword, which also reviews scholarship (among other things), provides a more conventional approach.

Ultimately, the choice of a translation for the classroom depends on the appeal of the style, which each instructor must judge, taking into account the students who will use the text and, doubtless, personal preference. To give a general impression of how each translator approached the problem of conveying both the sense and the subtlety of the original text while preserving to some extent the original alliterative verse form, here follows each translator's rendering of the passage that describes the Green Knight's precipitous entrance into King Arthur's great hall.

> For unethe was the noyce not a whyle sesed,
> And the fyrst cource in the court kyndely served,
> Ther hales in at the halle dor an aghlich mayster,
> On the most on the molde on mesure hyghe.
> (Waldron, lines 134–37)

(This passage was selected for demonstration purposes because instructors frequently singled out "aghlich mayster"—along with "cildgered"—as a place where students benefit from a commentary on the connotations of the poet's chosen diction.)

Marie Borroff translates these lines as:

> For scarce were the sweet strains still in the hall,
> And the first course come to that company fair,
> There hurtles in at the hall-door an unknown rider,
> One the greatest on ground in growth of his frame.

In Borroff's hands, the *aghlich* ("inspiring fear, terror, awe" related etymologically to Old English *aglaeca*, which is applied by the *Beowulf* poet to both Beowulf and Grendel; Tolkien and Gordon gloss as "terrible" and Waldron as "fearsome") becomes merely *unknown*, and *mayster* (from Old French *maistre*, 'lord,' 'knight,' 'master') is rendered as *rider*. While *rider* can perhaps by association with the German *Ritter* and the French *chevalier* convey the sense—implicit in *mayster*—of superior social status in the world of feudalism and chivalry, this association is not likely to occur to students reading the poem on their own. *Unknown*, of course, is a fairly neutral word that by itself does not have the sense of the alien, the strange, the awe-inspiring that *aghlich* has. The verb *hurtles* has to bear the burden of expressing how truly abrupt and unusual the intrusion of the Green Knight is, even in a world where King Arthur has always insisted on a marvel before dinner. *Hurtles* is perhaps slightly more vivid than the original *hales*, which means "hasten, rush." The last line quoted is an example of how Borroff takes pains to maintain the alliterative pattern of the original, even managing to retain the successive balanced and alliterating prepositional phrases, but certainly at the expense of fluency.

In his original translation Brian Stone gives us:

> But barely had the blast of trump abated one minute
> And the first course in the court been courteously served,
> When there pressed in from the porch an appalling figure,
> Who in height outstripped all earthly men.

If Borroff preferred to think of the *noyce* ("noise") of the banquet as *sweet strains*, Stone specifies the sound as the blast of a trumpet announcing the service of a course. Making no effort to retain the pattern of line 137, "On the most on the molde on mesure hyghe," Stone comes up with a rendering that rather accurately transmits the meaning of the original in a form more immediately accessible than Borroff's. When it comes to *aghlich mayster*, Stone obviously gave priority to conveying the overtones of *aghlich*, choosing *appalling* as his equivalent. But this choice gave him a problem. With the letter *p* as his alliterator, he selected *porch*, which more likely brings to mind the entrance to an American Gothic home on a tree-shaded street in the Midwest than the grand doorway to the banqueting hall of the Round Table. Stone must himself have felt uncomfortable with the line because the second edition has "When there heaved in at the hall-door an awesome fellow." This version gets rid of the unfortunate *porch* and changes *appalling* to *awesome*, which is both less judgmental about Arthur's unexpected visitor and etymologically equivalent to *aghlich*, but neither *fellow* nor *figure* conveys the social significance of *mayster* or indicates the tension between the somewhat contradictory connotations of the noun and its modifier.

Rosenberg renders the passage thus:

> But merely had the music melted into echoes
> And the opening course had been commanded and carved,
> When suddenly came crashing in a frightening great creature
> Terrible to look upon, tall as a forest tree.

Here the noise becomes music, which melts metaphorically, and *suddenly came crashing* provides a relatively uneconomic equivalent for *hales*. Indeed lack of economy characterizes Rosenberg's rendering of this passage, for *aghlich* becomes "frightening great . . . / Terrible to look upon." Like Borroff and Stone (on both tries), Rosenberg fails to make much of *mayster, creature* having more in common connotatively with *aghlich* than with *mayster*. The simile "tall as a forest tree" has no precedent in the original text, unless we stretch a point to find a cue in *on molde* 'on earth.' Of course, the arboreal image here looks ahead to the *overal enker grene* 'entirely bright green,' strategically located at the very end of the same stanza, and to the holly bob. But do we want the translator to look ahead when the poet was at great pains to conceal the knight's astounding verdancy until the last word of the bob and wheel?

Finally, Raffel, who feels least constrained to translate line for line and who is content to hint at the alliteration of the original rather than to attempt to reproduce it, comes up with:

> --the trumpets and pipes
> Were barely still, the drums silent,
> The first dishes set in place
> When a ghastly knight sprang through the door,
> Huge, taller than men stand, so square
> And thick from neck to knee, thighs
> So broad around, legs so long.

The additional lines were quoted to demonstrate Raffel's characteristic enjambment as opposed to the end-stopped lines of the original, which the other translators imitate. Raffel's rhythm, syntax and word choice all speak of the late twentieth century rather than the fourteenth. The gains and losses of Raffel's approach can perhaps best be shown by comparing his "Huge, taller than men stand" with Borroff's "One the greatest on ground in growth of his frame." Like Stone, Raffel specifies the noise as the music of trumpets, but he expands the idea to the stilling of pipes and the silence of drums, using the ubiquitous Old English stylistic technique of variation, which he had no doubt internalized after translating *Beowulf* and many other Old

English poems. The alliteration in this passage has dwindled to merely a whisper and an echo, "slant" alliteration if there is such a thing, having no structural function: *still-silent, stand-square,* and more orthodoxly *thick-thighs, legs-long.* Finally, our target phrase, *aghlich mayster,* becomes *ghastly knight,* making this the only translation of the four to catch the contrast between the dreadful and the courtly inherent in the original. What is lost metrically is perhaps here made up in diction.

Poetic Translations of More Than One Poem from Ms. Cotton Nero A.x.

Although as an allegorical dream vision *Pearl* has perhaps less immediate appeal for the typical contemporary undergraduate than does the racy narrative of *Gawain,* instructors frequently choose to teach this exquisitely beautiful poem in translation as a companion piece to *Gawain.* For those who wish to teach Modern English versions of more than one of the Cotton Nero A.x. poems, there are several possible choices of texts.

When J. R. R. Tolkien died, he left translations of *Gawain, Pearl,* and *Sir Orfeo* among his unpublished papers. These translations were published by his son Christopher Tolkien in 1975 along with brief introductions, that to *Gawain* taken from comments Tolkien made for a radio broadcast of a reading from the translation, that to *Pearl* from the introductory material he wrote for E. V. Gordon's edition of *Pearl,* originally planned as a Tolkien-Gordon collaboration. There is no introduction to *Sir Orfeo.* Christopher Tolkien has added a brief glossary of archaic and technical terms used in his father's translation (the necessity for this glossary gives some idea of the style of the translation) and included a brief translation of a lyric from the Vernon ms. entitled by his father "Gawain's Leave-taking." There is also an appendix on the verse forms of *Gawain* and *Pearl,* winnowed again from Tolkien's unpublished notes. A number of instructors use this volume, in part because they like the collocation of the three poems, finding the delicate magic of *Sir Orfeo* a fitting accompaniment to the more robust magic of *Sir Gawain* and to the finely wrought *Pearl.* Further, Tolkien was an exceptionally sensitive—and well-informed—reader of medieval literature. However, he chose to devote his time largely to the writing of fiction rather than to scholarship and criticism. One advantage of using his translations, then, is that by examining his handling of difficult, obscure, or controversial passages, one can infer Tolkien's scholarly opinion on these various thorny issues, opinion otherwise unavailable to succeeding generations of readers.

The late 1960s saw the almost simultaneous publication of two collective translations of all four Cotton Nero A.x. poems plus *St. Erkenwald* (which may or may not share common authorship with the other four poems), one by Margaret Williams and the other by the novelist cum medievalist John

Gardner. Williams's volume, *The* Pearl-*Poet: His Complete Works*, is now out of print, but several instructors apparently make the effort to gather up personal and library copies for use as classroom texts. In any case, this work is well worth placing on reserve for student consultation because of its extensive and valuable introduction. Among the topics Williams treats in a full and lively way likely to appeal to students are a description of the manuscript and its language (including an appendix giving a summary of morphology and two specimen Middle English passages from *Patience* and *Cleanness*), an overview of the Alliterative Movement, and an extensive summary of the various speculations about the author of the Cotton Nero A.x. poems (which includes a list of books identified as sources and analogues for the entire corpus). In a section on the backgrounds of the five poems, Williams does an excellent job of introducing students to medieval literary theory before commenting on each poem separately and concluding with a synthetic overview of the entire oeuvre. The introduction to *Gawain* covers diction and style, literary form, sources and analogues, courtly love, symbolism, and allegory. Appendixes are devoted to a technical description of the manuscript and its illustrations and to prosody. The volume also includes a substantial selected bibliography, now of course out-of-date, and several pedagogically useful annotated charts, including a tripartite time line of the fourteenth century correlating important events and trends in church history, English history, and cultural history and a schematic diagram that plots the setting (place and time), the structure, the narrative action, the themes and dominant imagery, and the sources and analogues against the divisions (parts, fitts, and stanzas) of *Gawain*.

John Gardner's *Complete Works of the* Gawain-*Poet* excites considerable controversy among those who use it as a class text. One instructor claims that it is "nearer to the original in subtleties," while another decries the "liberties" it takes with the text. What is a liberty to one reader is a "howler" to another. Gardner himself admits at the outset that his is a free translation, "exaggerating the poet's images and the connotative effects of his language in order to make images, puns, and the like available" with lines "quite drastically altered . . . in order to reproduce by indirection effects I could not get otherwise" (vii, viii).

One of Gardner's characteristic mannerisms as a novelist is the introduction (perhaps resurrection would be a better word) of obsolete medieval words—without comment or glossing. He also uses this technique in his translation of *Gawain*. Throughout the text words like *handsel, banderole, cates, blaunner, chaperon, brocatelle*, and *brochéed* appear unexplained and unglossed. On the one hand, this is appropriate, since the *Gawain* poet's vocabulary was highly technical and difficult even for his own time, but instructors should be prepared either to gloss these words themselves or to assign students lexical projects using the *OED* and *MED*. On the other hand,

Gardner from time to time incorporates silently into his translation what amount to footnotes. An example would be his rendering of the simplex *luf* 'love' (line 1524), which the lady uses in her second attempt to seduce Sir Gawain, as Courtly Love (p. 283), a term that was coined about a century ago by Gaston Paris and that carries with it by now the connotations of an elaborate medieval philosophy of love as reconstructed (or perhaps constructed) by modern scholars and critics.

Gardner's translation is prefaced by a six-part introduction and commentary of some ninety pages. The first, "The Poet," is largely a comparison and contrast of the personalities of Chaucer and the *Gawain* poet as revealed in their works. The section "Conventions and Traditions" cites parallels to *Gawain* from lesser-known works to illustrate the conventions of the Alliterative Movement and also discusses characteristic alliterative style and ornament, numerology, adaptation of sources, exegesis, allegory, and symbolism. In the third section Gardner sees the *Gawain* poet's vision of reality as mediated by feudalism, Neoplatonism, and courtly love, while the following section focuses on the poet's sense of the dramatic. Each of the five poems then receives a separate introduction—Gardner reads *Gawain* as a conflict between "human selfishness and the ideal of selfless courtesy" (70). He sees Gawain as a virgin knight who must pass both physical and spiritual tests, the spiritual test being divided into three temptations of his concupiscent, irascible, and rational wills respectively. The final introductory section is devoted to versification and form.

William Vantuono's *The* Pearl *Poems: An Omnibus Edition* is the only work combining the Middle English texts and facing-page verse translation; thus, it would seem to fill a real pedagogical void. Unfortunately this two-volume edition (*Gawain* appears in volume 2) is not suitable for routine classroom use because of its bulk, its elaborate scholarly apparatus, and above all its substantial cost. However, because this translation is supported by an extensive variorum commentary that at each crux explains Vantuono's translation strategy, instructors will find it worthwhile to consult Vantuono as a supplement to whatever inexpensive translation they choose.

While Tolkien, Williams, and Gardner are the only translations of two or more Cotton Nero A.x. poems mentioned in the survey of classroom use, instructors who adopt the Borroff and Stone translations should know that both translators have elsewhere published renderings of *Pearl* and that Stone has also translated *Cleanness* and *St. Erkenwald*. Stone's *Pearl* can be found in his *Medieval English Verse* and his *Cleanness* and *St. Erkenwald* in The Owl and the Nightingale, Cleanness, *and* St. Erkenwald. Borroff's rendering appears separately as *Pearl: A New Verse Translation*.

Once again personal preference concerning the translator's style will be an important consideration in choosing among these alternatives. Thus, we will return to lines 134–37 to examine the various approaches Tolkien, Williams, Gardner, and Vantuono take to the poem.

Tolkien gives us this translation:

> For hardly had the music but a moment ended,
> and the first course in the court as was custom been served,
> when there passed through the portals a perilous horseman,
> the mightiest on middle-earth in measure of height.

Tolkien's diction here associates *Gawain* with his critical theory of fantasy and with the practical application of that theory in his fiction. The keyword is *perilous*, which renders *aghlich*. For Tolkien *perilous* called to mind the Perilous Realm, Faërie, the Secondary World of Celtic folklore where beings like the Green Knight have their existence. Thus the use of *perilous* identifies the intruder as a fay, a word Tolkien applies to him (in the compound *fay-man*) in the bob and wheel of the same stanza. The decision to select *perilous* for its other worldly connotations forces *p* as the alliterator, thereby presenting Tolkien with the problem of finding an adequate equivalent for *hales*. He settled for *passed*, which has none of the urgency implied in the original. *Horseman*, given Tolkien's strongly philological bent, should almost certainly be read as the English translation of *chevalier*, thus preserving the aristocratic and chivalric overtones of *mayster*. The second important word here is *middle-earth*, which renders *molde* ("earth," with secondary meanings of "soil," "dirt," "clay," "arable," even "grave"). *Middle-earth* originally had cosmological and mythological significance, the human world sandwiched in between the world of the gods above and the world of assorted nondivine, frequently evil, and certainly perilous spirits below. The collocation of these two words then stresses the moment when the boundaries of this world and the other world touch and when it is possible for a being to cross over from one world to the next. This contact between the human and the faerie is what Tolkien termed fantasy, and his use of this concept and of the term *Middle-earth* will be well-known to many student readers of his fiction.

Margaret Williams renders this passage thus:

> For scarce had the festal sounds ceased for a while
> and the first course been fittingly served in court,
> then there flings at the door a gruesome fellow,
> the mightiest on earth, measured by his height.

When she chose to emphasize the bustle of the banqueting by interpreting the *noyce* as *festal sounds*, Williams apparently decided to link lines 134–36 with *f* alliteration: *for-festal, first-fittingly, flings-fellow*. (The *f*-pattern may indeed have been suggested by the last word in line 133, *life-food*.)

Thus in her hands *mayster* becomes *fellow*, perhaps losing its aristocratic overtones unless one reads *fellow* as stressing the likeness or fellowship between the Green Knight and his dramatic audience of the knights of the Round Table. *Gruesome* certainly stands in a state of tension with the connotations of *fellow* (which include both similarity and "jolly good"), and it is definitely more pejorative than *awesome*, the cognate of *aghlich*. *Flings* here is an appropriately precipitous verb.

John Gardner presents his reader with these lines:

> And strangely, almost as soon as that sound died out
> And the first course had been courteously served to the court,
> There haled through the door of that hall an ungodly creature,
> A man as enormous as any known on earth.

Gardner's translation of *aghlich mayster* as *ungodly creature* is interesting in the light of his commentary on the symbolic meaning of the Green Knight:

> It seems true (as Gawain himself thinks) that the Green Knight is the Devil's agent—and more: a symbolic summary of all that opposes the law of God. . . . But to view the Green Knight simply as an agent of the forces of darkness is to forget that the Green Knight serves God (as Gawain's priest-confessor) as readily as he serves the Devil. It therefore seems more satisfactory to view the Green Knight as a symbolic representation of the force of Nature. Like Nature, Bertilak is a jubilantly vital, changeable, more or less perpetual force.   (81–82)

Thus *ungodly creature* may be as oxymoronic as *aghlich mayster*, but in a different sense. The paradox here is not that of an uncouth courtier, but that of a being created by God (for surely *creature* implies a Creator) and yet ungodly, for given the force of Gardner's commentary above, *ungodly* here seems to carry the meaning of moral neutrality, neither God's nor the devil's creature exclusively. So, to follow Gardner's line of reasoning, the Green Knight, the "ungodly creature," is like nature, both created by God and both outside the moral realm.

Although William Vantuono's translation is not suitable for classroom adoption (unless the publisher issues an inexpensive paperback edition), a brief examination of its style seems worthwhile:

> For scarcely had the clamor ceased for a time,
> And the first course at the court been properly served,
> There rushed in at the hall-door an awesome master,
> The greatest in the land, tall in stature.

From these four lines it is immediately apparent that Vantuono has chosen to sacrifice a systematic re-creation of the *Gawain* poet's alliterative patterns in favor of an accurate rendering (based, as is clear from the commentaries, on complete command of the scholarly disputations that have, over the years, encapsulated each key word like so many layers of nacre). Thus *aghlich mayster* is rendered as *awesome master*, both words obviously chosen because they are the cognates of the original vocabulary. The commentary on this passage cites Philippa Moody's argument that the description of the Green Knight (134–50) establishes a "delicate relationship between the natural and the supernatural" (qtd. in Vantuono 247). The juxtaposition of *aghlich* and *mayster* clearly illustrates Moody's point, but, although etymologically correct, *master* may not convey the sense, which inheres in *mayster*, of the Green Knight's place in a particular human social order.

Anthologized Translations: Prose and Poetic

A few translations crop up occasionally because they are found in the anthology selected for a particular course. M. R. Ridley's prose translation can be found in *Medieval Romances*, edited by Roger Sherman Loomis and Laura Hibbard Loomis. *Medieval English Verse and Prose*, edited by Roger Sherman Loomis and Rudolph Willard, contains the poetic translation of Theodore Howard Banks, Jr., as do *The Literature of Medieval England*, edited by D. W. Robertson, Jr., and *British Literature*, Hazelton Spencer, general editor. George K. Anderson provided a prose translation for *The Literature of England*, edited originally (1936) by George B. Woods, Homer Watt, and George K. Anderson and revised most recently (1967) by George K. Anderson and William E. Buckler. The newest translation, by James J. Wilhelm, can be found in *The Romance of Arthur*, edited by James J. Wilhelm and Laila Zamuelis Gross.

While anthologies are chosen primarily because their tables of contents and apparatus best support the objectives of the course, nonetheless it may be helpful to look briefly at the style of these three translations. Ridley's prose translates our sample passage as follows: "But the notes had hardly died away when there swung in at the hall door a fearsome warrior, the tallest of all on earth." Prose provides the opportunity for a literal rendition, and yet Ridley entirely omits line 135: "And the fyrst cource in the court kyndely served." *Aghlich* here becomes *fearsome*, a reasonably literal choice, while *warrior* stresses the martial nature of the knight, a curious choice, since some stanzas later the Green Knight states that his intentions are not warlike, pointing out that he came to Camelot dressed in cloth, not steel.

Anderson's prose sticks noticeably closer to the original: "Scarcely had the hum of the banquet dwindled and the first course been served royally in the court, when there rushed in through the hall-door a terrible knight, the greatest in the world as to stature." If this does not have the beauty of well-wrought poetry, it does at least have relative accuracy, although *noyce* has become *hum of the banquet. Terrible knight* indeed comes near to the full connotative force of *aghlich mayster.*

Banks's poetic translation subtly changes the emphatic position of *aghlich mayster:*

> And scarcely the music had ceased for a moment,
> The first course been suitably served in the court,
> When a being most dreadful burst through the hall-door,
> Among the most mighty of men in his measure,

Both the shift of *being most dreadful* from the end of the line to the beginning and the choice of the pallid *being* water down the impact of the Green Knight's entrance, and the intrusion of the superlative *most* for which the original text has no precedent does not retrieve the situation. Further, *mayster* places the Green Knight firmly in the social system of the medieval world, while *being* indicates the uncharacterized alien: thus *being most dreadful* can be seen as tautological rather than oxymoronic. The omission of the sense of *on molde* from line 137 may also serve to obscure the essence of the Green Knight—he is both knight (a routine role in human society) and green (hardly a proper human hue, but characteristic of the inhabitants of Faërie).

Finally, Wilhelm's poetic translation gives these lines thus:

> For scarcely had the music ceased for a single second
> And the first course been courteously doled around the court,
> When there rushed through the door an extremely awesome rider,
> One of the greatest on earth, in measure enormous.

Wilhelm translates *aghlich mayster* here as *extremely awesome rider. Awesome,* of course, is entirely appropriate as the cognate of *aghlich,* while Wilhelm's choice of *rider,* a choice shared by Borroff, does have some chivalric overtones. However, the intensifier *extremely* lacks authority in the text and is perhaps unnecessary, since *awesome*—unlike *awful,* which has almost completely lost its force—still retains the sense of *awe-inspiring.* In the previous line, the original verb *served,* although perfectly clear in Modern English and not forming part of the alliterative pattern, has been replaced by *doled,* which with its overtones of rationing and grudging distribution (as in "on the dole") is at variance with the traditional atmosphere of liberality expected in a medieval court. Certainly *kyndely* ("fittingly, properly, done according to nature or true character") must be interpreted to mean that the food was served as it should be at a holiday feast fit for a king, not, one imagines, doled out in niggardly portions. Another interesting rendering in the stanza occurs at the end of the bob and wheel, where the narrator of the poem reveals what is most extraordinary about the knight, remarking almost as an afterthought that he is *overal enker grene*. Wilhelm translates this as *head to toe, ink-green*. *Enker* is an intensifier, meaning "very" or "extremely." Apparently the choice of *ink* to modify *green* was made purely on the basis of sound, since the knight is no ink-stained clerk, and *ink-green* (unlike, say, hunter green or bottle green) has no ready associations with any particular hue. (It is, of course, possible that this rendering was suggested by French *encre* 'ink.')

Anthologies

About half the instructors who responded to the questionnaire reported teaching *Gawain* from an anthology in one context or another. The advantages of using an anthology are, of course, economy and the convenience and flexibility inherent in mass-ordering a single text for multisectioned introductory courses. Some feel that students like to have their reading drawn all from one volume, while others report that students are reluctant to bring a large, cumbersome text to class, preferring individual paperbacks for sheer portability. The disadvantage of an anthology, in addition to its perhaps daunting bulk, is that an editor's choices rarely, if ever, coincide exactly with the preferences of the individual instructor.

Anthologies are most frequently used for the traditional sophomore survey of British literature. The overwhelming choice for this course is *The Norton Anthology of English Literature*, M. H. Abrams, general editor. The section devoted to the Middle Ages, edited by E. Talbot Donaldson, contains Marie Borroff's popular translation of *Gawain*. In volume 1 of the full-length edition, *Gawain* is surrounded by a number of medieval works that make interesting thematic comparisons and contrasts possible, such as Donaldson's prose translation of *Beowulf; The Battle of Maldon*; several of the *Canterbury Tales*, including the Wife of Bath's and the Franklin's tales; *Sir Orfeo*; *Pearl*; and excerpts from *Piers Plowman* and Malory's *Morte Darthur*. Borroff's version of *Gawain* also appears in the one-volume Major Authors edition accompanied by Donaldson's *Beowulf* and a more limited selection from Chaucer (which fortunately retains both the Wife of Bath's Tale and the Franklin's Tale). Instructors like this anthology because it contains Donaldson's introduction and Borroff's translation, but quite a few termed the interpretative footnotes "skimpy." The well-known physical format of the

Norton series of anthologies—bulky and thick, flimsy nonopaque paper, minimal margins— is seen by some as a barrier to student reading.

Primary competition for the *Norton Anthology* is *The Oxford Anthology of English Literature*, Frank Kermode and John Hollander, general editors. The section on medieval English literature, edited by J. B. Trapp, is available in volume 1 of the two-volume edition or bound separately. Those who use the *Oxford Anthology* had only favorable comments, citing its good selections (which include Brian Stone's revised translation of *Gawain*) and excellent notes and introductions. Special features that set this anthology apart are its well-chosen group of iconographically significant plates (those pertinent to *Gawain* include the Wilton Diptych; an illustration from ms. Cotton Nero A.x.; and the months of January, September, and December from the *Très riches heures du duc de Berry*, depicting a New Year's feast, an elaborate castle, and a boar hunt respectively) and its occasional inclusion of minor works that in some way shed light on the major ones. The editor also provides a substantial glossary and a good basic bibliography.

Two other anthologies occasionally adopted are *The Literature of England*, revised edition prepared by George K. Anderson and William E. Buckler, which contains Anderson's prose translation of *Sir Gawain and the Green Knight*, and *British Literature*, Hazelton Spencer, general editor, which prints Banks's poetic translation.

Several anthologies developed for more specialized courses also include *Gawain*. The fourth edition of *The Norton Anthology of World Masterpieces*, Maynard Mack, general editor, has added Marie Borroff's translation to its "Masterpieces of the Middle Ages" section, which is introduced by John C. McGalliard. Other medieval works printed in this volume are *The Dream of the Rood*; *The Song of Roland*; *Aucassin and Nicolette*; selections from the *Divine Comedy* and the *Decameron*; the General Prologue of the *Canterbury Tales* and the Miller's, Pardoner's, and Nun's Priest's tales; and *Everyman*.

Roger Sherman Loomis and Laura Hibbard Loomis edited a collection, *Medieval Romances*, for the Modern Library. In addition to Ridley's prose translation of *Gawain*, the selections, all presented in Modern English prose and some abridged or excerpted, are Chrétien de Troyes's *Perceval*, Gottfried von Strassburg's *Tristan and Isolt*, *The Youth of Alexander the Great*, *Aucassin and Nicolette*, *Havelock the Dane*, *Sir Orfeo*, and "The Book of Balin" from Malory's *Morte Darthur*.

D. W. Robertson's *The Literature of Medieval England* is unique in scope, presenting selections from all of the literary languages of the British Isles— Irish, Welsh, Latin, and Anglo-Norman, as well as Old and Middle English— from the earliest written records through the fifteenth century. The general introduction considers medieval life and ideals, astronomy and astrology, the medieval Bible, the character of medieval literature, and the literature of medieval England. As one would expect, the apparatus of this anthology supports Robertson's exegetical approach to medieval literature, and those who find this approach uncongenial will probably not be comfortable with this text. In addition to Banks's poetic translation of *Gawain*, a number of titles in the table of contents would support a study of the *Gawain* poet's achievement: the beheading episode from *The Feast of Bricriu*; an excerpt from Gildas; "Culhwch and Olwen" from *The Mabinogion*; portions of books 8–9 of Geoffrey of Monmouth's *History of the Kings of Britain*, which contain the story of Arthur; and passages from Froissart's *Chronicles*. There is also a unit on medieval literary theory, which stresses John of Salisbury, Dante, Boccaccio, and Richard de Bury, with brief commentaries from such authors as Bernard Silvestris, Arnulf of Orleans, Nicholas Trivet, and Alexander Neckam.

A few instructors report using Roger Sherman Loomis and Rudolph Willard's *Medieval English Verse and Prose in Modernized Editions*, although it is apparently out of print. This collection runs from Layamon's *Brut* to *Everyman* and includes Banks's translation of *Gawain*, as well as translations of *Pearl* and *St. Erkenwald*.

Filling the void left when Richard L. Brengle's *Arthur King of Britain* went out of print is a new anthology, *The Romance of Arthur*, edited by James J. Wilhelm and Laila Zamuelis Gross. Its table of contents includes excerpts from the chronicles and pseudohistories placed in context by recent archaeological discoveries, selections from early Welsh prose and poetry including *The Triads*, "Culhwch and Olwen," excerpts from Geoffrey of Monmouth, Chrétien de Troyes's *Lancelot*, *Gawain*, a condensed version of the alliterative *Morte Arthure*, and episodes from Malory's *Le Morte Darthur*. All medieval works, except for Malory, are presented in new translations.

The two anthologies containing *Gawain* in Middle English—Charles W. Dunn and Edward T. Byrnes, *Middle English Literature*, and Ann S. Haskell, *A Middle English Anthology*—that instructors mentioned are now both out of print (although a reprint of Haskell's book has recently been announced). Too recent for inclusion in survey responses is the anthology *Medieval English Literature*, edited by Thomas J. Garbáty, which prints *Gawain* in Middle English. Covering literature in England and Scotland from 1100 to 1500, its selections are for the most part in Middle English. Old English, Anglo-Latin, and Anglo-Norman works, however, appear in translation. A general introduction of roughly forty pages places each work in its medieval context. Linguistic problems are handled with a five-page discussion of language and with extensive marginal glossing for poetic works.

(Glosses of prose passages appear in footnotes.) The primary table of contents organizes the selections by genre, but pedagogically useful alternative tables also analyze the works according to dialect, motifs and themes, modes ("courtly," "popular," etc.), and chronology. Each genre (and each work) has a brief introduction and selected bibliography, and historical and critical footnotes are provided.

Readings for Students and Instructors

When instructors were asked both to suggest critical and background works with which anyone teaching *Gawain* should be familiar and to enumerate the collateral readings that they require or recommend that their students consult, the two lists were extensive and essentially overlapping. Roughly half the instructors asked students to read secondary sources, and most guided students to reading that would support their particular essay topics instead of assigning a core reading list to the class at large. Therefore it seems most helpful to group these secondary works by topic and scope rather than by audience.

Needless to say, the following citations do not list all that has been written about *Gawain* or about the context in which it was written. Rather, in most cases these are the works instructors deemed most helpful in preparing to teach *Gawain* and most frequently recommended to their undergraduate and graduate students. For additional bibliographic information instructors should consult the collective and serial bibliographies listed under "Reference Works." Also, many of the essays in this volume that discuss specific areas of background and teaching approaches provide specialized bibliographies of some depth. Further, the comments concerning each work are deliberately descriptive in tone and necessarily brief, meant primarily to give instructors and their students ready access to key works that provide an orientation to *Gawain* and to the medieval world from which it sprang.

Background Studies

Primary Sources

Medieval thought in general and medieval literature in particular were greatly influenced and shaped by a number of fundamental works, and students can enhance their understanding of medieval literature by reading the handful of books most important to the tradition in which the authors of the Middle Ages—including the *Gawain* poet—wrote. In addition to the Vulgate Bible, students and instructors might turn their attention to Boethius's *Consolation of Philosophy* and Saint Augustine's *On Christian Doctrine* and *Confessions* for philosophical and theological underpinnings. For insight into the medieval attitudes toward love and the relations between the sexes, it is helpful to read Andreas Capellanus's *The Art of Courtly Love*, the *Roman de la Rose* by Guillaume de Lorris and Jean de Meun, and Ovid's *Art of Love*. Other, less universally influential medieval works that present useful insights into the *Gawain* poet's world are Ramón Lull's *Book of the Ordre of Chyualry* and Jean Froissart's *Chronicles*.

The works that have been identified as analogues, and possibly as direct sources, of *Gawain* have been conveniently grouped in Elisabeth Brewer's collection *From Cuchulainn to Gawain*, which contains relevant excerpts in translation from—among other works—the *Feast of Bricriu, Caradoc, Perlesvaus, La mule sanz frain, Hunbaut, Yder*, and the Arthurian Vulgate Cycle. Seven other Gawain poems, including *Sir Gawain and the Carl of Carlisle* and *The Wedding of Sir Gawain and Dame Ragnell*, have been translated by Louis B. Hall in *The Knightly Tales of Sir Gawain* and are thus readily available for students studying the characterization of Gawain in medieval literature.

Historical and Cultural Background

A great difficulty facing the teacher of medieval literature is providing sufficient insight into context and background for the contemporary student to understand and appreciate that literature, written in a period when cultural assumptions differing radically from our own prevailed. Fortunately, many scholars have labored to provide us with a picture of the Middle Ages that grows more comprehensive and detailed with every year.

An excellent introductory guide to medieval culture as it pertains to medieval literature is Robert W. Ackerman's *Backgrounds to Medieval English Literature*, which conveniently covers the social and religious contexts of Old and Middle English literature, the English language in the Middle Ages, popular Christian beliefs, and the medieval worldview at a level suitable for students and general readers. A more recent work with similar objectives is A. C. Partridge's *A Companion to Old and Middle English Studies*, which provides social, economic, and political background for medieval literature, paying particular attention to questions of language and dialect. Translated primary sources to support these overviews can be found in A. R. Myers's *English Historical Documents, 1327–1485*, which has a copious bibliography and which prints documents relating to political affairs, law and all levels of government, the Church, education, and economic and social developments. The classroom-oriented volume *The World of Piers Plowman*, edited by Jeanne Krochalis and Edward Peters, presents primary sources, keyed, of course, to Langland's poem but nonetheless useful for students of all late fourteenth-century literature, as is Edith Rickert's similar compilation of documents, *Chaucer's World*.

A good collaborative history of the period is *Medieval England*, edited by Austin L. Poole, which contains treatments of topics important to the understanding of *Gawain*: "The English Landscape," "Arms and Armour," and "Domestic and Military Architecture." R. W. Southern's *The Making of the Middle Ages* discusses the development of medieval institutions and ways of life. Volumes 5–8 of the *Cambridge Medieval History* are also useful background for the Middle English period. Historical treatments of the fourteenth century in England include May McKisack's standard in the field, *The Fourteenth Century, 1307–1399*, the fifth volume of the *Oxford History of England*; Alec R. Myers's *England in the Late Middle Ages (1307–1536)*; F. R. H. Du Boulay's *An Age of Ambition: English Society in the Late Middle Ages*; Maurice Hugh Keen's *England in the Later Middle Ages*; Gervase Mathew's *The Court of Richard II*; G. M. Trevelyan's still useful *England in the Age of Wycliffe*; and, larger in scope, G. G. Coulton's *Medieval Panorama: The English Scene from Conquest to Reformation*. Barbara Tuchman's bestseller *A Distant Mirror: The Calamitous Fourteenth Century* is, despite its flaws, assigned to students with some frequency. This book is of special interest to readers of *Gawain* because its "hero," Enguerrand de Coucy VII, has occasionally been associated with the *Gawain* poet. Also of special note is Michael J. Bennett's recent *Community, Class and Careerism: Cheshire and Lancashire Society in the Age of* Sir Gawain and the Green Knight, which provides a detailed look at the social, economic, and demographic makeup of the *Gawain* poet's immediate community. Bennett postulates that the *Gawain* poet might have been one of the many ambitious men who left impoverished Cheshire and Lancashire to serve in the entourages of Richard II and John of Gaunt, duke of Lancaster, only to return home (ironically by the same route Gawain takes from Camelot to Hautdesert) after the accession of Henry IV. This book also includes several maps of the area that show the birthplaces of notable courtiers plotted against the boundaries of the Cotton Nero A.x. and *St. Erkenwald* dialects, with the conjectural locations of Hautdesert and the Green Chapel superimposed.

The standard work on medieval thought and intellectual history is Henry O. Taylor's monumental two-volume *The Medieval Mind: A History of the Development of Thought and Emotion in the Middle Ages*. Other works on medieval intellectual history and philosophy include Gordon Leff's *Medieval Thought: St. Augustine to Ockham* and, more immediately relevant, *The Dissolution of the Medieval Outlook: An Essay on the Intellectual and Spiritual Change in the Fourteenth Century*; William Brandt's *The Shape of Medieval History: Studies in Modes of Perception*; David Knowles's *The Evolution of Medieval Thought*; and the distinguished Thomist Etienne Gilson's *The Spirit of Medieval Philosophy*. Of particular interest in that it applies a study of medieval thought directly to the understanding and appreciation of medieval literature is C. S. Lewis's highly influential *The Discarded Image: An Introduction to Medieval and Renaissance Literature*. Ernst Robert Curtius's magisterial study *European Literature and the Latin Middle Ages* also looks at literature, in this case specifically Latin and not vernacular, in terms of its reflection of the intellectual climate of its times. Johan Huizinga's seminal work *The Waning of the Middle Ages*, while focusing on the intellectual and cultural backgrounds of fourteenth- and fifteenth-century art in France and the Low Countries, is nevertheless exceedingly helpful in understanding English literature of the same period.

Good overviews of English social and economic history in the late Middle Ages can be obtained from G. M. Trevelyan's *English Social History: A Survey of Six Centuries*, James W. Thompson's *Economic and Social History of the Middle Ages*, Henri Pirenne's *Economic and Social History of Medieval Europe*, Christopher Brooke's *The Structure of Medieval Society*, M. M. Postan's *Medieval Economy and Society: An Economic History of Britain in the Middle Ages*, and Geoffrey Barraclough's *Social Life in Early England*. More specialized studies relevant to *Gawain* include Marc Bloch's definitive work on feudalism, *Feudal Society*, Sidney Painter's *French Chivalry: Chivalric Ideas and Practices in Medieval France*, Georges Duby's *The Chivalric Society*, Maurice Keen's *Chivalry*, J. H. Baker's *An Introduction to English Legal History*, A. R. Myers's *London in the Age of Chaucer*, Terence Wise's *Medieval Warfare*, and Jean Gimpel's *The Medieval Machine: The Industrial Revolution of the Middle Ages*. Dorothy Hartley's *Lost Country Life* provides a fascinating introduction to the agricultural practices, unseen in the poem, that supported the leisure of the medieval aristocracy. Richard Barber's *The Knight and Chivalry* and *The Reign of Chivalry* are written on a more popular level and are copiously illustrated.

Easily accessible to students are *Medieval People* and *Medieval Women*, both by Eileen Power. Students' questions about the everyday lifestyle of knights and ladies can be answered by Joseph Gies and Frances Gies's *Life in a Medieval Castle*, Margaret Wade Labarge's *A Baronial Household of the Thirteenth Century*, Marjorie Rowling's *Everyday Life in Medieval Times*, William Stearns Davis's *Life on a Medieval Barony*, and Mary E. Whitmore's *Medieval English Domestic Life and Amusements in the Age of Chaucer*.

Background for the holiday feasts so prominent in *Gawain* can be obtained from F. J. Furnivall's *Early English Meals and Manners*, Bridget Ann Henisch's *Food and Feast in Medieval Society*, Lorna J. Sass's *To the King's Taste: Richard II's Book of Feasts and Recipes*, and Madeleine Pelner Cosman's *Fabulous Feasts: Medieval Cookery and Ceremony*. For information on costume, see Francis M. Kelly and Randolph Schwabe's *A Short History of Costume and Armour, Chiefly in England 1066–1800*.

To understand the visual world of the *Gawain* poet, instructors and students should consult the distinguished works of Emile Mâle, *The Gothic Image: Religious Art in France of the Thirteenth Century* and *Religious Art in France: The Twelfth Century*, and of Erwin Panofsky, *Studies in Iconology* and *Gothic Architecture and Scholasticism*. Frederick Pickering's *Literature and Art in the Middle Ages* makes the connections between the visual and verbal arts explicit. An excellent introduction to the architecture and construction techniques of the medieval castle is David Macaulay's *Castle*, which explains its highly technical subject matter in terms accessible even to older children and is replete with skillful (and humorous) architectural renderings. Other relevant books on art history include Hans Hofstätter's *Art of the Late Middle Ages* and Sabrina Mitchell's *Medieval Manuscript Painting*.

Literary History

In order to be understood and appreciated, *Gawain* must be read not only in the light of its historical and cultural backgrounds but also within its more immediate literary context. Perhaps the best place to send students needing an overview of Middle English literature and its place in the whole sweep of English literary history is *A Literary History of England*, edited by Albert C. Baugh. Book 1, "The Middle Ages," written by Kemp Malone and Albert C. Baugh, provides information on such topics as the Arthurian legend, the romance tradition, and the Alliterative Revival. Another general literary history students might consult is David Daiches's *A Critical History of English Literature*, which, however, does not present as detailed and comprehensive a picture of Middle English literature as does Baugh. The accessible *Guide to English Literature: From Beowulf through Chaucer and Medieval Drama* by David M. Zesmer is a useful introduction to medieval literature for students, particularly because it contains Stanley B. Greenfield's excellent annotated "core" bibliography (through 1960). Other surveys of medieval English literature include George K. Anderson's *Old and Middle English Literature from the Beginnings to 1485*, Derek Pearsall's *Old and Middle English Poetry*, Stephen Medcalf's *The Later Middle Ages*, and John A. Burrow's *Medieval Writers and Their Work*. Some still use W. P. Ker's *Medieval English Literature* (although Ker attributes the ms. Cotton Nero A.x. poems to Huchown, a now discredited position) and George Kane's *Middle English Literature*, which comments on the *Gawain* poet's visual imagery. Instructors also report assigning Francis Berry's essay "*Sir Gawayne and the Grene Knight*" in the collective history *The Age of Chaucer*, edited by Boris Ford. This volume also contains a small anthology of medieval poems (including *Sir Gawayne and the Grene Knight*) edited by Berry. Ford also edited the recently published volume *Medieval Literature, Part One: Chaucer and the Alliterative Tradition*. W. T. H. Jackson's *The Literature of the Middle Ages*, organized principally by genre, contains an extensive chapter on the romance. However, while Jackson devotes substantial space to discussions of the Continental romances, his consideration of *Gawain* is confined to a few passing superlatives.

John A. Burrow's *Ricardian Poetry: Chaucer, Gower, Langland, and the Gawain Poet* broke new ground by examining the major English authors of the latter half of the fourteenth century and finding in their works a shared outlook and style that Burrow postulates as characterizing the literature of this period. Charles Muscatine also looks at Langland, Chaucer, and the *Pearl* poet in *Poetry and Crisis in the Age of Chaucer* to consider the "relevance of poetry to cultural history" (35), judging as oblique the *Pearl* poet's response to the political, social, and economic crises of the late fourteenth century.

John Speirs's *Medieval English Poetry: The Non-Chaucerian Tradition* is the only critical work that attempts to cover the whole range of Middle English literature, exclusive of Chaucer. His reading of *Gawain*, perhaps the most extreme mythological criticism ever written about this poem, generated considerable controversy on publication, and many survey respondents indicated that they do not recommend it to their students.

While perhaps dated in some of its judgments (particularly on the identity and corpus of the Cotton Nero A.x. poet), the second volume of James P. Oakden's *Alliterative Poetry in Middle English* is still useful for its characterization of an alliterative school and its study of the diction and style of Middle English alliterative verse. A more recent attempt to define the alliterative school of Middle English poetry is Thorlac Turville-Petre's *The Alliterative Revival*, which discusses the origins and nature of the Alliterative Revival, meter, diction, and narrative technique. Other helpful works are Dorothy Everett's *Essays on Middle English Literature*, which contains a discussion of the Cotton Nero A.x. poems in the context of the Alliterative Revival (68–96); Derek Pearsall's "The Origins of the Alliterative Revival," in Levy and Szarmach's *The Alliterative Tradition in the Fourteenth Century*; and the collection of essays edited by David E. Lawton, *Middle English Alliterative Poetry and Its Literary Background*.

Literary Traditions, Themes, Techniques, and Special Topics

Gawain is universally acclaimed as the greatest of medieval English romances. Among the works that define and delineate the romance tradition are W. P. Ker's classic and still widely read *Epic and Romance*, Erich Auerbach's seminal study *Mimesis: The Representation of Reality in Western Literature* (esp. ch. 6, "The Knight Sets Forth"), and Northrop Frye's equally influential *Anatomy of Criticism*. Gillian Beer's slender volume *The Romance* provides a definition and brief history of the romance and discusses *Gawain* in the context of the medieval chivalric romance. *The Rise of Romance* by Eugène Vinaver, the great editor and interpreter of Malory is also useful background reading. John Stevens's *Medieval Romance* analyzes the body of medieval romances thematically, discussing *Gawain* primarily under the rubrics "Realism and Romance: Characters and Types" and "Realism and

Romance: Discourse of Love." Dieter Mehl's *The Middle English Romances of the Thirteenth and Fourteenth Centuries* also formulates generic criteria for the romance and examines *Gawain* at some length. Several useful articles on the Middle English romance as a genre and *Gawain* as a romance are Derek Pearsall's "The Development of Middle English Romance," Sacvan Bercovitch's "Romance and Anti-Romance in *Sir Gawain and the Green Knight*," Paul Strohm's "The Origin and Meaning of Middle English *Romaunce*," Mark E. Amsler's "Literary Theory and the Genres of Middle English Literature," and John Finlayson's "The Expectations of Romance in *Sir Gawain and the Green Knight*" and "Definitions of Middle English Romance."

Gawain is of course also a representative of the Arthurian tradition. Here the preeminent scholar is still Roger Sherman Loomis, whose works in this field include *Celtic Myth and Arthurian Romance*; *The Development of Arthurian Romance*, an excellent introduction to and survey of this field; and a posthumous collection of essays, *Studies in Medieval Literature*. He also edited the collaborative history *Arthurian Literature in the Middle Ages*, which is the standard in the field and which contains Laura Hibbard Loomis's essay on *Gawain*. Other useful works on Arthurian material include Richard W. Barber's *Arthur of Albion*, which devotes a chapter to the Gawain character in Arthurian literature; Lucy Allen Paton's *Studies in the Fairy Mythology of Arthurian Romance*; Jessie L. Weston's *From Ritual to Romance*, famous as the source for T. S. Eliot's *The Waste Land*; Edmund K. Chambers's *Arthur of Britain*; and Leslie Alcock's *Arthur's Britain* and Geoffrey Ashe's *The Quest for Arthur's Britain*, which both provide historical and archaeological background. Since it has recently gone out of print, Richard L. Brengle's *Arthur King of Britain* is no longer useful as a classroom text, but its combination of excerpts from the histories and chronicles (e.g., Gildas, Nennius, William of Malmesbury, Giraldus Cambrensis, Geoffrey of Monmouth) and from Arthurian literature (e.g., Wace, Layamon, *The Mabinogion*, the stanzaic *Morte Arthur* and alliterative *Morte Arthure*, Malory) and sixteen critical articles make it a worthwhile addition to the reserve shelf.

Medieval literary aesthetic is far removed from that of contemporary literature, and students need guidance as they encounter medieval symbolism and allegory. The neo-Augustinian exegetical approach to allegory is best typified by D. W. Robertson's highly controversial and highly influential *A Preface to Chaucer: Studies in Medieval Perspectives*, while Morton W. Bloomfield's "Symbolism in Medieval Literature" argues that Augustinian allegorical interpretations are not appropriate to all works of medieval literature. The point is further debated by E. Talbot Donaldson, R. E. Kaske, and Charles Donahue, in three articles under the general title "Patristic Exegesis in the Criticism of Medieval Literature." Other useful works on medieval allegory, symbolism, and literary aesthetic include James I. Wimsatt's *Allegory and Mirror: Tradition and Structure in Middle English Literature*, which includes a chapter "The Ideal of Chivalry: Gawain and Lancelot"; Rosemond Tuve's *Allegorical Imagery: Some Medieval Books and Their Posterity*, which does not treat *Gawain* specifically but does deal at length with allegory in general and allegory in romance in particular; and Judson B. Allen's *The Friar as Critic: Literary Attitudes in the Later Middle Ages*, which reviews the various allegorical readings of *Gawain* and proposes its own (145-50). The arcane subject of number symbolism as it pertains to medieval literature is discussed by Vincent F. Hopper in *Medieval Number Symbolism* and as it pertains to *Gawain* by A. Kent Hieatt in "*Sir Gawain*: Pentangle, *Luf-Lace*, Numerical Structure." The prominent color symbolism in the poem is elucidated by Joseph F. Eagan's "The Import of Color Symbolism in *Sir Gawain and the Green Knight*," William Goldhurst's "The Green and the Gold: The Major Theme of *Gawain and the Green Knight*," Robert J. Blanch's "Games Poets Play: The Ambiguous Use of Color Symbolism in *Sir Gawain and the Green Knight*," and W. Bryant Bachman's "*Sir Gawain and the Green Knight*: The Green and the Gold Once More."

C. S. Lewis's classic study *The Allegory of Love* certainly provides insight into the medieval use of allegory, but it also serves as an excellent guide to the medieval literary convention of courtly love. Among other important works on courtly love and the chivalric code as it is reflected in literature are Denis de Rougemont's *Love in the Western World*; Roger Boase's survey of scholarship *The Origin and Meaning of Courtly Love*, which has an extensive bibliography on the subject; Joan M. Ferrante and George D. Economou's *In Pursuit of Perfection: Courtly Love in Medieval Literature*; *The Meaning of Courtly Love*, a bibliography and collection of essays by Francis X. Newman; and *Patterns of Love and Courtesy*, the festschrift in memory of C. S. Lewis edited by John Lawlor, which contains Derek Brewer's essay "Courtesy and the *Gawain*-Poet." Margaret Adlum Gist's *Love and War in the Middle English Romances* also provides helpful background on this topic. *Chivalric Literature*, edited by Larry D. Benson and John Leyerle, contains, among other essays, "The Major Themes of Chivalric Literature" by John Leyerle and "Honor and Shame in *Sir Gawain and the Green Knight*" by Loretta Wasserman. Bernard O'Donoghue's anthology *The Courtly Love Tradition* provides texts and translations of classical and medieval love poetry from Latin, French, Arabic, German, Italian, and Georgian sources as contexts for late medieval English poetry.

Gawain is frequently read in the context of temptation, sin, and penance.

In this area Morton W. Bloomfield's *The Seven Deadly Sins* is indispensable. Donald R. Howard's *The Three Temptations: Medieval Man in Search of the World* provides an extensive analysis of Sir Gawain's failure at the Green Chapel, while W. R. J. Barron's recent book *Trawthe and Treason: The Sin of Gawain Reconsidered* examines Gawain's fault in the light of "medieval social, legal, and theological usages" (viii). For penitential aspects of the poem, see Robert W. Ackerman's "Gawain's Shield: Penitential Doctrine in *Sir Gawain and the Green Knight*," John A. Burrow's "The Two Confession Scenes in *Sir Gawain and the Green Knight*," Mary Flowers Braswell's *The Medieval Sinner: Characterization and Confession in the Literature of the English Middle Ages*, and J. R. R. Tolkien's lecture "*Sir Gawain and the Green Knight*." Robert L. Kindrick's "Gawain's Ethics: Shame and Guilt in *Sir Gawain and the Green Knight*" considers questions of social and personal ethics.

A number of works enhance our appreciation of the *Gawain* poet's literary techniques. Piero Boitani's recent *English Medieval Narrative in the Thirteenth and Fourteenth Centuries* examines the poet's handling of time, space, and characterization. Medieval narrative technique is also the subject of William Ryding's *Structure in Medieval Narrative* and John M. Ganim's *Style and Consciousness in Middle English Narrative*. Charles Sears Baldwin's *Medieval Rhetoric and Poetic (to 1400)* provides an overview of medieval literary theory with passing references to *Gawain*. The difficult issue of irony is treated by Dennis H. Green in *Irony in the Medieval Romance*. Pamela Gradon's *Form and Style in Early English Literature* examines the construction of the Middle English romance, including *Gawain*, in the context of other medieval genres. A fairly technical discussion of the alliterative meter of *Gawain* can be found in Robert William Sapora's monograph *A Theory of Middle English Alliterative Meter with Critical Applications*. Ronald A. Waldron has applied the Parry-Magoun oral-composition theory to *Gawain* in "Oral-Formulaic Technique and Middle English Alliterative Poetry," and R. F. Lawrence has also explored this issue in "The Formulaic Theory and Its Application to English Alliterative Poetry."

For the folklore elements of *Gawain*, see Francis Lee Utley's "Folklore, Myth and Ritual" and Charles Moorman's "Myth and Mediaeval Literature: *Sir Gawain and the Green Knight*." Albert B. Friedman's "Folklore and Medieval Literature: A Look at Mythological Considerations" examines the validity of folkloric and mythic approaches to medieval literature in general and *Gawain* in particular. An interesting modern folk analogue to *Sir Gawain and the Green Knight* read as a Christmas entertainment is Henry Glassie's *All Silver and No Brass: An Irish Christmas Mumming*. On a topic related to the reading of *Gawain* as a Christmas poem, Johan Huizinga's *Homo*

Ludens: A Study of the Play Element in Culture has had a significant impact on *Gawain* criticism. Three articles that apply Huizinga's insights are Robert G. Cook's "The Play-Element in *Sir Gawain and the Green Knight*," Martin Stevens's "Laughter and Game in *Sir Gawain and the Green Knight*," and John Leyerle's "The Game and Play of Hero."

The question of audience for poems like *Gawain* is examined in Richard Firth Green's *Poets and Princepleasers: Literature and the English Court in the Late Middle Ages*, Derek S. Brewer's *Chaucer in His Time*, and Elizabeth Salter's *Fourteenth-Century English Poetry: Contexts and Readings*.

A number of individual passages in *Gawain* can be better understood in the light of background information. Marcelle Thiébaux's *The Stag of Love: The Chase in Medieval Literature* reviews medieval hunting practice and the iconography of the hunt and applies that information to the hunt as it appears in medieval literature, including *Gawain*. For additional information on this subject see Glending Olson's *Literature as Recreation in the Later Middle Ages* (119–27). The beautiful description of the passing seasons and the many references to landscape in *Gawain* are placed in context by Derek Pearsall and Elizabeth Salter in *Landscapes and Seasons of the Medieval World*, which has many attractive plates. Background for Gawain's antifeminist outburst near the end of the poem can be found in Francis L. Utley's *The Crooked Rib*. Robert E. Kaske considers the nature and location of the Green Chapel in "Gawain's Green Chapel and the Cave at Wetton Mill," in *Medieval Literature and Folklore Studies*, edited by Jerome Mandel and Bruce Rosenberg. Helmut Nickel's "The Arming of Gawain" provides a clear explanation of the technical description of Gawain's armor and includes a useful schematic diagram of late-fourteenth-century armor. The figure of the knight in medieval literature is examined by Charles Moorman in *A Knyght There Was*, which devotes a chapter to Gawain as the "stained knight." For an overview of the heroic figure in the later medieval period, see Morton W. Bloomfield's "The Problem of the Hero in the Later Medieval Period." The female characters in *Gawain* are examined in Maureen Fries's "The Characterization of Women in the Alliterative Tradition" and in chapter 4 of Nikki Stiller's *Eve's Orphans: Mothers and Daughters in Medieval English Literature*, which also includes a brief bibliography of pertinent women's studies.

Finally, on the vexed question of the authorship of the Cotton Nero A.x. poems, a convenient place to review the various identifications made over the years is in the "Author" section of Margaret Williams's introduction to her translations. Perhaps the most recent effort to put a name to the *Gawain* poet is William Vantuono's "John de Mascy of Sale and the *Pearl* Poems," which contains a bibliography on the subject. Larry D. Benson's "The Authorship of *St. Erkenwald*" has effectively removed that poem from the *Gawain* poet's canon in the minds of most scholars and critics.

Critical Works

Works on *Sir Gawain and the Green Knight* and the *Gawain* Poet

A limited number of full-length studies of *Gawain* and the *Gawain* poet were repeatedly recommended as good starting points for anyone—instructor or student—wishing to approach this poem. Most frequently mentioned is Larry D. Benson's *Art and Tradition in* Sir Gawain and the Green Knight, which discusses sources, literary conventions, narrative and descriptive techniques, theme, and alliterative style. Also noteworthy on alliterative style and meter is Marie Borroff's Sir Gawain and the Green Knight: *A Stylistic and Metrical Study*. J. A. Burrow's *A Reading of* Sir Gawain and the Green Knight examines the poem fitt by fitt, stressing the thematic emphasis on *trawþe* and concluding that the poem represents a "medieval Christian mode of realism" (vii). In *The* Gawain-*Poet*, A. C. Spearing considers the cultural and literary milieus of the Cotton Nero A.x. poems, argues for their common authorship and examines each of the four poems, emphasizing structure and symbolism. Charles Moorman's *The* Pearl-*Poet*, in the Twayne English Authors Series, conforms to the well-known format of that series and provides a suitable introduction for students to the poem and to the critical issues surrounding it. Edward Wilson's slender volume *The* Gawain-*Poet* treats all four poems briefly, focusing the discussion about *Gawain* on games and their function and on the relation of romance and realism. W. A. Davenport also sees the poem as an antithesis of romance and realism, the ideal and the actual, in his recent work *The Art of the* Gawain-*Poet*. In *The Voice of the* Gawain-*Poet*, Lynn Staley Johnson concentrates on the poet's treatment of time, at once cyclic, degenerative, and regenerative. Two older works still deemed of value are Henry Lyttleton Savage's *The* Gawain-*Poet: Studies in His Personality and Background* (which associates the *Gawain* poet with the estates of Enguerrand de Coucy and which reprints in modified version Savage's seminal and much earlier "The Significance of the Hunting Scenes in *Sir Gawain and the Green Knight,*" on the symbolic links between the hunting and seduction scenes) and George Lyman Kittredge's *A Study of* Sir Gawain and the Green Knight, a pioneering source study. While not a full-length study, the segment on *Gawain* in A. C. Spearing's *Criticism and Medieval Poetry* provides an extended reading according to the methodology of the New Criticism.

Collections of Critical Essays

In the late 1960s three collections of critical essays with somewhat overlapping contents were compiled. Making readily available a number of seminal
articles, such collections are particularly convenient items to place on the
reserve shelf for student use. The most extensive of the three is *Critical
Studies of* Sir Gawain and the Green Knight, edited by Donald R. Howard
and Christian Zacher. Its twenty-three articles and excerpts from longer
critical works are arranged in five parts: introduction, "Critical Issues," "Style
and Technique," "Characters and Setting," and "Interpretations." Among
the key essays reprinted here are Morton W. Bloomfield's review of scholarship and criticism, "*Sir Gawain and the Green Knight*: An Appraisal"; C.
S. Lewis's "The Anthropological Approach," a response to John Speirs's
extreme mythological reading; Donald R. Howard's well-regarded "Structure and Symmetry in *Sir Gawain*," which is also reprinted in Fox and in
Blanch, Sir Gawain *and* Pearl; and Sacvan Bercovitch's genre study "Romance and Anti-Romance in *Sir Gawain and the Green Knight*." A sampling
of other entries includes Laura Hibbard Loomis on the relation of *Gawain*
to Celtic and other Arthurian literature, M Mills on Christian significance,
Larry Benson and Marie Borroff on style, Alain Renoir on sound patterns,
and John A. Burrow on *cupiditas*.

Denton Fox has prefaced his collection, *Twentieth Century Interpretations of* Sir Gawain and the Green Knight, with a brief introduction placing
Gawain in the context of late-fourteenth-century literature and providing
basic information on structure and theme. Part 1, "Interpretations," consists
of five articles including Dorothy Everett's "The Alliterative Revival," Gervase Mathew's "Ideals of Knighthood in Late-Fourteenth-Century England,"
B. J. Whiting's study of the character of Gawain as it appears throughout
romance tradition, John Speirs's highly controversial myth criticism, and
Donald R. Howard's "Structure and Symmetry." There are also excerpts
from three important longer works: Benson's *Art and Tradition in* Sir Gawain
and the Green Knight, Burrow's *A Reading of* Sir Gawain and the Green
Knight, and Borroff's Sir Gawain and the Green Knight: *A Stylistic and
Metrical Study*. Part 2, "View Points," contains brief commentaries from
Heinrich Zimmer, E. Talbot Donaldson, C. S. Lewis, A. C. Spearing, Cecily
Clark, and Ralph W. V. Elliott.

Designed primarily for undergraduate and graduate students, Robert J.
Blanch's critical anthology, Sir Gawain *and* Pearl: *Critical Essays*, contains
five essays on *Pearl* and six on *Sir Gawain*. In addition to Howard's "Structure
and Symmetry," Blanch selected John Burrow's "The Two Confession Scenes
in *Sir Gawain and the Green Knight*," which explores the penitential aspects

of the poem; Albert B. Friedman's "Morgan le Fay in *Sir Gawain and the Green Knight*," which concludes that Morgan le Fay's role of instigator is not well integrated into the narrative of the poem; Alan M. Markman's "The Meaning of *Sir Gawain and the Green Knight*," which focuses on the hero as a truly human figure rather than a symbolic one; Richard Hamilton Green's "Gawain's Shield and the Quest for Perfection," which investigates the symbolism of the pentangle; and Charles Moorman's "Myth and Medieval Literature: *Sir Gawain and the Green Knight*," which is largely a rebuttal of Speirs.

Reference Works

The recent publication of Malcolm Andrew's *The* Gawain-*Poet: An Annotated Bibliography, 1839-1977* has provided researchers with a convenient tool for approaching all the scholarship and criticism pertaining to ms. Cotton Nero A.x. that has accumulated since Frederic Madden published the first edition of *Syr Gawayne and the Grene Knyȝt* in 1839. This bibliography is comprehensive in its coverage of editions, translations, books, articles, and notes concerning any of the four poems and selective in its listing of reviews. It does not cover adaptations, children's books, records, tapes, or films, nor does it mention background works that do not specifically treat the Cotton Nero A.x. texts. Robert J. Blanch's bibliography, Sir Gawain and the Green Knight: *A Reference Guide*, also should prove to be a useful resource. Unlike Andrew's bibliography, its chronologically arranged entries include only interpretive or critical treatments of *Gawain*. The annotations tend to be fuller than Andrew's, generally giving the complete thrust of an author's argument. Other helpful features include a critical introduction discussing the manuscript, author, date, and dialect; an overview of recent research (1969-77) delineating critical trends and offering desiderata for further research; and a subject index (unavailable in Andrew). William Matthews's Goldentree bibliography, *Old and Middle English Literature*, provides a concise core listing useful to students. For access to background studies and works on topics related to *Gawain*, such as courtly love, the Alliterative Revival, and Arthurian romance, Walter H. Beale's selective bibliography, *Old and Middle English Poetry to 1500: A Guide to Information Sources*, supplies useful brief annotations, although it contains numerous inaccurate spellings and dates.

Current bibliographical information can, of course, be obtained from the *MLA International Bibliography*; the MHRA's *Annual Bibliography of English Language and Literature*; *The Year's Work in English Studies*, published by the English Association; the *Bibliographical Bulletin* of the

International Arthurian Society; and three interdisciplinary bibliographies: *International Guide to Medieval Studies, The International Medieval Bibliography*, and the *Quarterly Checklist of Medievalia*. Middle English research in progress can be found in *Neuphilologische Mitteilungen*.

Older works on Arthurian literature are accessible in John J. Parry and Margaret Schlauch's two-volume *Arthurian Bibliography* and in the serial bibliography of Arthurian critical literature covering the period from 1936 to 1962 in *Modern Language Quarterly* (1940-63). Recently published is a two-volume annotated bibliography, *Arthurian Legend and Literature*, compiled by Edmund Reiss, Lillian Horner Reiss, and Beverly Taylor. Volume 1 is devoted to the Middle Ages, and volume 2 to the period from the Renaissance to the present. "Twentieth-Century Arthurian Literature: An Annotated Bibliography," compiled by Mary Wildman, can be found in *Arthurian Literature II*, edited by Richard Barber. C. E. Pickford and R. W. Last have published volume 1, the author listing, of *The Arthurian Bibliography*, with entries through 1978; they plan to update at five-year intervals. *Quondam et Futurus: Newsletter for Arthurian Studies* (1980-   ), edited by Mildred L. Day, publishes calls for papers, abstracts of conference papers, authors' queries, brief pedagogical notes, and annotated bibliographies of new books. It can be ordered from Day at 2212 Pinehurst Drive, Gardendale, AL 35071.

Perhaps the greatest obstacle to the understanding and appreciation of *Gawain* is the difficult and unfamiliar dialect of the Northwest Midlands in which it is written. In addition to the notes and glossaries of the various editions of the poem, instructors seeking further information on the *Gawain* poet's lexicon can consult the *Oxford English Dictionary* (*OED*) and the *Middle English Dictionary* (*MED*). The latter, edited by Hans Kurath, Sherman M. Kuhn, and others, is being issued by the University of Michigan Press; currently (spring 1985) entries through *red-* are available. Two useful general histories of the English language that can be recommended to students wanting an overview of Middle English are Albert C. Baugh and Thomas Cable, *A History of the English Language*, and Thomas Pyles and John Algeo, *Origins and Development of the English Language*. Detailed discussion of Middle English phonology, morphology, syntax, and dialect can be found in Fernand Mossé's *A Handbook of Middle English*, which contains two excerpts from *Gawain* and one from *Pearl*, together with notes on their dialect and meter; and a treatment of Middle English phonology as it relates to the study of Middle English dialect, including the dialect of the *Gawain* poet, appears in Richard Jordan's *Handbook of Middle English Grammar: Phonology*. James P. Oakden also discusses dialect matters in his *Alliterative Poetry in Middle English: The Dialectal and Metrical Survey*, as does Charles Jones's *An Introduction to Middle English*. Norman Blake's

The English Language in Medieval Literature applies a knowledge of Middle English to the appreciation of literature.

Basic information on the plot, sources, and bibliography of *Sir Gawain and the Green Knight*, as well as on other Middle English romances featuring Sir Gawain, can be found in Helaine Newstead's chapter on Arthurian legends in volume 1 of Severs and Hartung's *Manual of the Writings in Middle English*, while volume 2 of the *Manual* contains Marie P. Hamilton's comments on the other three poems of ms. Cotton Nero A.x.

Other useful reference works include Barnet Kottler and Alan M. Markman's *Concordance to Five Middle English Poems:* Cleanness, St. Erkenwald, Sir Gawain and the Green Knight, Patience, Pearl; Robert W. Ackerman's *Index of the Arthurian Names in Middle English*; Charles Moorman and Ruth Moorman's *An Arthurian Dictionary*; and Coolidge Chapman's *An Index of Names in* Pearl, Purity, Patience *and* Gawain.

For surveys of past scholarship and research see Morton Bloomfield's "*Sir Gawain*," Robert W. Ackerman's "Middle English Literature to 1400," Donald R. Howard's "*Sir Gawain and the Green Knight*," and John H. Fisher's segment of *The Present State of Scholarship in Fourteenth Century Literature*, edited by Thomas D. Cooke, which surveys scholarship since 1962.

A monumental new reference work, *Dictionary of the Middle Ages*, edited by Joseph R. Strayer, began to appear in 1982. This set, when complete, will provide concise, authoritative entries on all aspects of medieval history and culture and will doubtless become a favorite starting point for student research.

Aids to Teaching

More than half the survey respondents report using some type of aid in teaching *Sir Gawain and the Green Knight*. Most frequently the aids consist of architectural slides (often made during the instructors' visits to England), slides or facsimiles of illuminated manuscripts (especially the *Très riches heures du duc de Berry*, the *Livre de chasse* of Gaston Phoebus, the *Luttrell Psalter*, and ms. Cotton Nero A.x.), diagrams (e.g., of the pentangle), maps (drawn on the board or copied onto handouts), and recordings of readings of the poems and of medieval music. Those who are fortunate in their location suggest field trips to museums with good collections of medieval art, the Cloisters in New York City being, of course, outstanding.

While no complete guide to audiovisual aids on medieval topics exists, instructors may find some useful information in Frederick E. Danker's article "Teaching Medieval Literature: Texts, Recordings, and Techniques." The *Schwann Record and Tape Guide*, published monthly, gives access to pertinent recordings. Of the recorded readings of *Gawain*, the most popular, Jess B. Bessinger and Marie Borroff's *Dialogues from Sir Gawain and the Green Knight*, is now available only on cassette. Charles W. Dunn reads excerpts from *Sir Gawain and the Green Knight* in *Early English Poetry*, and Jess B. Bessinger does likewise on Diane Bornstein's *A History of the English Language: A Discourse with Illustrative Passages*. Finally, a number of instructors use a tape made by Paul Piehler (Language Laboratory, Univ. of California, Berkeley), which is not available commercially. Because of the renewed interest in early music, quite a bit of medieval instrumental and vocal music, both secular and religious, has been recorded. Among the recordings mentioned as relevant to a study of *Gawain* (not all of which are currently available) are *A Medieval Christmas*; *Of Glad Tidings*; *The Medieval Sound*; *The Pleasure of the Royal Courts*; *Carols and Motets for the Nativity*; *Music of the Middle Ages*; *Instruments of the Middle Ages and Renaissance*; *Music of the Hundred Years War*; *In a Medieval Garden*; *Medieval Roots*; *Seraphim Guide to Renaissance Music*, an excellent survey of music from the thirteenth to the seventeenth centuries; *Music from the Court of Burgundy*; Guillaume Dufay (b. 1400), *Messensätze, Motetten und Hymnen*; *Music of the Early Middle Ages*; *Music of the Late Middle Ages and Renaissance*; *The Ars Nova*; and *Medieval English Lyrics*, which is of particular pedagogical interest because it contains many of the frequently anthologized Middle English lyrics, as well 'as the song Nicholas is said to sing so sweetly" in the Miller's Tale. For further information on recordings of medieval music, see *The Listener's Guide to Medieval and Renaissance Music*, by Derrick Henry.

Because the *Gawain* poet and Chaucer were contemporaries, books like Roger Sherman Loomis's *A Mirror of Chaucer's World* and Maurice Hussey's *Chaucer's World: A Pictorial Companion*, with their copious illustrations of life in late fourteenth-century England, would also be beneficial to students reading *Gawain*.

Although they have apparently not found their way into classrooms as yet, the University of Toronto Media Centre has an excellent series of videotapes available for rent or purchase. While none of their medieval titles, prepared with the University of Toronto Centre for Medieval Studies and the Poculi Ludique Societas, is specifically on *Gawain*, a number provide useful background: *The Fifteen Joys of Marriage* (an examination of medieval attitudes toward women), *King Arthur: From Romance to Archaeology*, *To Syngen and to Playe: Music and Instruments in Chaucer's Day*, *The Making of a Manuscript*, and particularly *Ceremony and Allegory of the Hunt in Late Medieval Europe*. Complete catalogs and ordering information can be obtained from the Distribution Office, Media Centre, University of Toronto, 121 Saint George Street, Toronto, Ontario, Canada M5S 1A1. Other helpful videotape presentations would be "The Great Thaw" and "Romance and Reality" from Kenneth Clark's BBC series *Civilisation*.

Further information on teaching aids and other pedagogical matters may be found in *Studies in Medieval and Renaissance Teaching* (*SMART*), published by the English Department, Central Missouri State University, and in Suzanne H. MacRae's pedagogical essay "The End Is the Beginning: *Sir Gawain and the Green Knight*."

Finally, many theatrical films with Arthurian or otherwise medieval subject matter could be used to stimulate student involvement in *Gawain*. This can prove a particularly good technique because of the poem's emphasis on visual imagery and the poet's almost cinematic treatment of the imagery. (For a discussion of the cinematic qualities of *Gawain* see Alain Renoir's "Descriptive Technique in *Sir Gawain and the Green Knight*.") These films range from such old-fashioned Hollywood epics as Richard Thorpe's *Knights of the Round Table*, Tay Garnett's *The Black Knight*, and Cornel Wilde's *Sword of Lancelot* to Garnett's version (the third) of Twain's *A Connecticut Yankee in King Arthur's Court* (starring Bing Crosby) to two very different adaptations of T. H. White's *Once and Future King*—the Disney cartoon *The Sword in the Stone*, directed by Wolfgang Reitherman, and the lavish musical *Camelot*, directed by Joshua Logan—to Terry Gilliam and Terry Jones's zany *Monty Python and the Holy Grail*. Of perhaps greater pedagogical interest would be Robert Bresson's *Lancelot du Lac*, Eric Rohmer's adaptation of Chrétien de Troyes's *Perceval*, John Boorman's popular *Excalibur*, and of course Ingmar Bergman's classic *The Seventh Seal*, an English translation of which is available in the Modern Film Scripts series. Although several respondents seemed to have dim recall of a film treatment of *Gawain*, having in some cases heard of a cartoon version, research was not able to confirm these rumors. The poem, however, practically cries out for dramatization, and perhaps such a film will one day be made.

Part Two

APPROACHES

INTRODUCTION

Surprised by Subtlety: A Survey of the Teaching of *Sir Gawain and the Green Knight*

Jane Chance

The enthusiastic response to *Gawain* by a student in my sophomore survey this fall surprised me: despite her initial trepidation about taking the course, she liked the poem so much that she had been reading aloud especially interesting passages to her bemused roommates. What is it about this complex and very medieval romance that prompts such a response? Perhaps its complexity and subtlety make it a pleasant game, a puzzle to work out, a Cracker-Jack box of surprises. The bursting in of the Green Knight, the lady's offering herself up secretly to her bed-bound (and vow-bound) but astonished guest, the oafishness of Gawain and the gentility of the Green Knight at the unmasking near the Green Chapel—these elements make it fun. Do the hero and his court realize the significance, if any, of his fall? Is it matter for laughter or matter for penance? This puzzle of a poem both perplexes and fascinates student and teacher.

The major purpose of this book is to distill this heady poem through the alembic of pedagogy. Understanding more of its backgrounds can only increase one's pleasure in reading and teaching it. Hence the volume focuses on pedagogy rather than interpretation (the latter can be pursued at length in the many articles, books, and bibliographies associated with this much-studied poem) and studiously avoids taking critical sides. Thus it hopes to respond to the need articulated so well by William F. Pollard:

For those of us who have taught *Gawain* and Chaucer for a number of years, the volume might touch upon how to "translate" the poet's vision of the world and man's response to its challenges in such a way as to capture the attention of the business major who may never again have the opportunity to reflect upon the value of literature. . . . It is often all too easy for us medievalists to be carried along with our own enthusiasm without communicating the sources and mechanics of that enthusiasm to the students. *Gawain* presents the teacher with an early opportunity in the survey course to demonstrate the richness of literature, the necessity of a comparative approach, and the virtue of what Keats called "negative capability." Here is a chance, two weeks or so into the course, to demonstrate the intrinsic value of an idea—living with and modifying hypotheses.

In this introduction I examine the issues related to the teaching of *Gawain* that were specifically discussed by the respondents to the Modern Language Association questionnaire. The information derived from this survey offers an interesting picture of how *Gawain* is actually taught today at both the undergraduate and graduate levels. Section I describes the courses in which it is taught, focusing specifically on other medieval and modern literary, historical, and religious works with which it is frequently taught; section II treats various classroom aspects of teaching the poem—the amount of time devoted to it in a semester, the apportionment of that time, and key issues and problem areas noted in its teaching; and section III outlines examination and paper questions and other project assignments that respondents felt tested and probed the key issues involved in teaching the poem. This composite description of approaches to teaching *Gawain* provides an appropriate context for the descriptions of various individual approaches that follow, an outline of which occupies section IV.

1. Teaching Gawain with Other Works

Although most responses to the questionnaire derived from the experience of teaching the work to undergraduates, one-fifth of the respondents described graduate surveys or seminars. In another encouraging sign for medievalists, one-sixth of the replies described undergraduate or dual-level (mixed undergraduate and graduate) surveys in Middle English or medieval English literature, and nearly one-sixth described courses in Arthurian or medieval romance. About a tenth focused on more specialized approaches in upper-division undergraduate courses: literary theory, literary schools (alliterative poetry), comparative literature (introduction to medieval studies), and special topics (thematic, generic, or individual-figure courses). It is not surprising that nearly a third of the questionnaires listed the introductory or sophomore survey of English literature for majors and nonmajors as the lower-division course most likely to teach *Gawain*. Finally, a handful of thematic freshman composition and literature courses (The Quest, The Hero, Fantasy, etc.), as well as a few world literature courses, rounded out the lower-division grouping of the survey.

The works taught in conjunction with *Gawain*, usually works of literature, divide chiefly into two categories—medieval and modern.

A. Medieval Works

In response to the question "If you teach other medieval works in conjunction with *Gawain*, state which, and how each enhances understanding of *Gawain*," respondents offered both conventional and unconventional answers, but even the conventional answers were often accompanied by unusual explanations. Teachers generally agreed with the response of John Ganim:

> I'm afraid I'd slightly reverse the question. *Gawain* tends to disrupt the flow of most of the courses it is placed in. It by no means fits into an Arthurian course as neatly as it seems—it tends rather to question the basis of most of the texts it is read against, although Chrétien perhaps best illuminates the art of the poet.

That is, as a work that shatters and inverts the medieval literary conventions, *Gawain* itself often sheds light on more conventional (and frequently less interesting) works. The poem has been taught to advantage with Arthurian materials, medieval romances, and other medieval and Renaissance masterpieces (such as the *Canterbury Tales* and *Piers Plowman*) that often appear in upper-division and sophomore surveys.

1. Arthurian Materials and Romances

In relation to the Arthurian matter that *Gawain* shares with other works, several types of literature illuminate the poem when taught concurrently. To demonstrate the continuity and transformation of the British tradition, instructors find useful not only the Arthurian pseudohistories (like Geoffrey of Monmouth's history of the kings of England) but also the Irish, Celtic, Welsh, and French analogues of the poem (e.g., those in Elisabeth Brewer). Specifically helpful suggestions include "The Vision of Sir Launfal," "Pwyll" (from the Welsh *Mabinogion*), and "The Feast of Bricriu." Other Arthurian materials by Chrétien, chiefly *Perceval*, emphasize the differences between the French and English views of Gawain. One explanation for the use of these Arthurian materials is presented by Sherron Knopp:

> I use Chrétien and the *Mabinogion* to illustrate the kinds of Celtic magic that find their way into Arthurian romance. Chrétien also provides a paradigm for courtliness and chivalry as well as romance plot structure. Gottfried von Strassburg illustrates one kind of transformation or development of the Chrétien model, and he introduces students to the possibilities of satire and parody in romance. Next to these works, I want students to see how stunning and unique *Gawain* is on every count—in the "magic" of the Green Knight, in the witty sophistication of its courtly and chivalric ethos, in the depth of its irony, and in the dazzling coherent compactness of its form.

Gawain is also taught in conjunction with other, frequently non-Arthurian romances, chiefly the native English *King Horn*, *Havelock the Dane*, and *Sir Orfeo*. Here the purpose in conjoining the works centers more on form—genre, in fact—than on content, as was the case with the Arthurian materials, but indeed,

> This allows for a sharp contrast in both form and content; students can easily see a developing tradition in the English romances, and are able to evaluate the contributions of the *Gawain*-Poet, especially in terms of his movement away from episodic, repetitive, formulaic structures, towards greater narrative concentration and the use of extensive description.   (A. J. Colaianne)

What students discover in this developing romance tradition is in Colaianne's phrase the "decomposition of the Arthurian romance," exemplified by *The Wedding of Sir Gawain and Dame Ragnell* and by Malory's "Book of Balin" or his treatment of Gawain. In addition, Malory, Chrétien (especially *Yvain*), and even *The Romance of the Rose* help define romance characteristics and in tandem with, say, the "Book of Balin," demonstrate the moral uncertainty of the romance hero. Such romances illustrate in different, frequently conflicting ways how the romance preoccupation with chivalric loyalty or courtly behavior pertains to love and courtesy. For Lauren Lepow, "the similar conflict in *Gawain* thereby becomes not only clearer, but also can be seen as an inevitality of the romance world." In a related approach to the romance's conventions, Katharina M. Wilson, who teaches a course in world literature, uses *Aucassin and Nicolette* and Marie de France's *Yonec* and *Lanval* as alternative literary models to the courtly-knight ideal and "to [the knight's] ornamental appendix, the courtly lady." By using these less conventional examples of courtly love, Wilson emphasizes *Gawain*'s inversions of such roles as lover/beloved, giver/receiver, action/reaction, and initiator/follower.

2. Other Medieval Works

In surveys of medieval literature, *Gawain* is taught as both part of a particular unit and part of an entire course with a thematic bias. Some instructors teach it either with other works of the *Gawain* poet or with *Piers Plowman*, not only to contrast the social consciousness of Langland with the "formalist" view of the *Gawain* poet but also to better illuminate the larger literary context of the Alliterative Revival. Others teach all the works of the *Gawain* poet to show how "medieval" *Gawain* is and to show—through style, theme, and imagery—either the common authorship of all his works (including *St. Erkenwald*) or variations in his subject and technique. One example of an unusual medieval English course is taught by Penelope Doob, who perceives *Gawain* as an example of Ricardian poetry that, with the *Canterbury Tales*, shares the values, techniques, and literary preoccupations of that age.

Two additional examples of how *Gawain* and Chaucer mesh: the *Book of the Duchess* shares *Gawain*'s concern with the problem of courtesy, the *Franklin's Tale* its concern with a definition of *gentilesse* or *trawþe* and with the "rash promise" topos. When *Gawain* is compared more broadly with other works, the theme of chivalry becomes more important—not only in *Beowulf* but also in the jousting-of-Jesus episode from *Piers* (passus 19, B-text), the Wife of Bath's Tale, and the "Piteous Tale of the Morte Arthur," in Malory. *Gawain* is also taught with Dante, Chaucer, and *Everyman* as a "lesson" book.

Other non-English medieval works with which *Gawain* is compared include Augustine's *Confessions*, on the dangers of seduction by worldly things, and Dante's *Inferno* and *Paradiso*, for an "interior, allegorical version of a spiritual quest which *Gawain* presents more literally" (Anne Howland Schotter).

In the sophomore survey, *Gawain* is frequently coupled with *Beowulf* or Chaucer, especially if the approach depends on a "masterpieces" focus. *Beowulf* provides parallels with *Gawain* through their common emphasis on history and genealogy at the beginnings of the poems, and Gawain himself has elements of both the epic hero Beowulf and the romance hero. An interesting progression from *Beowulf* through *Gawain* to Spenser traces variations on the *sapientia et fortitudo* motif. Changing attitudes toward women can be compared in *Beowulf*, Chaucer, and Shakespeare. One advantage for the students of the comparison with Chaucer is that "Chaucer opened them to the possibilities of humor in an age they imagine as dominated by a somber Church. . . . They could also compare two very different treatments of a Gawain-character [the other appears in the Wife of Bath's Tale]. And they were prepared to question the roles (sexual and social) of the characters" (Barbara Eckstein).

Several innovative thematic courses offer new perspectives on this poem by using a traditional medieval context. Clia Doty Goodwin has taught two courses in the humanities division, "Work and Play—The Game in Earnest" and "Fate and Freedom." In the former she teaches *Gawain* with the Wake-field *Noah* and the *Second Shepherds' Play:* "The focus will be on the in-terweaving of work and play: the guilds' involvement, the representations of work, and the comedy in the plays; the varieties of 'game' in *Gawain*, chivalry as the work of a knight, and the seriousness underneath the lightness of each." In the "Fate and Freedom" course she teaches *Gawain* along with *The Ruin, The Battle of Maldon, The Wanderer,* and *Njal's Saga.* Another unconventional perspective is Jane Chance's course on J. R. R. Tolkien, in which *Gawain* is taught in conjunction with *Beowulf* and *The Battle of Maldon* to demonstrate the differences between the heroic and chivalric ages as defined by Tolkien in his essay "Ofermod" (19-24 of *The Homecoming of Beorhtnoth Beorhthelm's Son* in *The Tolkien Reader*) and used in his three-decker novel *The Lord of the Rings.*

B. Modern Works

Question 9 asked respondents, "If you teach modern works in conjunction with *Gawain*, state which and how each enhances understanding of *Gawain*." Most courses in which *Gawain* and modern works are read can be summed up as thematic courses, whether freshman composition and literature or upper-division courses in fantasy and literary criticism.

1. Science Fiction and Fantasy

Modern literary works with which *Gawain* is taught range from science fiction works like *The Lathe of Heaven* or *Lilith* (used for comparing the generic properties and epistemology of *Gawain*) to works of contemporary fantasy like Tolkien's *Hobbit, Lord of the Rings,* and *Farmer Giles of Ham* or Richard Adams's *Watership Down* (used for revealing moral conflicts in a fantastic world). Often the heroic quest and hero in *Gawain* are compared to those of such modern films as *Star Wars* and *E.T.*, which, according to Sherron Knopp, provide

> a wonderful way to get students to imagine and visualize Gawain's extraordinary encounter with the Green Knight. At the same time I also try to get them to see how much more subtle, sophisticated, and ultimately satisfying the tensions and moral questions are in the me-dieval work and to break down any stereotypes they have about the Middle Ages as a period of deadening didacticism on moral issues.

Other works of fantasy with which instructors compare *Gawain* include the following, taught by Clia Dody Goodwin: Peter Beagle's *The Last Unicorn*, Lewis Carroll's *Alice's Adventures in Wonderland*, Kafka's *Metamorphosis*, C.S. Lewis's *Perelandra*, Kurt Vonnegut's *Sirens of Titan* (plus one volume of Ursula LeGuin's trilogy A *Wizard of Earthsea*, *The Tombs of Atuan*, and *The Farthest Shore*).

Why are such works so helpful in elucidating *Gawain?* They make the poem seem relevant: if the modern student insists that the world of this poem is alien, then it might be profitably compared with the image of the other world promulgated by Lewis in his essay "On Science Fiction," to suggest a fantastic creation similar to that of Lewis in *Perelandra* or of Frank Herbert in the *Dune* series—even of Doris Lessing in her most recent fiction or of John Barth in *Chimera*. A student, like Lewis, might come to see even the *Commedia* in its exploration of the physical and moral cosmos as "science fiction" and, like J. R. R. Tolkien, to see the Gospel, in its creation of a secondary world with its own laws and colors and ending happily with the Resurrection, as "fantasy."

2. Modern Adaptations

Works that translate or adapt medieval stories into modern guise can offer a provocative context in which to examine *Gawain*. Penelope Doob confesses that

> I have occasionally taught *Gawain* in conjunction with Fowles' *The Magus*, and always talk about the two together: similar "God-games," moral preoccupations, *bildungsromans*, structural elaboration, focus on process, link of reader and narrator or hero, meaning that we discover just as the hero does despite our being intentionally misled.

Another work with which the romance is compared for parallels and contrasts, especially in relation to the character of the hero, is John Fowles's *The Ebony Tower*.

Arthurian literature courses frequently compare *Gawain* with other modern Arthurian adaptations by Matthew Arnold, Alfred Lord Tennyson, William Morris, Algernon Charles Swinburne, Mark Twain, John Masefield, E. A. Robinson, James Russell Lowell, T. H. White, C. S. Lewis, Richard Monaco, and many others. "The perfection that Gawain sought is still being sought or is being despaired of," declares Judith Bronfman. One might also note in these works the continuing literary interest of medieval romantic themes. A particularly apt comparison between Gawain in *Sir Gawain and the Green Knight* (also the knight in Chaucer's *Wife of Bath's Tale*) and in Thomas Berger's *Arthur Rex* reveals the degeneracy of the modern age. For William F. Pollard, a comparison of *Gawain* with Tennyson's *Idylls of the*

King, Twain's *Connecticut Yankee*, and White's *Once and Future King* yields fascinating results about identity and the self:

> We explore the impact of the Arthurian matter upon modern English and American perceptions of the self—we also consider the extent to which the *Gawain*-Poet has an ironic perspective lacking in modern renditions of the material and the multilayered complexity of his early critique—whether or not the Hony Soit belongs at the end!

On the matter of romance and the form in which it exists today, some teachers turn to the gothic romance, in both its eighteenth- and nineteenth- and its twentieth-century incarnations, and to the soap opera. Others compare *Gawain* either with a picaresque novel such as *Huckleberry Finn* or *Joseph Andrews* or with a modern example of the romance such as *The Hobbit*.

3. Other Modern Works

Finally, *Gawain* is also frequently compared with modern works whose subject matter is neither fantastic nor Arthurian and whose form is not romance. The topics of comparison center on form and genre or on themes relating to the hero, the quest, the tension between Christian and pagan. To examine the hero in modern exemplars such as Joseph Conrad's *Lord Jim*, Emily Brontë's Heathcliff (*Wuthering Heights*), Arthur Miller's Willy Loman (*Death of a Salesman*), and Kurt Vonnegut's Billy Pilgrim (*Slaughterhouse Five*) allows students to see Gawain as a precursor of the antihero. In another unusual combination, Esther C. Quinn considers *Gawain* with Harold Pinter's *Birthday Party* for the idea of "menace as challenge, antihero and semi-hero." Along the same lines, in a course on rites of passage, Peggy A. Knapp compares Gawain's maturation with that of Stephen Daedalus in James Joyce's *Portrait of the Artist as a Young Man* and that of Daniel in E. L. Doctorow's *The Book of Daniel*. She explains, "Conflict with a father figure (even with Arthur, if you read the ending a certain way) binds the three together, and so does the plight of the youthful hero whose standards are higher than those of his society in general and particularly those he is answerable to." The quest theme is also used for comparison in works like Conrad's *Heart of Darkness*, Joyce's *Portrait of the Artist*, and T. S. Eliot's *The Waste Land*. Hermann Hesse's *Narcissus and Goldmund* is taught with *Gawain* to demonstrate the tension between the Christian and the courtly (or Christian and pagan) ideals.

In relation to the literary questions of form and genre, Gail A. Berkeley uses Tennyson's *Idylls of the King* and Eliot's *The Waste Land* "to raise questions about conventionality in modern literature, and hence to return to the *Gawain*-Poet's unique rereading of the given *matière*, and the continuity of the English tradition." Walter S. Phelan teaches *Gawain* in conjunction with John M. Synge's *Playboy of the Western World* and Eliot's *Murder in the Cathedral* to illustrate the contrast between comedy and tragedy together with the idea of martyrdom.

II. Classroom Aspects of Teaching Gawain

We asked respondents the following questions about their teaching:

- How much class time do you spend on *Gawain*, and how do you apportion this time?
- In terms of your course objectives, what do you consider to be the key issues involved in teaching *Gawain*?
- What aspects of the poem do you find most difficult to deal with in class?

A. Allocation and Apportionment of Class Time

The specialized undergraduate course or graduate seminar studying the work in the original requires an average of three to four weeks, with "one week" defined as three fifty-minute classes, although the extremes range from two two-hour sessions to eight weeks. The undergraduate survey course studying the work in translation requires on average one and a half to two weeks, although extremes range from one day in an introductory survey to five weeks for a specialized course doing close reading.

   To teach the poem respondents rely on a variety of methods ranging from complete lecture to complete discussion. Generally respondents commence with a lecture on the background of the poem (for example, the Alliterative Revival or the Arthurian legends) and then proceed with discussions, close reading, and/or translation, often selecting only problem passages if time is short. One example of an unusual lecture approach, dominated by a cultural and scientific context looking back to the past and forward to the future, is that used by Louis Brewer Hall:

> I always contrast *Gawain* with what went before. *Gawain* is an ideal account of another world. I use slides of Romanesque art and compare it with fourteenth century art, then look ahead to the fifteenth century and the development of scientific perspective. In survey I have stressed the influence of the *Aeneid* way of story telling (idealized characters, setting, story, where divine direction has become magic), and ordinary, everyday details of living are excluded. I stress *Gawain* as an alternate way of story telling whose techniques have survived in science fiction (Ursula LeGuin, Steinbeck, for two).

One example of the Socratic method is used by Carl Lindahl in a world literature course to reveal, first, the romance's literary and artistic backgrounds and, second, its folkloric underpinnings.

> After using *The Song of Roland* as an example of medieval epic, to highlight the concepts of feudalism and literary symmetry, and some medieval lyrics (e.g., "Qui Amore Langueo") to illustrate how religious devotion, feudalism and courtly love were combined metaphorically in art, I discuss the idea of romance with the students. I point out the major differences between romance and epic (e.g., the former's fiction of historicity; the two sides of heroism, courage and courtesy; fantastic elements; happy endings). Then I ask the students, for the next class, to look for symmetry in *Gawain*, to tell me if it has a happy ending, and to explain the connection between the two tests.

On the second day, Lindahl delves finally into the folkloric patterns:

> During the next day's discussion, after the structure is detailed, I ask if Gawain is a true romance hero, if he has passed the tests, and what was the true nature of each test (could the beheading game be a test of courtesy disguised as a test of bravery? Could the bedchamber scenes be a test of bravery disguised as a test of courtesy? Etc.) Then I ask the students to consider *Gawain* as a conflict between nature and culture and to explain what the Green Knight symbolizes. We discuss mumming traditions, May Day ceremonialism, and the solstice/Yule. We end by discussing the blending of comic and serious elements, by way of prologue to the General Prologue of the *Canterbury Tales*.

B. Key Issues in Teaching *Gawain*

Responses to the question "In terms of your course objectives, what do you consider to be the key issues involved in teaching *Gawain*?" reveal the undergraduate teacher as chiefly interested in describing adequately the poem's backgrounds and then, through a variety of pedagogical methods, stressing its literary issues—its narrative episodes, characterizations, themes, and artistry.

1. The Backgrounds

The main subjects covered in teaching the backgrounds to the poem fall under the rubrics of medieval culture and genre. What is most difficult to explain is how medieval culture differs from modern culture, what Miriam

Y. Miller terms the "alterity of the late Middle Ages." The poem is often taught as an exemplary work of medieval literature in its use of chivalry and courtly love, sin and repentance, didacticism and entertainment, and thus as "a fine compendium of medieval custom, attitude, belief, fear, hope" (Thomas Wright). Instructors discuss these and such other matters as social attitudes of the late Middle Ages, aristocratic life, tournaments, clothing and ornaments, and architecture.

Genre is the second main background subject. As romance, *Gawain* is placed within either the French and English Arthurian romance tradition or the more general English romance tradition. Occasionally it is analyzed as both epic and romance and placed within both traditions, that is, studied for its transformation of Irish epic material into courtly French and English material. Within the romance tradition, students can see how Gawain compared with Yvain, Tristan, Perceval. Generally, topics central to the romance—subject and structure, the quest and temptations, the "indoor/outdoor" or "inner (ethical)/outer (active)" dichotomy (as one respondent described it)—are compared to see how the *Gawain* poet has reworked conventional material.

Many instructors place the poem against the background of late medieval English literature—for example, how the work contrasts in values and style with a similarly alliterative work like *Piers Plowman* or with the homiletic poems *Pearl*, *Purity*, and *Patience* by the same author. Some also discuss the poet himself (was he a cleric?), the manuscript (why only one?), and the language (dialect, prosody, meter).

2. Literary Issues

In addition to teaching the cultural, social, and literary backgrounds of the poem, instructors also focus on more conventionally literary issues—narrative episodes, characterization, themes, and artistry. A major issue, especially in lower-division courses, is the literal comprehension of narrative episodes—the plot. Upper-level courses are more concerned with the relation and meaning of the beginning and ending and with events at the castle, the journey, the three hunts, the three temptations, and the Green Chapel meeting.

Since narrative reveals characterization, instructors focus particularly on Gawain, although they often include discussions of Arthur, Bertilak, the lady, Morgan le Fay, and the guide. On the most general level, Gawain's psychological development as a hero—for Nancy Patricia Pope, this is the "untying of Gawain's 'perfect knot' "—attracts greatest attention. Ultimately, Gawain's chief problem as a man is mortality, a conclusion summed up eloquently by Jack Selzer:

Gawain confronts and learns to accept his own mortality; he learns that he too is a part of the natural world—mutable, subject to time, imperfect, *green*. Sure, this is a Christian poem; but it's also supremely human. His "sins" ("cowardice and covetousness") are not just against God but against his own humanity. By taking the girdle (the magic delusion that we don't have to face limits) Gawain shows that he covets life over death; he refuses to acknowledge his own humanity.

As a romance hero, Gawain is also compared with other Gawains (as are Guenore, Arthur, and Morgan with their counterparts). How good is he? Is he behaving as the best representative of the Round Table should behave? How does his behavior compare with that of the knights of Malory or Chrétien? Do knights of romance normally encounter challenges—and opponents—like those of Gawain? Are Bertilak and his lady good or bad, and why is this question hard to answer? Why do the reactions of Gawain and the court differ so at the end? What does this tell us about knighthood at the end of the fourteenth century?

The third key issue is theme, divided by one respondent into "the three magics of Morgan, romance, and Christianity" or, loosely, into the Celtic, Arthurian, and Christian themes. Celtic, fairy, and supernatural themes include fate, play (games, rules, competition, joy, magic, myth, ritual, festival), art as a means of combating death, the impossible. Arthurian themes encompass truth telling and loyalty (*trawþe*), feudal ideals, Camelot's fatal flaw, the heroic ideal (especially when, in a world literature course, the work is contrasted with, say, the *Odyssey*), courtly love, the conflict between chivalry and courtly love, legal issues. Christian themes focus on mortality, appropriate Christian behavior, *amor Dei*, the conflict between the ideal and real in human experience, sin, and repentance.

But what many instructors consider more important than any one of these categories of thematic issues is the poem's attempt to juxtapose the values involved in all three, showing how religious, social, and moral codes impinge on and affect the individual. Which is more important, courtly love or *amor Dei*? Chivalry or courtly love? *Caritas* or *cupiditas*? Penitential or national aims? The poem's ambivalence and ambiguity and the shifting identities of its characters trouble undergraduate students and interest their instructors. In this the poem reflects a Gothic vision, according to William F. Pollard: "The subtle layering of Celtic, Arthurian, and Christian themes reflect off each other like the vision Gawain has of Hautdesert itself. The key issue is to view these three forces as competing for the attention of the reader no less than for Gawain."

The fourth and final issue involved in teaching the poem, especially in upper-division courses, is its artistry. Structure, use of variation and symmetry, imagery, allegory, symbolism (color, number, animal, pentangle), wordplay, wit, sophisticated tone, style, humor, complexity—all are revealed through a close reading of the poem.

C. Problem Areas in Teaching *Gawain*

Is it possible to communicate any of the delightfulness of the poem to a potentially hostile or alienated audience? The respondents' problems in teaching *Gawain* centered on authority, not so much in the pedagogical and social issues of the instructor's authority as on the authority of the text. When we asked instructors, "What aspects of the poem do you find most difficult to deal with in class?," they responded that four areas, listed in descending order, pose the greatest difficulty—language, medieval backgrounds, narrative and thematic aspects, and poetic form. When *Gawain* is taught in the original, language creates obvious problems because of the poem's Northwest Midlands dialect. The medieval backgrounds of the poem, however, create problems whether the poem is taught in the original or in translation.

Understanding the poem, students quickly learn, requires help with some medieval social concepts: courtly love, as it defines the love relation between knight and lady; the chivalric code, as it defines the political relation between knight and lord; and religion, especially medieval Catholicism, as it defines the moral relation between the human soul and God. But more specific aspects of these three cultural and literary assumptions of the Middle Ages also proved problematic. Listed in order of difficulty, they encompass the medieval "interpenetration of religious and secular values"; the position of the poem in the Arthurian tradition; its Christian values (symbolic and typological background, importance of Christianity and the medieval Church); the relation between courtly-love conventions and real life (especially the stylized behavior of the characters); customs (sport, games, *luf-talkyng*); medieval history (or at least a sufficiently profound sense of the historical context of Gawain's adventures); what Katharina Wilson labels the "idea of chance or random adventure; the mingling of religious, military, courtly, supernatural, and fairy-tale elements"; and, finally, medieval aesthetic theory.

Lois Roney offers one example of how the biblical background can resolve ambiguity in the antifeminist passage that occurs in the fourth fitt during the meeting near the Green Chapel. Gawain rather churlishly notes that it is no wonder he has fallen, since Adam, Samson, Solomon, and David also fell at the hands of a woman. Roney explains, "this is another instance of the wonderful medieval buck-passing topos—according to the Bible and standard interpretations of it, each of the four men is guilty, but the four women here are presented in order of increasing innocence, culminating

with Bathsheba, and who could be more innocent?" These are the terms of
the poem, the tools necessary to break its code, a priori definitions of a
world and a culture very different from ours. But students rapidly assimilate
those definitions and can ignore the differences between *Gawain*'s social,
sexual, and cultural values and their own in learning to enjoy this alien
poem.

Narrative and thematic aspects also create some problems. Simple comprehension of plot represents a hurdle for some students, particularly in
lower-division introductory courses for non–liberal arts majors. Episodes
causing particular difficulty include the introductory stanza, with its bits of
classical history and legend, and the ending (Why was Morgan le Fay involved? Was the Green Knight acting independently? What was the Green
Chapel? What was the motivation for the Green Knight's rule? How was
Bertilak the Green Knight?). The "bedroom conversations with their under-
meanings" (Thomas L. Kinney) perplex some students; others are unable to
understand why Gawain will not sleep with the lady.

Thematic ambiguity is another problem area. Here the instructors' chief
efforts are to forestall simplistic moral interpretations of what Gawain goes
through. In general the subtlety and artistry of the poem make interpretation
fascinating—for example, Terri Curran suggests that the "swift passage of
one year in two stanzas" conveys "how swiftly, psychologically, the year
passes for Gawain." John M. Ganim notes that the work is challenging
because it presents the "conscious manipulation of myth" rather than the
myth itself (in the same way, Ganim says that C. S. Lewis's essay on *Gawain*,
entitled "The Anthropological Approach," functions as a rejoinder to J. R.
R. Tolkien).

Poetic form ends the list of problem areas. Specific matters of concern
include alliteration, the bob and wheel, prosody, assonance, rhyme scheme,
and different kinds of metaphor. Given the constraints within which most
of us work, integration of all these aspects of background, theme, language,
and poetic form is no simple task. One remedy is to assign a project or essay
on one of these problems, particularly one that cannot be handled easily or
quickly in class.

III. Projects, Assignments, and Examination Questions

The material that follows was received in response to the following questions:
"What kinds of projects or assignments (e.g., term papers) do you require?,"
"If you encourage students to do any creative assignments, please describe
them," and finally, "What kinds of quiz or examination questions do you
give during or after completion of the study of *Gawain*?" The following

summary of answers to these questions is intended to serve as a practical and useful listing of possible topics for assignment and examination.

A. Projects and Reports

The length and type of projects and reports assigned depend on the level of the course (lower-division and introductory or upper-division and specialized), on the instructors' preferences (some use only examinations), and on the type of course (English literature survey, medieval literature, Arthurian romance). Answers fell into three major categories—background reports, papers on *Gawain* alone, and comparative papers linking the work with other works taught in the course.

1. Background Reports

The topics offered to students for background reports are of two kinds: philological and literary on the one hand, cultural and historical on the other. To the philological and literary category belong such suggested topics as

- the significance of a word from the poem as glossed in the *OED* or the *MED*;
- medieval bestiaries and beasts in the poem;
- the pentangle of Gawain's shield;
- the boar hunt in Arthurian literature;
- Gawain in France and England;
- the fairy element in the poem;
- its sources;
- a comparison of "The Grene Knight" (Hales and Furnivall 56-77) with *Gawain* from the point of view of implied audience; and
- (clearly an assignment intended for a graduate seminar) an assessment of the criticism on the poem in the manner of Beryl Rowland's *Companion to Chaucer Studies*.

To the cultural and historical category of suggested topics belongs an innovative project: a journal on *Gawain* and other medieval works that asks students to note characteristics of the Middle Ages that are reflected in its literature. Most other cultural and historical suggestions consisted of reports on such topics as

- the symbolism of armor in Ramón Lull's *Book of the Ordre of Chyualry*;
- *The Unicorn Tapestries*, by Margaret B. Freeman;
- panels in the *The Belles Heures of Jean, Duke of Berry* (Meiss and Beatson) and *The Hours of Catherine of Cleves*;

- chapters in David Knowles's *The Monastic Order in England* (chs. 26, 30), Wolfgang Braunfels's *Monasteries of Western Europe*, and volume 1 of *The Plan of St. Gall*, edited by Walter William Horn and Ernest Born;
- hunting techniques in the fourteenth century;
- the historical background of *Gawain* (Bede's *History of the English Church and People* and Geoffrey of Monmouth's *History of the Kings of Britain*);
- Romanesque and Gothic architecture and *Gawain*.

2. Single-Work Papers

Papers on *Gawain* alone seem to be assigned primarily in lower-division nonspecialist courses and focus primarily on conventional literary topics: character, theme, plot, structure, imagery and symbolism, and style or diction. Oddly, essay topics on character rarely examine a single character—for example, whether the Green Knight was good, evil, or both. Usually such assignments depend instead on comparisons of

- Gawain and Bertilak or Adam or the hunted beasts;
- Arthur and Bertilak (or the two courts);
- Gawain, Arthur, and Bertilak as representatives of knighthood and its ideals;
- Morgan and Lady Bertilak.

Theme papers cover some very broad topics—for instance, "How is this poem an 'imitation of life'?" Other general assignments range from

- What emotions are expressed in the poem?
- How do they contribute to the events, characters, atmosphere, etc.?

to

- What is the significance of 'truth' in the poem?
- Are there various definitions or interpretations and attitudes toward truth presented by the characters?

Values offer another approach:

- Discuss two or three major values in the poem and their significance for the historical period and to the character(s) who portray or display or lack them.

The same topic is sometimes broached in another way:

- Are there discrepancies and/or conflicts between ideals and realistic values and behavior in the poem (or are they identical or nonconflicting)?

One thematic question requests a demonstration of how the final moral is stated, alluded to, or portrayed throughout the poem. Another merely asks,

- How important is the theological stratum of the poem?

Approaching the same topic in a different manner, another question demands an analysis of any ten- to twenty-line passage as an illustration of an important theme or stylistic device. Several more complex (and specific) topics ask students to examine the poem as psychological parable, comedy, or game; others offer a theme for students to analyze—such as literalism, obligation, youth and old age, and gift giving.

Other paper topics concern structure and form, imagery and symbolism, and literary techniques and language. Topics on structure and form are surprisingly few: one assignment asks for an examination of the three bedroom and hunt scenes and the different meanings of each another for a discussion of structural parallels in the poem as a whole. Topics on imagery and symbolism either focus on a symbol (color, number, or season), on the significance of specific days, or on the turning of the seasons passage, or ask for a reexamination of the critical articles on the pentangle and girdle. Finally, suggested topics on literary techniques and language include

- the reader's expectations after reading the first strophe of the poem,
- one of the poet's literary techniques as exemplified in one passage,
- the dynamics of two or three contrasted stanzas,
- the ways in which the poet stimulates both admiration and sympathy for Gawain,
- the ways in which the poet creates suspense in the poem,
- the cinematic quality of the narrative,
- the kinds of ambiguity in the poem, and
- the relation of humorous passages to the overall meaning of the poem.

3. Comparative Papers

The third kind of project requires comparing the poem with one or more others taught during the course. Topics here reflect the subject of the course more than do those in the earlier categories. In the English literature survey, essays compare *Beowulf* and *Gawain* by examining the heroes, the women characters, the heroes' antagonists (Grendel and the Green Knight) and opening stanzas. In world literature courses, essays compare Gawain with heroes from other works (e.g., Gisli, Roland, and Agamemnon); the poem's structure with that of *The Song of Roland*; its view of women with those of classical, medieval, and Renaissance sources; and its theme of magic with that of the *Odyssey*.

In upper-division medieval literature courses, *Gawain* is frequently compared with Chaucer's dream visions, the *Canterbury Tales*, and *Troilus*. Topics center on the worlds of the General Prologue and of *Gawain*; the image of the prince in the Knight's Tale, *Troilus*, and *Gawain*; and the marvelous in one or more dream visions and *Gawain*. Other topics include

- the narrator;
- *trawþe, cortaysye, luf-talkyng,* and *daliaunce*;
- renown and reputation;
- history;
- the image of the court;
- games and playing;
- hunting lore and the symbolic hunt;
- symbolic landscapes or setting;
- architecture; and
- sounds and sound imagery.

Gawain is also compared with nonromance medieval works other than Chaucer's. One question asks for the major unifying device—thematic, rhetorical, structural, or stylistic—either in the works of the *Gawain* poet or in those of Langland, Chaucer, and the *Gawain* poet. Others suggest comparing *Gawain* with *Pearl* or arguing for common authorship of *Gawain*, *Pearl*, *Purity*, and *St. Erkenwald* by focusing on one or more shared characteristics—thematic, symbolic, structural.

Finally, *Gawain* is also compared with other Arthurian and non-Arthurian romances:

- Is Gawain unique as a romance hero when compared with Ywain, Tristan, Parzival, and the heroes of other Middle English popular romances?
- Which two of these three (Yvain, Tristan, Gawain) are more attractive as characters, and why?

The Green Knight is also examined as a romance antagonist: is he a "diabolical tempter" or a "benevolent trickster" in the context of the romance tradition? Some students are invited to discuss the idea of heroism in *Gawain*, Malory, and *Sir Orfeo* or the treatment of the feast or hunt in *Gawain* and Malory. Others are also asked to compare, in several romances, the roles of women, the dilemmas (or lack of them) created by the conflict between romantic love and honor, and the effectiveness (or lack thereof) of the magical elements of Arthurian stories.

4. Creative Assignments

"Creative" assignments are provided by a handful of instructors who teach primarily upper-division undergraduate courses, although one suggestion derived from a graduate course (editing a portion of the Cotton Nero A.x. manuscript in facsimile). While some respondents reply that criticism is creative and therefore, by implication, that unconventional assignments are unnecessary, others list three basic kinds of unusual or creative assignments—in literary criticism, creative writing, and the visual arts or other media.

Assignments in literary criticism include

- assigning literary characters like the Miller, the Wife of Bath, Sir Gawain, and Lady Bertilak to places in Dante's *Inferno*;
- writing a parody of *Gawain* that makes its hero into a stock character and then discussing the difference between the parody and the original; and
- keeping a journal of outside critical readings, including notes and a summary of the student's opinion.

Creative writing assignments favor the writing of alliterative verse, comparing translations of the poem, writing verse translations of the poem, writing short stories or poems on Gawain (like that of Yvor Winters), and, especially popular, rewriting the poem from Gawain's or Arthur's point of view (in the manner of John Gardner's *Grendel*). Visual arts and other media projects include

- illustrating scenes from *Gawain*, some with the aid of medieval manuscript illuminations;
- designing a dust jacket;
- designing a castle;
- designing costumes; and
- constructing a board game like "Monopoly" based on the journey of the hero in the four fitts.

Creative projects using other media involve writing a screenplay for *Gawain* (for example, for the opening beheading scene), dramatizing scenes from the poem, making short films on the journey to Hautdesert or on the pentangle, and preparing a medieval banquet complete with music, entertainment, costumes, and food.

4. Examination Questions

Finally, respondents also indicated the kinds of examination questions they used in teaching *Gawain*, normally determined by the level of the course. Examinations in lower-division surveys frequently employ identifications consisting of a character's name (e.g., Bertilak), a symbol (e.g., pentangle), an action (e.g., the whirring of an ax), or a passage from the poem. Examinations in upper-division courses, particularly in specialized seminars, often demand translation of and commentary on passages from the Middle English. The material presented here consists primarily of essay questions, some of which involve the poem alone and others a comparison of *Gawain* with one or more other works of literature, depending, again, on the course.

Identification questions might request the name of the *Gawain* manuscript, other works in the manuscript, the name of one or more of the poem's alliterative patterns, the definition and function of the bob and wheel, the meanings of *green* in the poem, the objects held by the Green Knight when he first appears and their significance, the mythic and ritualistic use of the pentangle, the biblical associations of the pentangle, the significance of the number five, the nature of Gawain's shield, the color of Guenore's eyes (and the convention on which that color is based), and the identity of Morgan le Fay.

Essay questions treating only this poem, used primarily in lower-division courses, begin with character:

- What is Gawain's "fatal flaw"? If his "fatal flaw" is his lack of faith, how is that symbolized in the poem?
- What is the significance of the Green Knight/Bertilak?
- Who are the lady, Morgan le Fay, and the guide?

They also concern theme:

- What are Sir Gawain's tests? virtues?
- What is the theme of *Gawain*, and how is it supported by imagery and plot elements?
- In what ways might it be termed a comic work? a serious work?
- Why does Arthur's court laugh at the end?

- What has Gawain learned at the end when he returns to Arthur's court wearing the green girdle? What has the court learned?
- Horace states that the purpose of literature is to teach and to delight: how does the *Gawain* poet accomplish this?
- Discuss the pattern of *Gawain* as a "comment on history and on the alternation between those two faces of history, *blysse* and *blunder*, that is, between order and confusion" (Muscatine 60).

Other questions focus on structural parallels (e.g., the hunt of the lord and the hunt of Gawain by the lady) and on symbols ("discuss the role of Bertilak's castle; examine the passage describing the turning of the seasons in the second fitt and relate its significance to the theme and structure of the poem"). And finally, other questions relate the poem to courtly love, religion, the romance genre, or medieval poetic techniques.

By far the greatest number of questions involve comparisons of *Gawain* with other works of literature. We turn first to the sophomore survey.

1. Introductory Survey of English or World Literature

The work most frequently compared with *Gawain* is *Beowulf*, particularly in relation to the visiting monsters and their respective motives, as well as to the poets' treatments of such visits. Other medieval and Renaissance works compared with the poem, like the Nun's Priest's Tale and *The Faerie Queene*, are used to illustrate the development of virtue. One approach invites students to define the romance and then look at *Gawain* and *The Faerie Queene* simply as romances, while another asks them to look at the endings of the two works and discuss why it is difficult for Sir Gawain to reenter his community but relatively easy for the Redcrosse Knight. Yet another analysis probes medieval and Renaissance drama as well as *Gawain* and *The Faerie Queene*: "choose two heroes and their opponents from *Gawain*, *The Faerie Queene*, *Everyman*, *Dr. Faustus*, and *Henry IV, Part 1*, and explain the type of temptation offered to the hero by the evil being, its relationship to the temptations in *Beowulf*, the tempter's reasons for thinking the temptation might work, the reasons it does or does not actually work, and why the hero (or tempter) is the stronger." Even seventeenth- and eighteenth-century authors like George Herbert and Jonathan Swift are compared and contrasted with Chaucer and the *Gawain* poet—for example, on the theme of "a virtue untested is no virtue at all" in the poetry of Herbert and *Gawain* and on the question of whether Chaucer, the *Gawain* poet, and Swift see humankind as good or evil. Finally, some students might be asked to define "genre" and then, after choosing two (epic, romance, drama, or poetry), to show

how their characteristics are manifested in the works of at least two authors covered during the semester.

2. Medieval English Literature

Most essay questions concerning *Gawain* derive from some type of survey of medieval literature. In the more introductory medieval course, *Gawain* is chiefly linked with *Beowulf*, the *Canterbury Tales*, and the *Morte Darthur*. Students are asked to compare the court and *comitatus* of *Gawain* and *Beowulf* or their landscapes (specifically Grendel's mere and the Dragon's barrow with the landscape through which Sir Gawain passes in quest of the Green Knight). They are invited to trace the theme of broken kinship or brotherhood bonds through works from *Beowulf* to Malory's *Morte Darthur*. Another question asks which knight is more ideal, Sir Gawain in *Gawain* or Sir Lancelot in the *Morte Darthur*, and why. One innovative question requests that students imagine Beowulf traveling forward in time to substitute for either Sir Gawain in *Gawain* or Sir Lancelot in *Morte Darthur* and describe which duties he would be prepared for and which would cause problems for him (also, which aspects of his surroundings would surprise him and which would be familiar). Finally, the atmosphere of Arthur's court in *Gawain* is compared to that of the Wife of Bath's Tale. Sometimes the questions are general enough to apply to any number of the works read in such a course: students are asked to examine two or three works studied during the semester for the paradoxical concept of love in the Middle Ages, for nature imagery, or for structural symmetry (as based on the medieval belief in planes of correspondence, typology in scripture, and the diptych and triptych in painting). Another such question allows students to pick only one work and investigate its allegorical or polysemous nature.

Questions on *Gawain* in more specialized courses often demand comparisons with other works of the *Gawain* poet (usually *Pearl*) or with other Middle English works. Questions focus on landscape, structure, decorative detail, or style and theme, despite possible differences in genre. Frequently students are asked to make a case for the single authorship of *Gawain*, *Pearl*, and *Patience*. *Sir Gawain* is also discussed with a variety of other medieval works—*Piers Plowman*, the romances of *Sir Orfeo* and Malory's *Morte Darthur*, Middle English lyrics, the debate poem *The Owl and the Nightingale*, Chaucer's Clerk's Tale, and various medieval plays (*Secunda Pastorum*, *Everyman*). Many questions invite a comparison of several of these works—the questions are not restricted to a single genre. The particular works selected seem less important than the idea or literary form being analyzed.

Most of the ideas in exam questions from specialized courses concentrate on characteristically medieval concerns: spiritual and Christian motifs, including miracles and the miraculous: antifeminism; contentiousness as the defining quality of fallen creatures; the inevitability of change. Another medieval concern in these examination questions stresses the secular and chivalric aspects of the concepts of the hero, heroism, and the quest.

Interestingly, the greatest number of questions touch on cultural attitudes as reflected in the literature:

- blind adherence to fixed ideals (but also "among the best poets an awareness of the vulnerability of the codes that governed their lives" [Martin Camargo]);
- "medieval ambivalence," including "a relish for the world alongside a disdain for it, a delight in the concrete and immediate (or the sensuous and the temporal) along with a reaching for the abstract and infinite (or the ideal and the eternal)" (Thomas Wright);
- the conflict between Christian and worldly values, or the contrast between the sacred and the profane, the "canny and the uncanny" (Susan Hilligoss);
- the contrast between the "Age of Certainty" in the High Middle Ages and the "Age of Ambiguity" in the fourteenth century.

Modern as well as medieval preoccupations are also demonstrated in the questions about

- effects on the probable audience;
- the uses of myth and folklore;
- the role of women; and
- the education of the hero.

Technical and aesthetic questions also explore

- the relation between the modern novel and the medieval romance;
- the conventions of romance, especially as derived from Jessie Weston's *From Ritual to Romance*;
- structure or structural balance;
- the relation between the part and the whole;
- the techniques, subjects, and aims of poetry;
- techniques of humor;
- literary qualities in medieval works composed by men that might have appealed to a feminine audience;
- transformation and conversion in place of character development; and
- comedy, laughter, and humor instead of seriousness.

In the rare graduate courses that require an examination, the emphasis falls much more on matters like the *Gawain* poet's use of sources—for example, Irish saga.

3. Romance

When the poem is studied in a romance course (or in a unit on the romance in a Middle English course), students are often asked simply, "Is Gawain a typical romance hero?," or they are asked to compare the treatment of either Gawain or the ideal knight in more than one work. But many questions are more complex. Courtly love in *Tristan* and *Gawain* is contrasted with the fabliau elements in each; or the treatment of Gawain in *Yvain*, *Parzival*, and *Gawain* is examined, with the corresponding differences in the moral significance of each work; or the narrative structure of *Gawain* is compared with that of "Pwyll" or "Culhwch." Alternatively, one question asks students to assess the role played by either courtly love or chivalry in a representative selection of romances. A similar question concentrates on the mythic rites of passage patterning individual experiences in at least two romances (the term "rites of passage" explained in the light of Charles Moorman's basic pattern of change in *A Knight There Was* [36] from the static world of childhood to rebirth in the adult world). Finally, several questions deal with a comparison of romances and their sources: one requested analysis of the English Arthurian romances (the alliterative *Morte Arthure*, the stanzaic *Morte Arthur*, and *Gawain*) as unique in their treatment of subject and form, in contrast to the French models of Chrétien. Another focuses on the differences among the accounts of Arthur in early chronicle, epic, and romance, as clarified through the changing emphases on prowess and courage, the ends the works serve, and the roles of the individual knight in each.

IV. Specific Approaches to Gawain

In the hope of aiding other teachers of the poem interested in pedagogical concerns, this description of the context and manner in which *Gawain* is taught today (chiefly in American colleges and universities) has outlined the pattern of interests expressed on the respondents' questionnaires. However, respondents to the *Gawain* survey, when asked what types of information they would most like included in a pedagogical sourcebook on the work, requested very practical and specific information. Again and again, requests were voiced for essay and examination questions as well as for study aids, syllabuses, and bibliography—for some way of sifting through the wealth of writing on the poem. The "Materials" section, this introduction, and the essays that follow represent a collective attempt to provide, in response to these requests, helpful information as well as useful teaching ideas.

Many survey participants requested a variety of background essays. Hence, the first five essays provide basic material on backgrounds identified by respondents as problematic for teaching *Gawain* to undergraduates, whether in specialized or nonspecialized courses: the Arthurian tradition (Maureen Fries), courtly love (Thomas L. Wright), chivalry (Louis Brewer Hall), religion and law (Robert J. Blanch), and medieval poetics (Richard Hamilton Green).

The remaining essays on approaching the poem in the classroom describe individual courses in which the poem is taught, selected according to two criteria: on the one hand, their collective applicability to a wide range of institutions, student abilities, and levels of instructions and on the other, their presentation of a range of innovative pedagogical techniques. These course descriptions extend from the lower-division undergraduate to the graduate.

Included in the first section, all using the poem in translation, are essays on the freshman composition course (John M. Fyler), the introductory survey for nonmajors (Rosemary Ascherl), the survey for majors (Sherron E. Knopp), and the world literature course (Katharina M. Wilson). The next section, also using translations, contains essays on upper-division undergraduate courses: a survey of medieval literature in translation (Peggy A. Knapp), Arthurian literature (Victoria L. Weiss), Tolkien and his sources (Jane Chance), and a course on literary criticism (John M. Ganim).

Essays on courses reading the poem in the original follow. Dual-level courses include a medieval studies course (Julia Bolton Holloway), a Ricardian poetry course (Penelope B. R. Doob), and a Scots and Celtic literature course (Jeffrey F. Huntsman). Graduate courses complete the contents with essays on a seminar in the *Gawain* poet and the Alliterative Revival (Anne Howland Schotter) and a course in alliterative literature that links Old and Middle English literature (Edward B. Irving, Jr.)

In the last section of the book, these essays are supplemented by essays on four specific teaching issues—oral performance of the Middle English text (Marie Borroff), visual aids (Donald K. Fry), visual projects (Judith Bronfman), and the medieval banquet (Patricia A. Moody)—designed to enhance any syllabus that features *Gawain* by engaging students not only intellectually but also sensuously.

Through these individual course descriptions we hope to provide, first, practical guidance for both beginning instructors and experienced generalists seeking background information and methodologies and, second, new and stimulating ideas for seasoned medievalists desiring a fresh approach for advanced undergraduate and graduate courses.

Just as it would be impossible to settle on one interpretation of this wonderfully ambiguous, continually shifting poem, offering as it does so many perspectives on the issues it raises, so, too, the instructor would find it impossible to fix this work solely in one specific context. *Gawain* is so universal a poem and so crafted a masterpiece that it seems to achieve its own decorum in whatever pedagogical context it appears. Yet if the survey and this collection intensify interest in this marvelous and surprising poem and stimulate its teaching in many different ways, they will have served their purpose well.

TEACHING THE BACKGROUNDS

Teaching *Sir Gawain and the Green Knight* in the Context of Arthurian and Other Romance Traditions

Maureen Fries

Teaching the backgrounds of *Sir Gawain and the Green Knight* as they are found in Arthurian and other romance traditions is a difficult and fascinating, frustrating and rewarding experience. One must initiate one's students into materials known—or perhaps only conjectured—to be related to the poem. This variety of traditions includes the national and international, chronicle and romance, learned and "lewd," biblical and folk; Latin, Irish and Welsh, French and native English; and, ultimately, universal heroic myth. It includes especially a consideration of convention versus innovation: for instance, the poet's choosing for his hero a thoroughly conventional Arthurian personage of ancient lineage—Gawain, king's sister's son to Arthur—and then casting him in a relatively unconventional role. That same blend of tradition and the individual talent appears in his framing his narrative with the Trojan context that had for hundreds of years been used to give authority to Arthurian chronicle and romance.

I begin my discussion of the sources and analogues of the *Gawain* poet's romance with a brief introduction to universal heroic myth as it is reflected in that genre. The call to adventure, supernatural aid, the meeting with the goddess and/or temptress, the conflict with the (often supernatural) Other, and the return (with the perilous journeys that separate and reunite the hero and his own society) are all apparent in *Gawain*. Here, as elsewhere, I use chalkboard diagrams and/or class handouts to schematize the narrative. Outside readings most often recommended are Campbell and Frye. But I also make clear the poet's departures from the classic pattern, such as the double struggle with Bertilak and his wife and the qualified praise of Gawain at the end of the poem, to which I return while discussing the narrative proper.

Proper and further caveats, of course, stress the particular as opposed to the general sources and analogues. Here the poet's indebtedness to Arthurian tradition itself, particularly French and Celtic but also his own English alliterative tradition, necessitates a discussion of the classic *Artusroman*. In scholarly theories about the work of such disparate (in style as well as language) writers as Chrétien de Troyes, Hartman von Aue, and the poet of *The Awntyrs off Arthure at the Terne Wathelyne*—for example, see Köhler, Kuhn, and Spearing (Gawain-*Poet*), respectively—this form emerges as duple in structure. Divided at the hero's crisis and depending on narremes of quest and (errant) adventure, with bride winning and social service as their object, such stories culminate in the hero's reintegration into his applauding society in the Continental versions—although their duple structure has recently been cogently put in question by Schultz. A further qualification is Fichte's contention, which he uses *Sir Gawain* to demonstrate, that the Middle English verse romance is a modified type of the usual Arthurian model. In both form and matter, he contends, most English authors exhibit different concerns, although he finds the *Gawain* poet closer to his Continental models than is any other British Arthurian writer. Fichte's article goes on reserve along with the other secondary sources I have mentioned. In class I stress the similarities and differences between *Gawain* and its classic predecessors, including its inversion of the bride quest and the questioning of Arthurian values it shares with a few Continental predecessors but strikingly with poems from its own tradition, such as the contemporary *Awntyrs off Arthure* and alliterative *Morte Arthure*.

Gawain adheres to the classical Arthurian pattern of dupleness in spite of the quadripartite form suggested by the large capitals in the manuscript, but it focuses almost entirely on quest with only incidental use of random adventure. Further, unlike French and German romances modeled on Chrétien, its moral crisis comes late in the second half of the narrative instead of concluding the first, and its final festivities seem inconclusive, its hero's victory questionable. To suggest to one's students that this development is unique to *Gawain* would be misleading: Erec, Yvain, and Perceval all face similar crises and make wrong decisions—"By acknowledging and accepting their mistakes [they] turn them into a special distinction" (Schultz 39), such as the *Gawain* poet's green lace. But these earlier knights err early enough in their narratives to make their amends seem more complete; this is why the usual Arthurian crowd scene's welcome of Gawain is less convincing in this poem, although as usual the hero's society refuses to blame him as he conventionally blames himself. Thus the *Gawain* poet's twos (beheadings, even if mock; perilous journeys; brilliant courts; tempting ladies; and so forth) work toward a more tenuous glorification of his already ambivalent hero than is usual. And they contrast with the threes (days' entertainments; hunts; concurrent temptations; exchanges; and so forth) of myth, folklore, fairy tale, and religion that are the core around which the double (real or threatened) beheading moves.

This structural source study leads students into the first of the three mythic subtexts underlying the poem: a version of the beheading game, in the Old Irish *Fled Bricrend* (Henderson). In two episodes, the great Ulaid hero Cuchulain (a king's sister's son like Gawain, and solar-connected, as is Gawain in a number of narratives) keeps a beheading appointment—the "champion's bargain"—which his older brothers, alone the first time, and then with another of Conchubur's courtiers the second, fail to honor because of fear. In both the unwitnessed first occasion about which his brothers lie and the witnessed second occasion about which they cannot, Cuchulain escapes harm by his qualities of "courage and skill and honour," which make him "the supreme warrior of Ériu," as his last challenger, the Otherworld king Cú Rui, tells him (Gantz, *Irish Myths* 255). Both Cú Rui and Úath, the first challenger, are shapeshifters like the Green Knight; both pretend to strike but do not; and in the Úath episode there are even three feints of the ax. But there is no temptation or bride quest in reverse in this saga of the Ulster Cycle in which the heroes strive for the "champion's portion"—a question of precedence—which Cuchulain at last wins; nor is there any question of an exchange of winnings. Nevertheless, since it is readily available, fairly cheap, and in its other stories as well as *Fled Bricrend* extremely useful for whichever of the several courses I teach *Gawain* in, I put the little Gantz Penguin translation in the bookstore among the optional books as well as on my library reserve. For this and all other sources discussed in class, I recommend as outside reading Bruce, Benson (*Art*), Elisabeth Brewer, Fletcher, Kittredge, and Laura H. Loomis.

Other sources are not lacking, in other languages, for the beheading, which is one of many signs of the widespread journeyings of Celtic motifs throughout Europe (Roger S. Loomis, "Oral Diffusion") and of Arthurian romance's ubiquitous tendency to draw unto itself narremes originally unrelated. Here a diagram of the apparent course of this borrowing helps. In French there are *Caradoc* (Roach), *La mule sanz frain* (Paiens de Maisières), *Hunbaut* (Stürzinger), and *Perlesvaus* (Nitze and Jenkins); in German, *Diu Crône* (Türlin; perhaps also Colin and Wisse's *Parzifal*); in English, besides *Gawain* itself, *The Grene Knight* and *The Turk and Gawain* (both in Hales and Furnivall). All these are discussed in Roger S. Loomis's invaluable *Arthurian Literature in the Middle Ages*, to which students are referred. In class I discuss only three. *Caradoc*, interpolated into volume 1 of *Continuations of the Old French* Perceval (Roach) in three variations and extant also in a sixteenth-century prose text, is the most important. The hero, Arthur's nephew, responds to a tall, strange, singing knight's challenge to a beheading game with a year's interval and receives a harmless return blow when the stranger returns to court, after which he praises Caradoc for courage and troth and reveals he is Caradoc's natural father. Thus *Caradoc* both looks back to *Fled Bricrend* and, in its refinement of the theme of a beheading game as proof of one's bravery and honor, forward to *Gawain*'s major and framing narreme, even to the year's interval and a mixed revelation.

But since my own theme in discussing these sources is the alteration of tradition by the individual talent, I also tell and show—again by means of comparative diagrams—two other French analogues. In *La mule sanz frain* we have Gawain's first appearance under his own name in the role previously filled by Caradoc. His nonfatal opponent is a churl (a real one and not disguised like Cú Rui in the Old Irish), who carries a *giserne*—the specific kind of ax borne by the Green Knight. A churl is again Gawain's opponent in *Hunbaut*, where the (here) unchivalrous Arthurian champion prevents a return engagement with his challenger's ax by seizing the *vilain*'s body to keep it from retrieving its head, until it dies. This parodic reduction to farce of the heroic motif is a good illustration for students of how structure changes with the alteration of any component. With its fabliau ambience it also helps introduce the second mythic subtext, the temptation.

Temptations of heroes are far more plentiful in romance, and indeed in general literature of all sorts, than are beheading games. Students also seem to understand the temptation narreme more easily—it is perhaps closer to their own experience. In Arthurian romance especially, there are statistically more sexual frauds—including disguised, incestuous, or merely unrecognized partners—than in any other branch of medieval narrative. I begin my treatment of this subject with a discussion of Morgan le Fay and her movement from archhealer to archtemptress of Arthurian story, not illogical since the plot is supposed to turn on her and partially on her manipulations of Bertilak's wife to be her puppet surrogate. As early as the twelfth century, and later especially in the prose *Lancelot* (Sommer) and in Malory, Morgan is the medieval vamp nonpareil—if often so unsuccessful as to be ludicrous. Her *val sans retour* is a sensual trap for good knights (the only kind she wants, though she often consorts with bad ones), and even Lancelot must do his time in her dungeon in the long prose romance that bears his name. But she was also tester of chastity, especially by the famous horn of the thirteenth-century prose *Tristan* (Løseth), and her judgments seem to have been just. Since her late appearance in her own name in *Gawain* often puzzles students, this attention to her reputation helps explain both her triadic nature and her relevance (for fuller discussion, see Faton).

Specifically relevant temptation motifs are thus not so necessary as beheading motifs (Elisabeth Brewer 3), but a few prove fruitful in discussion, using the same comparative methods as above. I would choose to look at six or seven. In the Welsh "Pwyll, Prince of Dyfed" (Evans and Rhys; Gantz, *The Mabinogion*, and Patrick Ford have translated the work), the strong bond that binds the hunting hero to assume the form of the hunting King Arawn of the Celtic Otherworld, to sleep every night with Arawn's wife for a year, and then to defeat his enemy Hafgan is implicitly related to Pwyll's chastity, as the same virtue is more explicitly related to Gawain's only partial defeat. In *Lanzelet* (Zatzikhoven), German with an Anglo-Norman original, the pre-Guineverian knight accepts the sexual proffers of Galgandreiz' daughter after they are refused by his more honorable companions, is challenged to a knife duel by her father—whom he kills—and accepts her further offer of herself and the kingdom. A closer analogue, in the prose *Lancelot*, has Morgan sending her damsel to lure Lancelot, with whom she has three times initiated an unsuccessful seduction—a possible parallel to the situation in *Gawain* and, as with Bertilak's wife, resulting in three further fruitless attempts on an implacable virtue. *Hunbaut*, that romance of the trunkless head, offers a host who urges Gawain to kiss his daughter after she has indulged in a forthright banquet-table flirtation similar to that of Bertilak's wife; who objects to four kisses instead of one and threatens to blind Gawain; and who is cheated anyway when the girl succeeds in bedding her hero, who quickly retreats at dawn. In *Le chevalier à l'épée* (Armstrong), where Gawain is offered his host's daughter with prior knowledge of dire results should he seduce her, he decides it would be a slur on his honor should he not; and he is wounded by a preannounced sword on the skin, but not severely (like Gawain's nick), so that he "quite lost all his desire" (Elisabeth Brewer 66).

Another, usually highly touted source, the Anglo-Norman *Yder* (Gelzer) has—like the Welsh "Pwyll"—the advantage of having a wife in the temptress slot. The hero agrees with Ivenant that his knighting depends on his resisting the advances of the latter's queen (who will attempt to seduce him); he endures her wiles until he ends the temptation by kicking her in the abdomen, which causes much amusement to the whole court and satisfaction to the king, who further knocks his wife to the floor. This ludicrous and indeed gross episode is no more consonant with the end result in *Gawain* than is the understatement of "Pwyll"—less so in terms of subtlety. Romances combining beheading and temptations are few and tenuous: *Lanzelet*,

Hunbaut, and *Le chevalier* all combine the functions of sex and death in an aesthetically unsatisfying way, as students recognize; none presents the integral, unified structure of *Gawain*, and none offers exchange of winnings as a binding motif in, say, the way "Pwyll" (in its somewhat disjointed way) does. The one exchange-of-winnings tale usually advanced—the Latin *Miles gloriosus* (Pontas du Méril)—is for sharing and not exchanging, has a fabliau plot resembling somewhat Chaucer's Shipman's Tale, and does not seem at all relevant to our poem. One must in honesty tell one's students that Kittredge was right, years ago, to say that "no such compact occurs in any other version of the Temptation . . .[or] elsewhere" (113).

But there are folklore analogues the poet might have known: in fairy tales (e.g., "Rapunzel" and "Rumpelstiltskin") where the contract is made with an evil other, the stake is a human (admittedly a baby's) life; the contractee may ultimately escape full consequences of the bargain, but an outside releaser is necessary. There are also agreements with the devil, with whom the Green Knight has been identified and with whom Morgan is said in the *Suite du Merlin* to have had relations (Tolkien and Gordon 130). Modern analogues to match the most famous medieval one—in which Faust wins back his youth in exchange for his soul—include "The Devil and Daniel Webster." Analogous medieval bargains, in a different context, could include the infamous if misunderstood ones in Chaucer's Franklin's Tale. Morgan le Fay, the ultimate bargainer in Arthurian romance by the time the poem was written, is a possible source for the compact. These analogues still do not explain the use or success of the motif; perhaps the poet was—as perhaps was Layamon—a lawyer, much given to the study of contracts.

Characterization depends more surely on Arthurian sources: the people in *Gawain* are largely conventional. We have Arthur as *roi fainéant*; Guinevere as nonadulteress (one of her two phases)—her usual role in the alliterative tradition, except for the alliterative *Morte Arthure*; such favorites of the alliterative writers as the ubiquitous bishop Baldwin, as a bit player; the Green Knight as a refined development of the familiar Celtic-French challenging churl and/or noble, but only here green (though parti-colored faces are characteristic of many Irish sagas) and perhaps a fertility figure, a "green man" (Roger S. Loomis; Weston; Speirs, *Medieval*). At Bertilak's castle there are also the lady, the stereotyped eager female of English romance, even more forthright than the French (Harris); and Morgan in her "loathly lady" phase, but unwooing and unlikely to be disenchanted, as are her analogues Dame Ragnell and the hag in the Wife of Bath's Tale.

And then there is Gawain.

In the felicitous phrase of the most encyclopedic of Gawain watchers, I announce to my class that "I will not treat of Gawain before Gawain" (Whiting 195)—if they will excuse a small *occupatio*. In perhaps the most inconsistently suggestive career of any Arthurian—or indeed any—hero, Gawain has been traced to the sun-god (his solar strength) and to Cuchulain (also a solar figure and king's sister's son in the European tradition of champions); curiously, both Gawain and Cuchulain are small in stature, perhaps to emphasize further their achievement over giant foes. Also conflated with the Welsh Gwalchmei, who appears independently in the Welsh *Triads* (Bromwich), Gawain plays only a small part in *The Mabinogi* (Evans and Rhys)—for instance, he aids the young Arthurian knight Culhwch in his bride quest as only one of a number of heroes summoned by the king. The vexed question of dating *The Mabinogi* (Charles-Edwards, Hamp) has thrown into doubt the supposed earliness of its tales, but there is no question about the date of another probably Welsh-authored work the *Historia regum Britanniae* of Geoffrey of Monmouth written in the 1130s.

Carefully examined (Fletcher 49–115), Geoffrey's sources—both fiction and chronicle (and I remind my students that at this time the difference between the two was often minimal) as well as historical, mythical, folkloric, and contemporarily societal—when combined with his successors and imitators, Wace and Layamon, provide in their imaginative reworking all the positive and at least one of the negative characteristics of the romance Gawain. As Arthur's nephew, probably an intentional parallel with the (fictional) Roland-Charlemagne relationship (Gerould), he is courageous and loyal (in contrast to the cognate Mordred); his reputation is almost on a level with his king's, and his only fault is rashness, as with the Romans. Service as a page to Pope Sulpicius probably began his reputation for courtesy, which is expanded by the Anglo-Norman *Brut* (Wace); and Wace also—in Gawain's speech praising love as better for knights than war is—gives us the first hint of Gawain the lover, a characteristic significantly suppressed in the alliterative tradition both by the earlier English *Brut* (Layamon) and the later alliterative *Morte*. These traits of loyal warrior, courteous knight, and ardent lover were to be the hallmarks of Gawain's subsequent career (Whiting)—mostly. Because of the importance of the chronicles, I put Thorpe's translation of Geoffrey and the *Arthurian Chronicles* (Evans) on reserve. I also mention an early anti-Gawain tradition—for instance, in 1147, Thomas de Loches's use of an anonymous French author's contention that Arthur's nephew caused his king losses in the Roman war by his "impetus et stultitia" (Fletcher 123). This double view of Gawain's character and worth was to assume an enormous importance with the growth of Arthurian literature.

Gawain's emergence as a romance hero is due to that only begetter of (extant) Arthurian romance, Chrétien de Troyes. While he never gives Gawain a tale of his own, the French author sees him as a pattern of brave and courteous knighthood: he is first on the list of knights in *Erec*, in *Cligés* and *Yvain* the touchstone to the hero's prowess, aider of the new hero in *Lancelot* and of Perceval in his eponymous tale. Everywhere he is a passionate but light and fickle lover of women. And, while his adventures rival in number those of Perceval and he emerges as "the type of perfection of the worldly knight," he is finally only a foil to "the knight who has a mystic function to perform" (Bruce 1: 250). Even if he had been the original Grail hero (Weston), he has by this time declined from that high spirituality (at least in the French—there is a German romance of about half a century after Chrétien, *Diu Crône*, in which he achieves the blessed ceremony unconvincingly). Suggested reading includes Chrétien (*Arthurian Romances*), Roger S. Loomis (*Arthurian Tradition*), and Nitze ("Character of Gauvain").

After Chrétien, Gawain becomes a central figure of many romances in verse and the later, lengthy prose products. His reputation always precedes him in the former, where, as is usual in chivalric literature, he is often not immediately recognized. Finding who has defeated them, other knights honor him; discovering his identity, amorous ladies who have loved him from his reputation alone seek his love and—denied it—do not believe that he is Gawain, as Bertilak's lady does not. This honor and love, I underline for my students, is echoed at least seemingly in Gawain's reception at Hautdesert. In the prose romances his reputation ranges from mixed to downright bad. In the *Vulgate* (Sommer), the most influential, he declines from a queen's knight to a (literal) ladykiller; from a brave fighter to second or worse to Lancelot to sneaky slayer of good knights because of senseless feuds; from Grail quester to murderer of eighteen of the twenty-two Arthurian knights who die questing; from friend of Lancelot to implacable enemy and eggeron of Arthur to the monstrous feud that destroys the Round Table forever. One prose romance, *Perlesvaus* (Nitze and Jenkins), shows us a Gawain on quest who refuses a wooing lady's advances—sensing the even pre-Christian link between chastity and spiritual strength; it is an exception, but one that the poet seems to have known and the potential of which he certainly exploited. Mostly the prose Gawain is pictured as a lecher rather than an ideal lover; as a murderer rather than a gallant fighter; as a rude rather than a courteous knight (especially in the prose *Tristan*, where his sins range from killing to gain a woman, to impoliteness to an unattractive damsel, to laughing at Tristan's haircut—no mean violation of courtesy). One must point out, here, to one's students the notorious French prose romancers' custom of running down one hero to exalt another, which resulted in the eventual displacement 'of Gawain by Lancelot even in the English Malory. And one must add the caveat that Gawain is never completely bad, as when he refuses to join his brothers' plot to trap Lancelot. Suggested reserve reading includes Micha on the French verse romances and, for the prose, Pickford, Frappier, Bogdanow, and Busby's two works.

Thus the reputation of Gawain must have come to our poet as totally inconsistent, for we know from his poem that he had read widely in Arthurian romance. We must stress to our students that he made deliberate choices, drawing the concept of warlike champion from chronicle inspiration and of pattern of knighthood from early romance tradition, mainly French. A chaste Gawain draws authority from the *Perlesvaus*, but he is rare and may also have to do with general behavior on a quest—or the wish to counterpoise one tradition against another. Courtesy is the exemplary virtue one remembers: it is the quintessential Gawain, in spite of his supposed antifeminism (Dove). The suppression of the "bad" Gawain is intentional, as is his incomplete spiritual success.

Also intentional and consonant with his own alliterative tradition, which shared his mostly positive attitude toward his hero is the poet's use of Troy as a framing device to begin and end his work. Here one should briefly discuss the *historia* by which a fictional Brutus—already conflated from a Roman consul in Eusebius-Jerome and an eponymous Italo-Celtic ancestor in a pre-Nennian chronicle (Bruce 2: 51–53) into a descendent of Aeneas (either grandson [Nennius] or great-grandson [Geoffrey])—led Trojan colonies to found the British state. At the centerpiece of Geoffrey's *Historia* was the career of Arthur, that genre as a traditional literary form allowing for pretended along with actual events (Strohm, "*Storie*" 348–52). Verisimilitude was achieved through various means: direct quotations from the Bible (Hammer 311); the sparing use of dates—only three in all (for example, Arthur's retirement to Avalon in 542 AD); compositely historic Roman names (Tatlock 215); cognate references to Palestine, Greece, or Italy (Parry 317); and a prescribed "historical" style. So convincing was Geoffrey's argument that, much later, Polydore Virgil was berated for suspecting Arthur's existence, and Milton for a long period considered Arthur for the hero of a proposed national epic (Heninger 380, 383). This Troy "matter" seems to have had patriotic as well as poetic significance for the alliterative poets, the alliterative *Morte* author back-framing his work and the *Winner and Waster* one (Gollancz) front-framing his with it.

What students must be made to see is that for the *Gawain* poet the full-framing with Trojan reference was both aesthetically and structurally necessary. Like other alliterative writers, such as those of the alliterative *Morte*, the *Awntyrs off Arthure*, and *Golagros and Gawain*, he viewed the Arthurian ethos with as much criticism as admiration; and this double view must have been supported by what each writer learned from *historia* as much as from French and Celtic romance. Additionally, since their hero was so often Gawain—still the great English Arthurian hero if now the more or less tarnished champion of French vogue—they had inherited a complex doubled protagonist whom, while they praised him, they must also have seen as flawed. Every aspect of the beheading-temptation-exchange plot is bent in that direction. But the reference to "Brutus bokez" as bearing "wyttenesse" to his "aunter," even if no one any longer believed it had happened "in Arthurus day" (and many undoubtedly did), allowed the unknown maker to reaffirm the historicity of his material at the same time as he gave expression to its faults and problems, as exemplified by the individual caught up in a basically flawed (in the Augustinian sense of original sin) society where fame may supersede *trawþe*/truth. Troy was truth as the poet knew it; and the truth at the heart of his poem, however fictional both he and we know it to be, moves him beyond his sources and into our own hearts.

Luf-Talkyng in *Sir Gawain and the Green Knight*

Thomas L. Wright

Teachers of *Sir Gawain and the Green Knight* are likely to find that students respond readily to the poem's heroic aspects—the exciting adventure of the beheading game, the arming of Gawain and his journey. the confrontation at the Green Chapel. But the poem's courtly aspect offers a less familiar narrative experience. As a comedy of manners it concerns—besides role reversal in the attempted seduction of Gawain—such issues as Gawain's reputation as the father of fine manners, his obligations as a guest, and the tensions inherent in Gawain's service to a Christian chivalry that embraces the spiritual and social ideals fixed so firmly in the pentangle. Gawain is involved in comic as well as possibly fatal complications, and much of the comedy of his social entanglement depends on an awareness of the conventions and decorum of courtly love. Even the duel of words in the temptation scenes is a version of the elegant speech commended to lovers in the poetry of courtly love. Students need both information and guidance if they are to share in the poet's delightfully ironic treatment of courtly manners and ideals. A good place to begin an examination of this aspect of *Sir Gawain and the Green Knight* is the second fitt, in which Gawain finds refuge in a castle where he is welcomed amid exclamations on his fame as exemplar of refined manners and sentiments of court. The following discussion begins at this point and offers one means of approaching the poem's courtly dimension.

When Gawain is comfortable in the castle where he seeks refuge, his armor removed and his horse stabled, the company gathered there for Christmas discover that this guest is a famous man—"Wawen hymself," as they excitedly put it. So Gawain hears himself acclaimed not as a questing Round Table knight renowned for his prowess but as the "fyne fader of nurture," the chief exponent of fine manners and noble speech, whose skills can reveal the "menyng of manerez mere" and the art of "luf-talkyng" (Andrew and Waldron 915–27). Gawain's courtesy is praised in its social aspect, as the term *nurture* and the references to manners and talk suggest. *Nurture* keeps company with terms like *courtesy* and *chivalry* and denotes qualities we think of as courtly: careful grooming and dress, *debonairté* ('an agreeable demeanor"), *mésure* ("moderation"), education, good speech, the pursuit of worthy deeds. These are qualities praised in the courtesy books (Bornstein, Furnivall), and they are cited by Bertilak's lady as she sums up Gawain's traits: "bewté, debonerté, blyþe semblaunt" (1273). But as we know from the discourse on the pentangle (619–65), Gawain's courtesy comprises more than this. It is a composite of military, religious, and social qualities, none separable from the others, and among them are his faith (*afyeunce*) and his

79

purity (*clannes*). The acclaim Gawain hears must therefore sound slightly awry in its emphasis on manners and courtly cheer. Yet whether to take exception to the incongruity is hard for Gawain to know. Already an unsettling ambiguity has informed some events—the grim challenge put forward as a Christmas game; the journey with no known destination; the barbed, forbidding castle that opens with welcome and joy.

Gawain denies none of the tributes to his *nurture*, and Christmas passes with feasting, games, good manners, gentle talk. Through it all Gawain carries himself with debonair ease and seems the embodiment of courtesy. There is little reason to think twice about the disregard of his prowess and faith and the emphasis on manners until the host proposes the exchange-of-winnings game, which requires Gawain to take his ease in the castle while the host goes off to the hunt, their winnings to be exchanged at the end of the day. Acceding to this jovial proposition is an obligation, for Gawain can hardly accept hospitality unresponsively. Yet to accede is to be vaguely entrapped: it is simple to imagine what may be won on a hunt, but what can be won in the castle? His own good manners draw Gawain into another game, with new stakes, new rules, new uncertainties.

However unexpected this shift in the terms of Gawain's testing may be, for the *Gawain* poet's sophisticated audience the adjoining of good manners and hunting can only hint of one thing—the pursuit of love as a hunt, a traditional narrative frame in the poetry of courtly love (Thiébaux, Freeman, Boase, Henry Kelly, Newman). Thus the poet turns his attention and ours to a comic evocation of courtly love and its ritual of yearnings, sorrows, stealth, and ennoblement. Of what this love involves the audience is fully aware, because it has long been a grand subject of romance and song. Love strikes unbidden through the eyes on sight of the beloved: thenceforth the lover serves the god of love. He yearns to make his love known to his lady and to obtain her recognition of his service in her honor. He keeps his love a secret because he thinks himself unworthy or she seems inaccessible, and he falls into a lover's malady of fevers and chills, sleepless nights, weeping, sad songs, and loss of appetite. He is in danger of death from love unrequited. Eventually the lover may approach the lady directly or be helped in his appeal by a friend who bears letters and arranges meetings. The lady resists, perhaps rejecting the affair altogether for a time, but finally she yields, speech is begun, gifts are exchanged, and the love is fulfilled, sometimes in open or in secret marriage. To this experience of love only the noble nature is susceptible: it is "of the court," not for the lowborn. And with it comes refinement of the lover's nature beyond the ordinary: not only passion but humility, generosity, sympathy, inspiration, a new awareness of the world, of time, and of destiny.

We await the turn of events, then, when the lady enters Gawain's room on the first day of her lord's hunting, and she soon confirms our suspicion and surprises Gawain by calling him first a careless sleeper "taken" unawares and later a knight whom she has "caught." The hunt of love is under way, but expected patterns are reversed: it is the lady who takes the initiative with genial aggression, sitting on the bed in which Gawain remains unclothed, offering both compliments and herself as servant. Her aim is seduction, and Gawain may succumb or phrase polite evasions. Such a seduction, of course, would seem a sure "winning" to almost any knight, and it is far from failing to appeal to Gawain—we have seen his kiss and his light embrace of the lady when they met. Besides, would any but a craven knight refuse a lady's favor? Yet the lady is the wife of Gawain's host, and her sexual favors are hardly what he should "win" and then exchange at the end of the day for whatever the deer hunt yields. Like a beast of venery, Gawain is trapped in a narrow net of courtesy woven from strands of his own reputation—*luf-talkyng*, merry manners, and fondness for women. What we enjoy now is the amusing and dangerous game of temptation played out for three days between Gawain and the lady.

The temptation is a strategy of gesture and speech, of calculated opportunities that invite Gawain's consent. Physical movement is minimal if suggestive, and it belongs to the lady: she enters, she sits on the bed, she lies down beside Gawain, she sallies out laughing, she "cachez hym in armez" (1305) and bends over to kiss him; more urgent on the third day, she "felle ouer his fayre face" (1758) for a first kiss and for another "sykande ho swe3e doun" ("sighing, she swung down" [1796]).[1] But Gawain receives, not gives, these kisses, and he must counter the lady's "spechez of specialté" ("expressions of fondness" [1778]) with responses that ward off her offer of service and readjust the relation so that he may be *her* servant and yet without insult do none of the things she invites. But seducing Gawain is not a question of gesture alone, as the lady must know when she suggests that he take her by force. His cleanness (*clannes*) will not fall so easily, and seduction must involve not the body only but the mind and its confident store of scruple. The dialogues are amusements, but they are struggles too. On the first day, laughing that Gawain is her captive, the lady "lauced" ("loosed") her jests as a huntress might loose dogs on the scent. The next day Gawain is "frayned . . . and fondet" ("tested . . . and probed" [1549]) by the lady and "defended hym . . . fayre" (1551), and the third day with "smooth smylyng" they "smeten into merþe" ("smote into mirth" [1764]). The undertone of menace is inescapable, and it ties the muted sounds of droll civility to the horn blasts and shouts in the quests and kills of deer, boar, and fox that enclose the bedroom scenes. Thus while her physical beauty and provocative gestures are well deployed, the lady's most dangerous resource is her skill with words—those "spechez of specialté þat sprange of her mouth" (1778). A fifteenth-century treatise on *nurture* pithily evokes this double-edged situation: "With fayre speche þou may haue þe wille, / And with þy speche þou may þe spille" (Furnivall 264).

Against Gawain words are an apt weapon. Our first impression of him comes in his well-turned address as he offers King Arthur "counseyl" and asks to be given the task of exchanging blows with the Green Knight. This speech (343–61)—and Gawain's gesture itself—shows us what sort of man he is. As Gawain speaks we like his deference to Arthur and Guinevere, his indignation at the cowering silence of "bolde" knights on the bench, his self-deprecation. He has spirit and control, and he seems justified when he ends his speech with his own challenge to the court: "if I carp not comlyly let alle þis cort rych / Bout blame" ("if I speak unfittingly let all this noble court blame me" [360–61]). We have no comparable example of the lady's mastery of "talkyng noble" before the bedroom scenes, but we get an early hint of it in her entertainment of Gawain at the Christmas feast "þurz her dere dalyaunce of her derne wordez" ("through the pleasing dalliance of her secret words" [1012]).

It is the competitive *luf-talkyng* of Gawain and the lady that ties *Sir Gawain and the Green Knight* to other poems in the courtly-love tradition. The notion that success in love requires the learning of accomplished speech reaches far into antiquity, but for medieval writers on the subject—both poets and exegetes—Ovid was the ultimate secular authority. The *Ars amatoria* advises the lover to write letters and to learn how to plead because women may be conquered by eloquent words, and the *Amores* offers many examples of words and gestures used as implements of the lover's art. In a chapter of *De arte honesti amandi* (*The Art of Courtly Love*) on ways of acquiring love, Andreas Capellanus includes eight model dialogues that would-be lovers may study. In Guillaume de Lorris's *Romance of the Rose*—which praises Gawain's courtesy and condemns Kay the Seneschal for gossip and mockery—the God of Love enjoins the dreamer to avoid base talk and confers on him, along with Sweet Thoughts and Sweet Looks, the gift of Sweet Talk. Jaufres Rudels, Bernard de Ventadorn, and other troubadours sang of love in seductive dialogues, debates, and visions of *fin' amors* (Topsfield; Wilhelm, *Seven Troubadours*). And Chaucer's Criseyde, considering Pandarus's suit on behalf of Troilus, lets slip her interest when she asks, "Kan he wel speke of love?" and then adds, "I preye / Tel me, for I the bet me shal purveye" (Robinson 407). The dreamer in the *Book of the Duchess*, listening to the Man in Black tell the course of his love, is also interested in how he spoke to Fair White (Robinson 277):

But wolde ye tel me the manere
To hire which was your firste speche,
Therof I wolde yow beseche;
And how she knewe first your thoght,
Whether ye loved hir or noght.

By the time *Sir Gawain and the Green Knight* was written, the question of speech between lovers, or between tempter and prey—How did the talk begin? What course did it take?—had become one of the great themes in the ritual of literary love.

But the *luf-talkyng* in *Sir Gawain and the Green Knight* is unlike that of many lovers in romance, whose speeches make pleas of merit and pledges of honest intent and long service. The talk here envisions only the present, and its intent is to disrupt the pentangular coherence of Gawain's courtesy. There is in the lady's second temptation a dizzying demonstration of how speech may ensnare. This instance (1508–34), a sort of verbal temblor of shifting rhetorical turns, descends from a peak of acknowledged principle and text through vistas of brave love to mere petulant, demanding carnality. The lady poses a question ("What is the purpose [*skylle*] of your knighthood and courtesy?"), but at once this turns into claims about doctrine in the game of true love, about what knights always do, about Gawain's renown, about how she has come twice to Gawain in two days and yet heard no word of love—nor is this all. She settles at last on accusation: Gawain's neglect insults her by implying she is too dull to learn. Syntax disintegrates in the sweep of the lady's speech, and with it coherence and plausibility (some editors repair this passage with punctuation); yet we see with Gawain, who cites her reliance on "talez of armes" (1541), how she can shape a maze, shift from point to point, suspend logic, and end implying a mutual consent to all that has gone before. The idea is to unsettle Gawain's certainty and to draw him into a petty version of courtesy that would see it as nothing more than amorous adventures from romance, ladies who risk all for love, knights who avenge them, and happiness in the bower (Barron 59; Mills). These elements are some part of Gawain's courtesy, indeed, but not all; for him they represent a partial, diminished, and self-centered code, bereft of faith, cleanness, fellowship.

Words capable of such reductive work do seem peculiarly empowered. The lady's "speeches of specialty" are not the first or the only instance in the poem of the mischief that words can do. The first occasion belongs to the Green Knight when his challenge to Arthur's court is answered with silence (309–15):

"What, is þis Arþures hous," quoþ þe haþel þenne,
"þat al þe rous rennes of þurȝ ryalmes so mony?
Where is now your sourquydrye and your con-
    questes,
Your gryndellayk and your greme and your grete
    wordes?
Now is þe reuel and þe renoun of þe Rounde Table
Ouerwalt with a worde of on wyȝes speche,
For al dares for drede without dynt schewed!"

"What, is this Arthur's house," said the man then, "whose fame runs through so many realms? Where is your pride now, and your conquests, your fierceness and your anger and your great words? Now is the revelry and renown of the Round Table overwhelmed with a word of one man's speech, for all cower in fear without a blow shown!"

The Green Knight's scornful taunt carries its own interpretation of the response to the challenge: the pride of Camelot is but a boast, and to bring it down and shape disaster for Gawain requires but one man's speech. And with this must fall the joy and confidence of all who have believed in Brutus and Britain and the Round Table. Yet if words may conjure our doom, they also may sustain, for before all else the world was created with a word (Andrew and Waldron 194; Colish; Gallacher): "And God said: Be light made. And light was made" (Gen. 1.3, Douay Version); "In the beginning was the Word, and the Word was with God, and the Word was God" (John 1.1, Douay Version). Gawain's words are sometimes prayers, as on his journey from Camelot (753–58):

I beseche þe, Lorde,
And Mary, þat is myldest moder so dere,
Of sum herber þer heȝly I myȝt here masse
And þy matynez tomorne, mekely I ask,
And þerto prestly I pray my Pater and Aue
And Crede.

I beseech thee, Lord, and Mary, mildest mother beloved, of some lodging where I might devoutly hear mass and matins tomorrow, and thereto I earnestly pray my Pater and Ave and Creed.

With the added benediction "Cros Kryst me spede" (762), Gawain's words seem by miracle to deliver him to the shelter of that unexpected castle in the wilderness. In the interviews, too, faith is never out of mind. From the

first morning the dialogues are strewn with Gawain's casual oaths—"By
God," "Kryst yow forӡelde," "In goode faytħe," "so saue me Dryӡtyn," "By
sayn Jon"—as if his invocation might disperse a malevolent spell. But they
do not daunt the lady. On the first day she claims, perhaps in furtive derision,
that Gawain has become her captive "þurӡ grace" ("through grace") of "þat
ilke Lorde þat þe lyft haldez" ("that same Lord who holds the heavens"
[1256]), and she answers his "Mary yow ӡelde" (1263) with "Bi Mary" (1268)
and shows that she too may invoke the Virgin. One of her strongest assaults
slyly alludes to God's role in the contest of talk (1291–93):

> And as ho sto ho stonyed hym wyth ful stor wordez:
> "Now He þat spedez vch spech þis disport ӡelde yow,
> But þat ӡe be Gawain hit gotz in mynde!"

And as she stood she stunned him with stern words: "Now He who
prospers each speech repay you this pleasure, but that you are Gawain
must be doubted!"

The poet sums up the course of the dialogues in the closing lines of a wheel
(1506–07): "Much speche þay þer expoun / Of druryes greme and grace"
("Much they expounded there of trouble and bliss in love"). The dialogues
themselves are "greme and grace," threatening and pleasant, wounding and
assuaging, and they extend the poem's various shifts between "blysse and
blunder" (19) and deepen its ambiguities. The poem's steady interest in
"wich spede is in speech" ("what fortune is in speech" [918]), in "þe teccheles
termes of talkyng noble" ("the faultless terms of noble talk" [917]), in "grete
wordes," makes us watchful of confessions and judgments as Gawain's trials
come to an end. And we are troubled by words that go unspoken in a poem
so aware of language—those absent in Gawain's confession to the chapel
priest after the third temptation, where nothing is heard of the girdle (1876–
84). Is this oversight or intention? Is this a silence that speaks? We are more
comfortable with Gawain's confession at his last meeting with Bertilak, where
he sees the girdle as a "luf-lace" and himself as "fawty and falce" (2438,
2382). Bertilak is tolerant because he has proved that Gawain is "on þe
fautlest freke þat euer on fote ӡede" ("one of the most faultless men who
ever went on foot" [2363]). Gawain failed in truth because he loved his life,
and a man is not blamed for that. This accounting seems full and just.

The lady's third temptation turns on the exchange of gifts, a ritual of lovers
that often concludes the first phase of *luf-talkyng*. When Gawain asserts that
he has no lover and no plans to find one, the lady makes her desire for a
"drury," a lover's token, seem a sentimental gesture of withdrawal and
despair. But Gawain easily resists a commitment so evidently trivial yet

binding, and his speech is flawless as he refuses to give or to receive. He has had his warning on the evening before. Then, having tried him twice and found him faithful, his host says, "'þrid tyme, þrowe best'—þenke on þe morn" (1680)—the third time's the charm. And we see on that morn that Gawain cannot resist the offer of the girdle that might save his life. In this moment, as Bertilak says, Gawain "lakked a lyttel" (2366). He accepts the girdle, hides it as a secret gift, and so betrays his truthful speech and his courtesy. Artful though his words have been, in the course of *luf-talkyng* Gawain is at last undone. And peerless as Gawain is—in Bertilak's phrase, "as perle bi þe quite pese is of prys more" ("as a pearl beside white peas is worth more" 2364)—he stands but a man.

NOTE

[1]All translations from *Gawain* are mine.

BIBLIOGRAPHIC NOTE

In addition to the works cited above, there are a number of texts useful for the study of courtly love and courtesy. Among the classical and medieval texts and translations are Boccaccio, *Filocolo*; Caxton, *The Book of the Ordre of Chyualry*; Goldin, *Lyrics of the Troubadours and Trouvères*; Hill and Bergin, *Anthology of the Provençal Troubadours*; Lowanne E. Jones, *The Cort d'Amor*; and Pisan, *The Epistle of Othea*, ed. Bühler.

Also of interest are the following secondary works: Dodd, *Courtly Love in Chaucer and Gower*; Donaldson, "The Myth of Courtly Love," in his *Speaking of Chaucer* (154–63); Dronke, *Medieval Latin and the Rise of the European Love-Lyric*; Ferrante, "*Cortes' Amor* in Medieval Texts"; Ferrante and Economou, *In Pursuit of Perfection: Courtly Love in Medieval Literature*; Douglas Kelly, *Medieval Imagination, Rhetoric and the Poetry of Courtly Love*; Lawlor, *Patterns of Love and Courtesy*; Leonard, *Laughter in the Courts of Love from Chaucer to Spenser*; Lewis, *The Allegory of Love*; Moore, *Love in Twelfth Century France*; Robertson, *A Preface to Chaucer*; and Smith and Snow, *The Expansion and Transformation of Courtly Literature*.

The Breakdown of Chivalry in the Fourteenth Century

Louis Brewer Hall

The recognition that the Middle Ages had some of the same problems as the twentieth century, yet provided alternative solutions, has combined with the spreading application of interdisciplinary studies to new areas of the curriculum and attracted students with differing backgrounds—the natural and physical sciences, the social sciences, engineering, and business—to courses in medieval literature. These students, as well as English majors, are pleasantly surprised to learn that the interdisciplinary approach has long been prevalent in medieval studies, and when the methods of other disciplines are brought to the literature of the period, all students respond with new interest to the many threads of commonalty between the Middle Ages and this century. Some students had their interest aroused reading Barbara Tuchman's A Distant Mirror. Although this popular history has perpetuated some old misconceptions of the Middle Ages, these errors are easily corrected during class discussions.

On the first day of class I ask the students to read Sir Gawain and the Green Knight casually and for pleasure. They always respond to the poem as a good story, but in discussions they adopt an amused and superior attitude, interpreting the poem as a realistic picture of the fourteenth century—sans technology, sans economics, sans psychology.

Students are then made aware that what they have read is not a picture of daily life but a picture of a world idealized for a special audience hearing (for it is being read to them) descriptions of ideal landscapes, ideal castles, ideal knights and ladies acting in an ideal manner as their conduct and standards are being tested (Curtius 182–202; Huizinga, Waning, 37–50, 67–84).

Reading on their own, many students have already been transported from the world they know to the idealized world of science fiction, to the world of Ursula Le Guin in The Left Hand of Darkness and The Dispossessed or of Isaac Asimov in the Foundation series. These students perceive the duality of the two worlds, but they usually comment that the world of science fiction is the world of the future, whereas the world of Sir Gawain and the Green Knight returns to the past, to Camelot. Then they recall that we use the phrase "Once there was a Camelot" with the same connotation: an ideal world already made. I can then explain the philosophical reasons behind the Gawain poet's use of history and show that the future, as the poet interpreted it, would end with the Apocalypse.

The move that students make from their world to that of science fiction is not absolute. In their own minds they carry a foundation of information and assumptions to guide them in that idealized world, so that both consciously and unconsciously they contrast the two worlds. Recognizing this necessary connection between the two worlds, students are convinced that they must go back to the fourteenth century to establish as far as possible that same kind of foundation for the ideal world of *Sir Gawain and the Green Knight*. Of course, the foundation for the medieval audience contains too many unknown stones to be reconstructed completely, but selected details will provide a basis, and the more information that can be referred to it, the more the foundation will serve as a guide to the ideal.

From Jean Gimpel's *The Medieval Machine* the student reads the assigned chapters, "The Energy Resources of Europe and Their Development," "Mining the Mineral Wealth," "Environment and Pollution." Technological development and its practical applications in water mills for grains, trip mills for fulling cloth and forging iron, and other changes that affected everyday life must all be taken into consideration. As part of the classroom discussion, engineering students are always glad to report on the development of power sources like the crank and gears (Lynn White 79–134), and the mills, mining, and machines can be illustrated with slides from Delort's *Life in the Middle Ages*.

Reading and discussing Gimpel and White establish in the students' minds a similarity between the twentieth century and the fourteenth. That similarity is strengthened by a survey of the economics of the Middle Ages with its cycles of collapse, depression, and recovery. A sharp inflation affected especially the price of crafted goods like armor and lowered farm prices, so that supporting a court of knights and ladies took more land than formerly (Peters 247–48). The students are interested that the *Gawain* poet comments on the cost of Guenore's dias (79).

After the technology and economics have laid something of a foundation as a guide to the ideal, the students add more specific detail by ascertaining the backgrounds of an audience of knights and ladies. The knights had been directly affected by technology and inflation. After the thirteenth century the use of steel plates of armor to fit all over the body had increased. The pieces around joints were articulated by lamination. This development is easily shown from any collection of brasses like that of James Mann or from a history of armor like Ashdown's. English metal workers had not the skill needed to mold the plates and articulate the lamination, and armor was being imported from Milan and Florence through brokers (Origo 11–13). Sir Gawain's armor is idealized, of course, but the description is basically that of the best fourteenth-century tournament or dress armor and is illustrated in Mann (pl. 5, 6). Each knight paid for his own equipment including horses (he usually had three), and the armor was contingent on what he could afford. The opulence of Sir Gawain's would be striking, but for this very reason the knights of the audience would be alert to the danger of his being ambushed and slaughtered on the trip through the wilderness. The audiences would also notice that Sir Gawain was protected by the Virgin Mary, another example of idealization.

The personal wealth of the knights varied greatly. As a mercenary a knight could rise from any social class except that of a farm laborer. By the fourteenth century mercenaries were the backbone of the army, paid by the day for a specific campaign when a lord needed them. At the beginning of his career, the mercenary likely had no money, and he had to purchase his armor and horses from a dealer on credit or from another knight who could no longer use it, because of injuries or of age. The mercenary bought only the minimum of plate to give maneuverability because he generally fought not on horseback but on foot. If he fought well, he was knighted with little ceremony by his employer (not the king) and was then addressed as "sir," though in his lord's castle he would be treated as a servant (Terry Jones 13–25). Still, as a knight at the court the mercenary must be considered as part of the audience for the poem.

A degree above the mercenary stood the indentured knight. What had been for many centuries the traditional obligations, especially the pledge for military service, were giving way to monetary payments and written contracts. The indentures varied, but they were usually contracts for life providing a fixed wage and other emoluments, perhaps food and fuel (Derek Baker; Terry Jones 7–8).

When called for his military service the indentured knight was expected to provide not the minimum of armor but a complete set of plate, good weapons, and good horses. Some indentured knights had enough money for this outlay; others would have to borrow, like the mercenary. The indentured knight was not a mercenary, however, did not consider himself one, and was not treated like one by his lord. He would remain in the great hall listening to *Sir Gawain and the Green Knight*.

The third classification of knight, the aristocratic knight, was landed and possibly had an inherited title. He could still be poor, however, a victim of inflation or of some unexpected calamity (Terry Jones 25, 242). The aristocratic knight with enough productive land to afford his knighthood is the more traditional figure. If he inherited a prestigious title, he would usually serve as an important commander during wartime. The social distance between the aristocratic knight and the other categories beneath him was large, but all three categories probably had war experience in common during this period of recurring conflict, and this experiment certainly colored their interpretation of *Sir Gawain and the Green Knight*.

Only one modern reconstruction attempts to reproduce the effect of what the medieval soldier experienced on the field of combat: John Keegan in *The Face of Battle* did just that for Agincourt, a battle close enough to the period of *Sir Gawain and the Green Knight* to be a valuable addition to the foundation. Keegan's description is detailed, unglorified, bloody, and it provides a contrast between the knight as veteran and the knight as audience for the romance (79–116).

Keegan's reconstruction of Agincourt, accompanied by selected illuminations, helps the student understand the confusion, agony, and brutality of medieval warfare. The subject matter of fourteenth-century illuminations is portrayed without depth perspective, but the student used to modern, nonrealistic art quickly adjusts and discovers that the flatness of presentation intensifies the feeling of battle experience.

The final component of the castle audience consisted of the women. The students are always interested that women, as contributors to the economy, managed the daily routine of the castles, and their executive abilities can be judged by the size of the fourteenth-century Château de Saumur pictured on the September page of the *Très riches heures*, a castle that closely resembles Sir Bertilak's. In other illustrations women can be seen helping defend a castle under siege, directing the sowing in the spring, harvesting in the autumn, and accompanying the lords on hunts.

The students now notice that the foundation they have built contrasts with the picture of life in the two idealized courts of the poem. They also perceive that the ethical standards that motivate Sir Gawain differ from those of knights in battle or those exhibited in the economic life of the times. They are glad their perceptions were supported by medieval writers like Eustache Deschamps, Alan Chartier (Barber, *Knight* 328–29), and Caxton, who advised reading the grail adventures of Lancelot, Perceval, Gawain, and other knights (Caxton 121–25; Allmand 29).

The contradiction between the two worlds—one set of standards preserved in the ideal world of history, the other developing as social values changed—was perceived also by the knights themselves. To help resolve the contradictions, they formed into ceremonious orders that revived the values of the past (Barber, *Knight* 307–09; Huizinga, *Waning* 85–107). Edward I proposed the Order of the Round Table; the Order of the Star was established in France; the Order of the Golden Fleece in the Duchy of Burgundy; the Order of the Sash in Spain. The most famous for us was the Order of the Garter, its motto inscribed at the end of *Sir Gawain and the Green Knight*.

Less well-known orders were formed, some on special occasions to celebrate festivals or tournaments. In all of them, the knights created an ideal world with special dress, ceremonies, rules of conduct, tests for valor, and penalties for failure (Allmand 25–27; Barber, *Knight* 399–444). The world of the orders was as divorced from the world in which the knights lived as was the world of *Sir Gawain and the Green Knight,* for the orders consciously imitated that world of romance. The orders created an ideal world that was realized physically; the poem created an ideal world realized imaginatively.

The students now read and discuss the chapters assigned in Huizinga's *Homo Ludens,* and they discover the psychological connection that extends from the wars the knights fought to the orders they joined and the poem they heard. From Huizinga the students understand that playing the game is not trivial but very serious (13). They need only recall a football game or the Olympic Games to agree that the game absorbs the player and spectator intensely and completely and that during the game both are separated from the world in which they live, the player physically, the spectator mentally.

The students discern how in the orders these roles are reversed. The knights become players in a game with similarities to battle—even more so during tournaments—and, listening to *Sir Gawain and the Green Knight,* they become spectators of a game, one also with special dress, rules of conduct, tests, and penalties. The student has now developed an empathy with the fourteenth-century audience that the intellectual construction of the foundation alone did not provide.

The two experiences, the empathy and the intellectual understanding, have brought the students a long way from their first superficial reading. Even if they have had no formal literary training, they will be receptive to a literary analysis of *Sir Gawain and the Green Knight,* and they have acquired a wide comprehension of the Middle Ages.

Course Outline
(A Six-Week Module)

Required Texts:
Marie Borroff, trans., *Sir Gawain and the Green Knight: A New Verse Translation*
Jean Gimpel, *The Medieval Machine*

On Reserve:
Johan Huizinga, *Homo Ludens*
John Keegan, *The Face of Battle*

Week
1   Read *Sir Gawain and the Green Knight.* Discuss the ideal world of the poem, establishing a foundation guide.
2   Read Gimpel, chs. 1, 3, 4, 5, 6, 9. Report on Lynn White, ch. 3. Discuss industry in the Middle Ages.
3   The economy of the Middle Ages. The history and the economy of armor.

4   Read on reserve: Keegan, "Agincourt" (79–116). The battles of Crècy, Poi-
         tiers, the siege of Calais. Discuss medieval warfare.
5   Read on reserve: Huizinga, *Homo Ludens*, chs. 1, 2, 3, 5, 7, 12. Discuss
         the knightly orders and tournaments as they illustrate elements of the game
         from *Homo Ludens*. Show women's role at the castle with slides.
6   A careful reading and discussion of *Sir Gawain and the Green Knight*. The
         foundations of fourteenth-century civilization in operation.

Religion and Law in *Sir Gawain and the Green Knight*

Robert J. Blanch

For those instructors and students who are approaching *Sir Gawain and the Green Knight* for the first time, this elusive Middle English romance appears to offer a bewildering variety of conventions and cultural perspectives as well as a dazzling array of interwoven motifs, symbols, and images. Although an elucidation of two important elements—the religious and legal traditions of the Middle Ages—will not resolve all the complex questions raised by *Gawain*, such an examination should contribute to our understanding of the poem. In short, if we scrutinize the religious and legal underpinnings of the narrative—the cultural bonds that shape Gawain's Christian and chivalric behavior—we shall perceive how and why Gawain's violation of spiritual and legal obligations is intertwined with the motifs of sin, penitence, and rebirth. Background materials on religion traced in this essay will include, then, the cycle of the ecclesiastical year—especially the liturgical significance of the Feast of Fools, Lent, Michaelmas, All Saints' Day, All Souls' Day, Christmas Eve, and the Feast of the Circumcision; the invocation of particular saints—Saint Julian the Hospitaller, Saint Peter, Saint Giles Aegidius, and Saint John the Evangelist—and the role played by the Virgin Mary; the three temptations at Castle Hautdesert; and the two confession scenes. Supplementary information on law, however, will highlight the tie between the *Gawain* poet's legal formulas and the phraseology of medieval contracts. This essay, likewise, will call attention to the background of the medieval contractual system, particularly the concepts of contract, covenant, surety, tally, and "year and day" in English juridical procedure and common law.

Rooted in the legal strictures and covenants of Judaism as well as in Christ's institution of the Eucharist and his directive to the apostles—"Do this in commemoration of me" (Luke 22. 19)—the celebration of holy days and seasons in the Christian liturgy initially springs from Sunday, the day of the Lord, as the period most closely linked with the Eucharistic sacrifice and with the memory of Christ's life, death, and Resurrection (Staley 6–7, 20–21). In time, however, Easter is pinpointed as the most important Sunday of the Church year, for that day commemorates both the Last Supper and the rising of Christ from the dead. With Easter perceived as the center of the Christian liturgical year, then, a series of movable or seasonal feasts—"the Proper of the Season" (Denis-Boulet 47–48)—is established; radiating from the placement of Easter in the Church calendar, such feasts (Ascension and Pentecost) are interlaced naturally and symbolically with the revolutions of the moon, for ". . . the rotation of cyclical time . . . gives man an image of the eternal" (Denis-Boulet 10). Fixed feasts (Christmas and New Year's Day), on the other hand, are associated with particular days in the solar year and constitute the "sanctoral cycle" of the liturgy (Denis-Boulet 50).

Apart from a reference to Christmas (line 37), the Mass celebrating the Circumcision of Christ (1 January) as well as the Feast of Fools (62–65) constitutes the first depiction of the liturgical cycle in *Gawain*. Conducted by subdeacons (minor clerics), the Feast of Fools represents a noisy burlesque of sacred Christian ritual (Savage, "Feast" 537–42). More significant allusions to the liturgy of the calendar, however, appear in a passage (498–535) portraying the changing seasons—a passage that provides both imagery of natural flux and a reminder of the instability of earthly life (Ann Matonis 43–45). Lent, the first holy season noted (502–03) in the description of nature's cyclical pattern, comprises the forty weekdays preceding Easter. Commemorating both Christ's forty-day fast in the desert (Matt. 4. 1–2) and the forty-hour period between Good Friday and Easter Sunday (Staley 191–92), Lent is a time of fasting (no meat and one full meal daily)—a penitential sign of mortification of the flesh. In *Gawain*, however, the reference to Lenten fare may suggest Gawain's ultimate self-abnegation and spiritual rebirth (Keenan 34), or perhaps it represents an ironic foreshadowing of his need for humility at Castle Hautdesert (860–900)—a world of lavish feasts camouflaged as self-denial (Blanch, "Games Poets Play" 77–78). Michaelmas, the second feast mentioned (532–33) in this passage, honors the archangel Michael and all the angels, particularly Michael's battle (Rev. 12.7–9) in heaven against Lucifer and the other fallen angels (Durandus VII.12.290). Traditionally celebrated on 29 September, Michaelmas may be identified with "the testing and judgment of Gawain" (Keenan 34) or with a "quarter day," an appointed time for settling accounts (Pace). For Gawain, then, the feast may represent a reminder of the "winter pledge" (533), the "wage" of his beheading, to be paid to the Green Knight on New Year's Day (Pace).

Immediately following the references to Lent and Michaelmas, two additional feasts—All Saints' Day (536–38) and All Souls' Day (566–67)—are noted as the poet delineates Gawain's preparations for his quest of the Green Knight. All Saints' Day (1 November), a feast that stems from Pope Boniface IV's seventh-century transformation of the Roman pantheon into a Roman Catholic church venerating the Virgin Mary and all the Christian martyrs (Durandus VII.34.297–98; Brewster 470–71), is traditionally designated in the liturgical calendar as a general celebration honoring God's saints and martyrs. Inasmuch as King Arthur regularly holds court on that day (Tolkien and Gordon 88, n. 536), his convocation of the illustrious representatives of chivalry for an All Saints' Day festival exalting Gawain may link Gawain with all the virtuous Christian knights (Levy 87–88) or may suggest Gawain's reward for true Christian living on earth (Keenan 34–35). All Souls' Day (2 November), however, commemorates all the faithful deceased. Solemnized through the celebration of three Masses for the eternal rest of the departed (*Missale Romanum* 781), All Souls' Day calls attention to the themes of mortality and fear of death in *Gawain* (Neaman), underscores the likelihood of Gawain's fall (Longo 72), and intimates, perhaps, Gawain's future confrontation with spiritual death (the three temptations at Castle Hautdesert).

The final allusions to the cycle of the Church year—Christmas Eve and the Feast of the Circumcision (New Year's Day)—are linked with Gawain's arrival at Hautdesert and with the Green Chapel tableau, respectively. Originally connoting an evening "watch" devoted to prayer and contemplation (Hampson 2:387; Staley 181), a solemn preparation for the joyful Feast of the Nativity (Durandus VI.12.179), the Vigil of Christmas or Christmas Eve became marred increasingly by elaborate meals and drunken revelry. By the fifth century, however, all vigils of holy days—including the Vigil of Christmas—were transformed into fast days (Hampson 1:354, 2:387). In the opening scene at Bertilak's castle, Gawain is served a fish banquet (889–93) because of the traditional Church regulation on the Advent fast. Although Gawain perceives this rich meal—a symbol of pride and a possible foreshadowing of his future spiritual blindness—as a feast (894), the lord's servants ironically depict the dinner as "penaunce" ("penitential fare" [897]) that will "amende" ("improve" [898]) in the future (Blanch, "Games Poets Play" 77–78 and "Game of Invoking" 244–45)—penitential terms that signalize Gawain's ultimate need for judgment and confession at the Green Chapel.

The climactic Green Chapel scene itself, moreover, takes place on 1 January, the Feast of the Circumcision of Christ. Conventionally represented in medieval iconography by a hatchet (Brewster 50), perhaps the religious counterpart of the Green Knight's ax (2222–26), the Feast of the Circumcision (1998–2010) memorializes "the first shedding of blood by Christ, a foreshadowing of the Crucifixion" (Longo 75–77), and symbolizes the remission of humanity's sins (Durandus VI.15.183–84). In terms of the narrative of *Gawain*, however, the Circumcision motif—the blood flowing from Gawain's wound in the neck (2313–15)—suggests the knight's spiritual rebirth through penitence (Levy 69–71; Neaman).

Additional evidence that serves to highlight the religious coloring of *Gawain* may be found in the traditions identified with four saints invoked in the narrative—traditions that illuminate the themes of sin, penance, and rebirth embedded in the poem. Julian the Hospitaller, the first saint mentioned in *Gawain*, is often depicted in medieval art and legend as a courteous nobleman, hunter, and generous host to weary travelers (Blanch, "Game of Invoking" 237–40). Inasmuch as Julian, through an error of judgment, kills his parents, he performs acts of charity in order to atone for his sin. Gawain invokes Julian's courtesy and nobility (774–75) when he seeks "good lodging" (776) at Castle Hautdesert, the setting for the knight's fall, but he ironically overlooks the significant motifs of penance and contrition in the Julian tradition (Tamplin 406–07)—themes that ultimately play a vital role at the Green Chapel. Saint Peter, the second saint noted in *Gawain*, is often represented as a celestial gatekeeper, for he bears the keys of the heavenly kingdom (Matt. 16.13–19). Linked with the concepts of sin, absolution, and redemption, the keys suggest Peter's ability to free humanity from the bonds of sin (Blanch, "Game of Invoking" 241). Even more significant, perhaps, is Peter's traditional identification in the Bible with the cock (Mark 14.30, and John 13.38), a symbol both of Peter's triple denial of Jesus and of his subsequent remorse and pardon for his faithless conduct (Blanch, "Game of Invoking" 241–42). In *Gawain*, on the other hand, the Peter tradition is elicited by the porter's invocation (813–14) once the knight arrives at Hautdesert, the stage for Gawain's "binding" and judgment. Further evidence emphasizing the tie between the Saint Peter oath and Gawain may be found in a series of cock images. For example, a reference to three cockcrows (1412 and 1415) on Gawain's second day of temptation is reminiscent of the rooster crowing during Peter's triple repudiation of Christ. Somewhat later (New Year's Day), however, Gawain's sleep is disturbed, for he warily acknowledges the judgment of fate, his engagement with the Green Knight at the Green Chapel. Hearing three cockcrows (2006–09), then, Gawain carefully prepares himself for the impending doomsday. Inasmuch as the cock is associated with Peter through various symbolic motifs—spiritual watchfulness (Mark 14.32–42), especially because of the approach of the Last Judgment; penance (confession); and the promise of spiritual renewal—a clear connection between the Saint Peter legend and Gawain's behavior at the Green Chapel is established (Blanch, "Game of Invoking" 245–48).

The traditions evoked by the remaining saints' oaths (Giles and John the Evangelist) reflect, likewise, the themes of sin, penance, and redemption in *Gawain*. Giles (1644–45), for instance, is portrayed in medieval legend and art as a humble recluse who, during his three-year life in a cave, is nourished by the milk of a hind. While Flavius, the king of the Goths, and his hunters track the hind for three consecutive days, the animal seeks refuge in Giles's cave. At the conclusion of the third day, however, Giles is wounded by an arrow shot by one of the king's archers. Such an incident parallels the situations in *Gawain*, for the three-day chase in the Giles legend is symbolically analogous to the three hunts-temptations at Hautdesert. Furthermore, the wound suffered by Giles foreshadows Gawain's injury (2313–15) at the Green Chapel (Blanch, "Game of Invoking" 250–51, 253).

In another significant incident in the Giles tradition, the Mass of Saint Giles, the saint is depicted as a confessor—an intercessor for King Charles (France) who has committed an "unmentionable sin." Once Giles gives Charles a scroll delivered by an angel, a letter that exposes the king's unconfessed sin and offers him forgiveness if he is truly contrite, the king repents and is thus pardoned by Christ. In *Gawain*, the symbolic affinity between the Mass of Saint Giles legend and the Green Chapel episode is clearly traced. After the Green Knight discloses Gawain's "unconfessed sin," the knight's failure to offer Bertilak the green girdle during the third exchange of winnings (2356–59), Gawain admits his faults to the Green Knight as secular confessor (2374–88), is penitent, and is thus spiritually redeemed (Blanch, "Game of Invoking" 251–52, 254).

Saint John the Evangelist, the last figure in the procession of Gawain's saints, is represented in Christian legend and iconography as a mystic who repudiates worldly vanity, as the virginal "disciple whom Jesus loved" (John 21.7, 20), as a courageous follower of Christ, and as the loyal protector of the Virgin Mary (John 19.26–27). Furthermore, John is identified with the concept of penitence, for the Emperor Domitian exiles the saintly apostle to Patmos, an island in the Aegean Sea and the backdrop for John's life of self-denial and fasting. In *Gawain*, Gawain's invocation of Saint John (1788, 1790–91) underscores the knight's chastity during the third temptation. At the same time, however, the Saint John oath ironically suggests Gawain's faults and his need for the qualities conventionally attributed to the apostle (contempt for earthly things, courage, and loyalty). Once Gawain experiences shame and humility during his confession to the Green Knight, Arthur's chaste knight is offered the hope of spiritual rebirth—a release from the allurement of worldly bonds (Blanch, "Game of Invoking" 254–61).

Although the traditions identified with the four saints constitute an important part of the religious background of *Gawain*, the figure of the Virgin Mary, likewise, plays a significant role in the narrative. Conventionally arrayed in white (truth) and blue (fidelity), Mary gave birth to Christ without violating her virginity. Especially venerated among women because she was chosen to be the mother of God, Mary was conceived free from the stain of original sin, Adam and Eve's disobedience in the Garden of Eden. Inasmuch as the Virgin Mary's holiness contrasts sharply with Eve's disloyal behavior toward God, Mary represents both a foil to Eve and an appropriate mediatrix between God and humanity. In *Gawain*, moreover, the Virgin Mary shapes the knight's behavior, for she safeguards Gawain's chastity (1768–69) when he is threatened by Lady Bertilak's sexual advances. Thus protected by the Blessed Virgin, an image of whom is depicted on the inside of his shield (649–50), Gawain's courage in knightly conflict is energized. While Gawain often prays to Mary (736–39, 754–58) for physical shelter and guidance before he arrives at Castle Hautdesert, the five joys (644–47) of Mary—the Annunciation (the angel Gabriel's announcement that Mary will be the mother of Christ), the Nativity, the Resurrection of Christ, the Ascension (Christ's bodily ascent into heaven forty days after Easter), and the Assumption (the heavenly ascent of Mary's body and soul after her death)—act as spiritual underpinnings for Gawain's courage.

The final religious strands entwined in the narrative of *Gawain* are the three temptations at Hautdesert and the two confession tableaux. The three temptations at Bertilak's castle, first of all, spring from the conception of the world as explained in 1 John 2.16: "For all that is in the world, the lust of the flesh, and the lust of the eyes, and the pride of life, is not of the Father, but is of the world." According to medieval Christian tradition, then, the temptations outlined by John—the flesh (gluttony), the eyes (avarice), and pride (vainglory)—are identified with the devil's three temptations of Adam in Eden (Gen. 3.1–7) and of Christ in the wilderness (Matt. 4.1–11, Luke 4.1–13). Gawain may thus be compared to Adam (Howard, *Three Temptations* 43–56, 215–54), for he indulges a craving for rich food both at Camelot and at Hautdesert, covets a worldly object (the green girdle), and falls prey to "pride of life." In a similar vein, Gawain is identified with Adam through the use of the *felix culpa* motif (Haines, "Allusions"; Sims; and Haines, *Fall* 74–177), the theme that depicts Adam's sin as a "fortunate fall" because his expulsion from Eden for disobedience creates the need for a redemptive second Adam (Christ). Gawain's fall, however, is especially significant, for once he shamefully acknowledges his faults—disloyalty, covetousness, cowardice, and pride—he is spiritually renewed. Finally, Gawain's and Camelot's inordinate preoccupation with decorative bindings of the earth (plaits, loops, nets, links, ribbons, cords, knots, and snares) is emblematic of pride and worldly values (Blanch, "Imagery").

Gawain's ambiguous confession to the priest (1876–84), however, raises some vexing questions, especially since the confession scene follows his "faithful" concealment of the lady's green girdle (1874–75). We may wonder whether the retention of the girdle constitutes a minor offense against God or a violation of the chivalric code (disloyalty or *vntrawpe*), for the third exchange of winnings between Bertilak and Gawain still has not taken place. While the *Gawain* poet's portrayal of the confession is disarmingly swift and straightforward, the question of Gawain's intention blurs the total effect of a sincere admission of guilt (Burrow, "Confession Scenes" 73–79 and *Reading* 104–10; Barron, *Trawthe* 85–103). Furthermore, in order to make a valid confession, signalized by the priest's absolution (forgiveness of sin), penitents must acknowledge their sins, feel genuine sorrow (contrition), make proper restitution, and resolve to sin no more; if these conditions of the sacrament of penance are met, the stain of guilt is washed away, thereby recementing the penitents' relation with God. In *Gawain*, however, the duties of confession are not fulfilled, for Gawain seemingly intends both to be pardoned for his sins and to violate the third bargain with Bertilak by retaining the lady's girdle, a clear failure to make restitution. Because Gawain neglects to carry out his confessional obligations, he is alienated from God and thus needs the spiritual salve of a valid confession.

In the second confession scene (2374–88), on the other hand, Gawain shamefully recounts his sins to the Green Knight as lay confessor and flings the girdle at him—Gawain's demonstration of restitution. Once the Green Knight offers both "absolution" (2390–94) and the green girdle to Gawain, Arthur's chastened knight vows to sin no more, for he will wear the *luf-lace* as a penitential reminder of his faults and the weakness of the flesh.

Although religious traditions play a major role in *Gawain*, medieval legal conventions—the concepts of contract, covenant, surety, tally, and "year and day"—contribute significantly, likewise, to the shaping of the narrative. Limitations of space, however, preclude a detailed discussion of the legal coloring of *Gawain*.

Marked by a formal bargaining process, the medieval contract represents, first of all, a voluntary negotiation between debtor and creditor as well as a debt liability that constrains only when one party's half of the agreement has been fulfilled. In many instances, moreover, the typical medieval agreement is termed "express," an agreement wherein contractual conditions are specified (orally or in writing) once the contract is framed; failure to complete the terms of the agreement within a year of the initial transaction triggers the debtor's liability for damages. The enforcement of such a contractual obligation is associated with the doctrine of quid pro quo. The quid, a valuable concrete thing or a symbolic representation, is given to the debtor, and in exchange for the benefit (pro quo), the contractor incurs a debt liability. Finally, if the contract entails a promise to perform some action in the future, such an obligation is construed as a covenant, a special kind of "express contract" (Blanch and Wasserman 599–600). In *Gawain*, the Green Knight's challenge (285–300) echoes both the arrangement and the phraseology of medieval contracts, for his offer to exchange blows constitutes an employment of the quid pro quo concept. Inasmuch as the challenge is perceived as a carefully constructed agreement between two people, the Green Knight demands that Gawain reiterate the covenantal terms (Gawain's assumption of indebtedness) and declare his name (378–80). Once Gawain fulfills these two conditions, the knight asserts that Gawain's interpretation of the covenant, the obligation for the rendering of services, is complete.

After Gawain pledges faithfully (403) to perform the covenant and decapitates the knight, the "couenaunt" is molded into a unilateral agreement, for Gawain now constitutes the only debtor who must offer a promised payment.

The medieval concept of surety, however, necessitates an oath or public affirmation before one witness to the covenant, a person who will guarantee the debtor's completion of the agreement and who will assume the liability if the debtor defaults. After King Arthur receives the Green Knight's ax (330) and extends it to Gawain (368–69), Arthur plays the role of the surety, the third party who authenticates the pact and guarantees the faithful behavior of the debtor (Blanch and Wasserman 600–01).

Interlocked with the motifs of surety and public pledging is the creditor's formal delivery of a tally—conventionally a notched stick, spear, or rod—to the debtor. Emblematic of the covenantor's free acceptance of indebtedness, the tally stick is usually offered by the creditor to the debtor at the moment when "credit" is granted. In *Gawain*, the tally is represented by the *giserne*, a battle-ax bestowed by the Green Knight as a gift and as a reward for partaking in the exchange of blows. Since the ax is linked with graphic descriptions of entanglement (215–20), this weapon represents a symbolic counterpart of the tally, Gawain's memento of legal obligation. Thus, after the Green Knight leaves Camelot, his ax is hung up conspicuously (477–79) as a sign of Gawain's unfulfilled covenant (Blanch and Wasserman 600–01).

The "year and day" concept, the final legal convention, is identified with judicial or regal force in Germanic juridical procedure and in English common law. Representing a legal "court day," an occasion for pleaders to outline their cases in court, "year and day," likewise, constitutes a significant common-law provision in the determination of murder. If a victim dies within a year and a day after receiving bodily injury, the assailant is guilty of murder. While this "year and day" principle for deciding murder cannot be invoked in *Gawain*, because the Green Knight's beheading does not result in death, a subtype of homicide may be relevant. Mayhem, a crime involving the loss of a bodily part, requires an identical penalty for attacker and victim. Inasmuch as Gawain is entangled both by the beheading-game covenant and by the legal punishment for mayhem, his beheading at the Green Chapel seems doubly certain. Finally, because any type of falsification (*vntrawpe*) may be punished by loss of life or of bodily member, Gawain's perfidious conduct at Hautdesert clearly foreshadows his possible fate at the Green Chapel (Blanch, "Legal Framework").

From the preceding discussion, it seems clear that religious traditions and legal conventions represent important parts of the background of *Gawain*. Encircled by emblems of Christianity—the liturgical calendar, saints' lives, the Virgin Mary's role as protectress, the temptations of Christ, and confession—Gawain is constantly reminded of his need for *trawpe*, particularly an

unwavering faith in God. At the same time, however, Gawain is enmeshed
in the medieval contractual system, for he must fulfill his obligations to the
Green Knight and to Bertilak. Thus bound by spiritual and legal covenants,
earthly reflections of God's order and rule, Gawain ultimately perceives that
the quest for knightly perfection is rooted in loyalty and fidelity to one's
pledged word.

Medieval Poetics

Richard Hamilton Green

In recent years I have begun my courses in Middle English literature, from graduate seminars to sophomore surveys, by handing my students copies of a thirteenth-century German poem by Der Wilde Alexander that begins, "Long ago, when we were children." I give them Peter Dronke's admirable translation, in his *The Medieval Lyric*, and Robert Lowell's version, published in his *Imitations*. I do this partly to show some things that happen to medieval poems in Modern English but mainly to illustrate the differences between the pleasures of immediate response to a strangely disturbing lyric and the riches of reference and resonance in the text when it is read as a *medieval* poem. The students at first are mystified by the images, then begin to see the child's passage from innocence to experience, a journey marked by warnings and danger, even the suggestion of blood. The words and figures stir imagination and memory; then, as the rich content of biblical allusion is explored, something of the original power of the poem is revealed, an experience that expands and enhances perception and enjoyment.

Everyone who has taught *Sir Gawain and the Green Knight* has noticed the poem's extraordinary attractiveness for even the most inexperienced reader. Its brillant surfaces, its evocation of the legendary history of Arthur and his knights, the symmetry and perfect closure of the story, and the dark mysteries relieved by comic excesses and pervasive ironies make *Gawain* accessible in the way much of Chaucer is, more accessible than, say, *Pearl* or *Piers Plowman*. It yields at once, in translation, to that naive understanding and pleasurable recognition which are the preconditions for a later, deeper understanding of the medieval Christian views of human aspiration and weakness. Indeed, the literary qualities of the poem are so attractive—and the hero's predicament seems so universal—that some very good criticism of the poem has not stressed its peculiarly medieval qualities. But the text-world of the poem is medieval and was made in historical contexts—literary, intellectual, religious, and social—that profoundly affect the poem's meaning and strongly differ from our own experiences. Because the best criticism of the poem is so good—and so abundant as to have become repetitious—I believe future study will profit from more attention to its historical backgrounds, in literary theory as well as social and religious practice, than these have so far received.

Some specific matters of obvious importance to the understanding of *Gawain* are the legendary history of Britain and of King Arthur as part of the unfolding, divinely ordered history of humankind from the beginning of time; the moral concerns of a hierarchical society that nostalgically recalls an earlier era of chivalry perceived as more perfect, yet itself flawed by the seeds of moral failure; the cycles of the year and week and day, measured by the ecclesiastical calendar of liturgical seasons and feast days as figurative reenactments of salvation history; ideas of the life of every individual as a journey, a quest, fraught with dangers and temptations.

Modern scholars have noted the figurative power of these traditional elements in the poem. Larry Benson calls attention to the romance tradition that lends *Gawain* "an authority and range of reference unmatched by any modern genre" and stresses the importance of what the audience knows as a key to interpretation (*Art and Tradition* 3–10). John Burrow observes that the hero is presented not only as a knight among his peers but "a man among men, a representative of *humanum genus* without distinction of social class— as an Everyman, in fact, whose experiences though in many ways fantastic and out of the common, are in many ways central to common experience" (*Reading* 33). Burrow provides a thorough analysis of the pentangle as a sign of *trawþe* based on the medieval idea of similitude, a reading that treats the pentangle as more than a symbol sufficiently explained in the text itself (41– 51, 187–89). Donald Howard, in his study of the medieval theme of temptation in three great medieval poems, the third being *Sir Gawain*, insists on the difference, the pastness of a poetry that demands of the reader its own learning, its own kind of reading; when he writes of the hero's adventures as likenesses of human life, he is reading the poem in its medieval ethical context (*Three Temptations* 250–54).

An acquaintance with the general medieval view of the meaning of the created universe and of humankind's place in it, and with medieval ways of interpreting human experience and representing it in literature, provides the modern reader with the basic poetic that underlies *Sir Gawain and the Green Knight*. To do full justice to this background requires a formidable program of reading, especially of original materials, but also of a vast body of historical scholarship. Still, students can and should be introduced to as much as pedagogical circumstances allow in the hope that all of them will read the poem with greater understanding and that some will go beyond the generalities of class and seminar—and the reading of modern criticism— to discover new ways in which general contexts can illuminate particular signs and events in the text of the poem. Among the books I find most useful for introducing students to this background are R. P. Miller's *Chaucer: Sources and Backgrounds*, C.S. Lewis's *The Discarded Image*, and D. W. Robertson's *A Preface to Chaucer*.

I base the sketch that follows on two twelfth-century books by Hugh of Saint Victor, *Didascalicon: On the Study of Reading* and *On the Sacraments*. Together they synthesize the patristic and Neoplatonic thought that preceded them. Both remain authoritative for medieval interpretation of experience and books through the fourteenth century. Both are in print in excellent translations, and both belong with Saint Augustine's *On Christian Doctrine* and Boethius's *The Consolation of Philosophy* as indispensable introductions to medieval intellectual and literary history.

Medieval education was, in the broadest sense, preparation to read, to interpret, two divinely made books: the book of nature, in which the Creator expressed the ideas of his mind in the works of creation, and the Sacred Scriptures, in which God expressed in his Word made flesh the works of redemption. In the first, the Creator revealed himself in all the things that he made, most perfectly in the human person made in his image. Through this revelation, in the sacramental natures of the things that were made, human reason could discover at least something of the Maker. Such discovery was possible through the similarity (*per similitudinem*) of visible signs to the invisible truth that they expressed. In discussing the water of the sacrament of baptism Hugh says:

> Now all water has from its natural quality a certain similitude with the grace of the Holy Ghost, since, just as water washes away the stains of bodies, so the other cleanses the iniquities of souls. And, indeed, from this inborn quality all water had the power to represent spiritual grace, before it also signified the latter by super-added institution [of the sacrament of baptism].   (*Sacraments* 155; bk.1, pt. 9, ch. 2)

The book of nature, the work of creation, would have been sufficient had not the human intellect been darkened by the Fall, and it continued to provide access to at least a partial understanding of the *invisibilia Dei* for the authorities of pagan antiquity (Plato, Aristotle, Cicero, Vergil, Ovid, and others), enabling them and their readers to achieve a kind of wisdom— Hugh's words are "quaedam sapientia"—to know God, "for the invisible things of him, from the creation of the world, are clearly seen, being understood by the things that are made" (Rom. 1.20). The other book, the divinely inspired Sacred Scriptures, was read as a second and more accessible revelation in which humanity's fall from grace and the history of its redemption by Christ's death were recorded. The history and doctrines of the old law were seen as prophetic figures of the new; the history of the Church since the coming of Christ was seen as the fulfillment of God's promises to his people. The words were fraught with the mysteries of the things, persons, and events they signified, and the duty of the Christian was to discover the invisible truth made manifest in its visible signs.

In his *Didascalicon*, Hugh speaks first of the method of analyzing texts that belong to philosophy—the arts of the trivium and quadrivium and the appendages of those arts, which include the songs of the poets, fables, and histories. "Exposition," he says, includes three things: the letter, the sense, and the inner meaning [sententia]. The letter is the fit arrangement of words, which we also call construction; the sense is a certain ready and obvious meaning which the letter represents on the surface; the inner meaning is the deeper understanding which can be found only through interpretation and commentary. (92; bk. 3, ch. 8)

Later, in book 6, he presents a clear synthesis of the standard method of interpreting the Bible developed over the preceding thousand years. Sacred Scripture has three ways of conveying meaning—namely, history, allegory, and tropology (Hugh omits anagogy, usually the fourth way). In the midst of sensible cautions about understanding the letter of the text and its historical meaning before venturing into spiritual interpretation and about the need for restraint and the dangers of rash interpretation, he presents the familiar steps of historical, allegorical, and moral exposition. In one of many traditional analogies, he compares the wholeness of spiritual meaning with the rich resonance of the lyre when its strings are plucked. Hugh's method is modified by later commentators, especially in its approach to the literal meanings of the text, but his account remains a sufficient place to begin.

Though the medieval method of reading was most fully developed in its application to the Bible, numerous commentaries attest that the reading of the poets, pagan and Christian, followed an analogous method. But with a crucial difference: the Scriptures were divinely inspired, and therefore true, both in the historical events they recounted and in the prophetic and moral meanings they enclosed. The works of the poets, even the most religious, were fictions, though the fictional narrative inevitably recalled the persons and events of sacred history and the moral truths of religion.

If we attempt to put a modern reading of *Sir Gawain and the Green Knight* within this broad, and oversimplified, framework of medieval assumptions about human experience and their representation in poetry, some useful considerations emerge. First, we should be clearer than we have been about the terms *allegory* and *allegorical interpretation* as they are applied to the poem. Second, we will find that a larger view of the historical contexts within which the language of the poem was heard by its original audience will enlarge our perception of its meaning. Third, we may be encouraged to let the informed imagination play with possibilities in a playful poem, with fewer constraints imposed by New Critical assumptions. Finally, and perhaps most important, we may open up new historical contexts that have so far been neglected.

The terms *allegory* and *allegorical interpretation*, because of their modern suggestions of a narrative with a continuous system of moral equivalents, have had an unnecessarily limiting and confusing effect on much criticism of *Gawain* in the past thirty years. The term *symbol*, too, is so blurred by common usage that it usually fails to reflect the medieval sense of relations based on real similitude between the visible thing and invisible truth. Other terms for the way things mean, terms with equal medieval authority—figure and figurative, sacrament and sacramental, spiritual, analogical, typological—serve as sharper reminders of the special claims of medieval poetic language. Erich Auerbach's seminal monograph *Figura*, published originally in German in 1944, and available in Ralph Manheim's English translation since 1959, traces the linguistic history of the term from Greek and Latin antiquity to "the strangely new meaning of *figura*" (28) in the Christian world of the church fathers. He analyzes Saint Augustine's usage to emphasize the phenomenal and ethical reality of the *figurae* of Scripture as well as the spiritual reality of their fulfillment, an attitude that gives the doctrine of the fourfold meaning of Scripture its realistic and historical character.

How should these medieval ways of interpreting the phenomenal world and of reading the figural prophecy of the Bible guide a historical reading of *Sir Gawain and the Green Knight*? Abelard demands of Héloïse and the nuns of the Paraclete a response to his liturgical hymns identical with that of biblical interpretation. We know that a closely analogous method was used by the medieval commentators on the poetry of Ovid and Vergil. And Dante's testimony about the differences between the allegory of poets and the allegory of theologians in his *Convivio* reveals a traditional way of reading his own poetry and that of the Latin philosopher-poets of the twelfth century, such as Alan of Lille and Bernardus Silvestris. But what of an English romance made by a learned and entertaining poet in the late fourteenth century? It would be foolish to apply the methods of biblical exegesis in any systematic way to the poem. As Judson Allen puts it in his remarkable *The Ethical Poetic of the Later Middle Ages*, "What the fourfold schema of exegesis defines for literature is not a range of possible meanings of a text, considered referentially, but rather a range of possible kinds of reality a text may assimilate because of the interaction of words and the world, past and present and future" (214). To read the poem in terms of medieval assumptions about the meaning and the value of human experience and in ways similar to those applied by medieval commentators to other literary texts will surely bring us closer to the expectations of the poet and his audience.

Allen's fourth chapter, "Assimilatio and the Material of Poetry," is especially valuable in taking us beyond the customary terms of biblical exegesis to the language of the commentator on poetry. In poetry, Allen observes, something *is*—the words evoke a species of existence; and in the later Middle Ages the most fundamental term for this phenomenon is *assimilatio* 'likening.' The term

> denotes not the state of existence of an entity but the result of the achievement of a relation. . . . What we call poetry exists in the Middle

Ages only because of and in terms of some larger complex of relationships and significances. The very stuff of which poetry is made—the
stories and descriptions which are, literally, the words which poems
are—cannot be taken as merely and in isolation themselves. The key
definition of the words, stories, figures, and statements of which poems
compose themselves is a definition, not of a thing, but of an act—an
act, moreover, whose actors and objects inhabit a larger world than
the poem itself. (179–80)

It is that larger world which a study of backgrounds seeks to explore, in this
case for the story of a legendary hero who undertakes a quest that tests the
limits of his perfection.

Three recent studies illustrate the variety and utility of approaches to the
poem based on the figurative power of traditional elements; all three derive
from genuine learning, open up historical contexts, and point to new possibilities in the text of the poem. None constrains our assent; each enlarges
our field of vision. The first, "Gawain's Girdle as Traditional Symbol," by
Albert B. Friedman and Richard H. Osberg, is conventional in its argu-
mentative approach to the meaning of the green girdle but remarkable in
the range and amplitude of the information it provides. The authors wish
to show the reader how "the phantom generic narrative in the background . . . shows through to give objects like the girdle their effective
meaning in the plot and their symbolic valence" (309). To show that the
girdle in the poem is a sexual symbol, they review its uses in folklore and
literature from classical and biblical antiquity to Renaissance England. To
get at "what the girdle meant to the poet's hearers and how they would
understand it to be operating in the poem," Friedman and Osberg then
focus on "the romance conventions and narrative patterns which would have
conditioned their reaction to the events of the poem" (307). When they are
finished, our reading of the symbol—and of the poem—has been enlarged
and improved. Though we will not agree with their treatment of everything
in the text (the pentangle, for example), we have learned a great deal, and
this is the point of good historical criticism.

The second study looks at different backgrounds, and, while it is less
assertive in its conclusions, its suggestions carry the weight of its author's
long familiarity with medieval texts. Robert E. Kaske's essay "Sir Gawain"
focuses on the biblical context of the poem's governing theme of *lewte* and
its virtual equivalent *trawpe*. He finds a pattern in the manifestation of this
virtue "in the beheading game through courage, and in the temptation
episodes through wisdom." The medieval commonplace of wisdom and fortitude as one definition of the heroic ideal—invoked by Gawain in his modest
denial, "I am the wakkest, I wot, and of wit feblest . . ." (354)—provides a
context within which the hero identifies the girdle, at the end of the poem,

as "the token of untrawþe þat I am tan inne," the token of his "cowardise" and "covetyse" (2508–09). Within this general and, for the poet's audience, familiar moral ambience, Kaske tests his thesis in brief but carefully documented analyses of many of the poem's puzzles: emblematic correspondences between the animals hunted by Sir Bertilak and the dangers faced by Gawain in the bedroom encounters with the lady, the thematic importance of the Troy allusions, the question of the hero's two confessions, a rather full analysis of the five fives of the pentangle, the enigmatic possibilities of the Green Knight and the two ladies. The issue is not whether one agrees with Kaske's suggestions in detail; the importance of historical criticism is to remind us of what the medieval audience knew and to suggest ways that their experience might have affected their response to the voice of the poet.

The most original and impressively researched effort to place the poem in the world of the late-fourteenth-century audience is R. A. Shoaf's *The Poem as Green Girdle: Commercium in* Sir Gawain and the Green Knight. In an argument far too complex to summarize here, Shoaf reads the poem as an attempt to reconcile the claims of old traditions and new economic and legal realities. His analysis shows the pervasive effects of sacramental theology and liturgy on the language and events of the poem. His book enlarges our awareness of historical contexts that inform the text and illustrates how the Latin of medieval learning affects the language of vernacular poetry.

A final caution. Students sometimes find the medieval formula for interpreting the text of the Bible—and related formulas for reading the literature that medieval scholars found worthy of commentary—inordinately appealing because of its apparent simplicity. Their efforts to apply this method often result in a grossly oversimplified search for correspondences that are not justified by the text. What I have tried to describe are certain assumptions about the meaning and value of the things and events of human experience as represented by the words and contexts of a medieval poem. From these assumptions arose a habit of reading that we try to approximate through familiarity with as much medieval literature as we can master, but the justness of our interpretation must depend on the accuracy with which we read the poetic text. Likenesses between the sign and the signified enlarge our understanding of the poem only when they are verified by the poem as a whole.

APPROACHING THE POEM IN THE CLASSROOM

Weavers and Wordsmiths, Tapestries and Translations

Julian N. Wasserman

Teaching a modern English version of a poem such as *Gawain*, one can easily understand Cervantes's assertion that reading a translation is much like viewing a tapestry from the reverse side. There amidst the knots and seams and stitchery one perceives the rough outlines of images, drawn without the subtlety, exactness, or vibrancy that cause us to value the original as a work of art. Thus, the first order of business is to point out to students that they are viewing the tapestry from its reverse side—to stress how much is lost in translation, since the poem, in manuscript, appeals not only to the intellect but also to the eye and the ear. Clearly, the visual and aural dimensions of its stanza forms as well as the poet's reliance on puns (again, both visual and aural), changing cadences (from the second hunt to the second temptation or the narrative intrusion at the end of the first fitt), and onomatopoeia (the drums and trumpets in Arthur's hall) all demonstrate that the poet was not only conscious of his medium but adept at manipulating it to his own artistic ends. One of the best ways to alert students to the complexities of the poet's use of language is to explain briefly the use of stanza-linking words in *Pearl*, where the repetition of key words and phrases at the beginning and ending of the stanza serves both as a "structuring" device and as a visual illustration of the poem's theme that "The first shall be last." As in *Pearl*, the form of *Gawain*, especially its language, is part of the poem's content, and a translation must of necessity obscure as well as facilitate meaning. For example, the pun on the Green Knight as "gome" ("man") and "game" ("game, riddle") cannot be rendered in modern English. Similarly, the skillful play on the juxtaposition of the formal and familiar second-person pronouns in the challenge scene is not apparent in translation and is well worth noting in the original. However, despite such obvious problems, it is still possible, even in translation, to trace throughout the fabric of the poem the rich threads of the poet's thematic repetitions of key terms for volition/will, noise, debt and repayment, knots, and marvel/wonder.

Of course translation has little or no effect on the poem's structure as a romance. The poem may be treated both as an example of medieval romance (John Stevens) and as an archetypal adventure consisting of separation, initiation, and return (Campbell, Frye). Analogies to the structure and conventions of the Wife of Bath's Tale are helpful here. If *Beowulf* has been taught earlier in the semester, a discussion of the distinction between epic and romance (Ker, *Epic and Romance*) can point to the differences between the chivalric code of romance questers and the heroic code of epic heroes. An unfailing topic of discussion is "How would Gawain fare in the court of the Geats? How would Beowulf make out in the courts of Arthur and Bertilak?" There also exist other points of comparison, such as the similarities of the Scyld Scaefing and Trojan prehistories in their respective poems as well as their essentially binary structures (youth/age; beheading/temptation). The very rare Middle English terms "gryndellayk," "gryndelly," and "gryndel" (*Gawain* 312, 2299, 2338)—though usually translated as "fierce"—are perhaps best thought of as "Grendel (like)," providing a tantalizing suggestion that the poet was familiar with *Beowulf*. Another source of class discussion is the fact that this unusual term is applied to Gawain rather than, as one might expect, the menacing Green Knight.

The difference between John Stevens's approach to romance as an artifact of a particular culture (the "medievalness" of medieval romance) and the more archetypal approaches of Campbell and Frye introduces another important issue that can be successfully treated in translation: the problem of how a poem can and will be read by a modern audience. To this end, I have found it extremely helpful to assign the Middle English lyric "The Maiden in the Moor Lay" with the excerpts from essays by Robertson, Donaldson, and Speirs contained in the Norton Critical Edition of *Middle English Lyrics* (Luria and Hoffman). These three critics are used as archetypes for the three general approaches most frequently encountered in discussing medieval literature as a whole and *Gawain* in particular. In regard to the lyric, Robertson sees the unusual qualities of the maiden as generating an *aenigma* best explained through application of patristic exegesis. Donaldson responds that the poem makes a type of sense on the surface and that the enigmatic aspects of the maiden are usually afforded a certain amount of supernatural treatment. Speirs appeals primarily to the traditions of myth and folklore and discusses the maiden as a well or water spirit. It then becomes a matter of asking how each of these critics might view the equally supernatural color of the Green Knight. Robertson would, no doubt discuss the iconography of "Satan the Fowler"; Donaldson might note that the color green is no doubt significant in a general way but that supernaturally decorated challengers are a commonplace in such romances and require no specific exegesis. Speirs might find a vegetation god at work here. Students, like critics, seem to drift naturally into one camp or another, so that much of the class time devoted to the poem consists of calling on individuals or groups to provide what they think one of the three "archetypal" critics might have to say about the pentangle, Morgan, or any of the poem's equally ambiguous elements, including the following issues or cruxes:

(a) The poem's opening and closing lines present a stylistic signature that links the poem with the others in the Cotton Nero ms. Yet they may, to the patristically minded, also present a view or concept of history as a series of fallen kingdoms, cities, or leaders, of which fallen Camelot, in this tale told in the past tense, may be a member. By implication, the poet's contemporary society with its New Troy (London) may be next. This cyclical theory of history may be viewed in the light of the poet's seemingly apocalyptic description of the passing of the year. Does our understanding of the poem's opening lines change by the time we see them again at the end of the poem? Does the fall of Camelot seem more understandable or even more tragic (in the modern sense) because we have come to know and perhaps even like one of the people affected by it? This latter question raises the problem of how we are supposed to respond to the characters. Are they supposed to be flat? By exploring the "personalities" of such characters, are we doing a disservice to the poem akin to demanding Giotto-like fullness from aesthetically complete but deliberately one-dimensional characters? In short, are we to respond intellectually and/or emotionally to the poem? Finally, is one of these responses more "medieval" than the other, and if so, what are the virtues and drawbacks of attempting to view the poem from a medieval point of view? Is such an approach even possible, and if not, should it be attempted anyway?

(b) The description of Arthur's court deserves explicit and careful explication, since the judgment of the court (ranging from merely high-spirited to worldly to seriously flawed to downright sinful and doomed) is probably the chief factor in shaping one's reading of the poem as a whole. Is the emphasis on the religious aspects of the season, or is it on the mechanics of the celebration? Are we presented with a paradigm of courtly manners or a moral yardstick for judging the subsequent action? For example, how does one interpret the fact that these celebrants are in their "first age"? Are they youthful and innocent revelers of mythological prehistory, or are they childish? Many translations tend to make Arthur "boyish" in a mildly pejorative way. The language of the original suggests a much more serious fault.

(c) Is Arthur's request for a tale a relatively harmless foible or a rash promise in the tradition of the many rash promises made by Arthur in romances such as Chrétien's *Erec and Enide*? Or is it an indication of his moral myopia, especially in the light of the first lines of the second fitt? Is Arthur's request unusually violent, or is that a modern concern?

(d) In the description of the Green Knight, the color of the knight's raiment and eyes—as well as his size, beard, and the bevy of knots that appear in his portrait—may be significant in our assessing his status as a threat or a benefactor as well as in placing him within Celtic tradition. Also, what are the immediate reactions of Arthur and his men to the appearance of the knight? What assumptions do they make?

(e) The challenge, like the initial description of Arthur and his court, deserves close reading—especially since it is repeated three times, so its exact wording is emphasized. Translations usually do not emphasize the legalistic or contractual nature of the challenge. What *exactly* is the challenge? What *exactly* is the role of the ax? Does Gawain *have* to use the ax to deliver his blow? Why does Arthur accept the challenge? What are the insults with which the intruder provokes Arthur's wrath? Can they, like beard wagging, be found in other romances, or are they significant in some other fashion? For example, is riding a horse into a hall either unusual or insulting? What at first seems a breach of decorum in fact turns out to be a fairly common occurrence in romance and ballads.

(f) The technical aspects of Gawain's arming are usually not afforded a close reading in class, but the passage is discussed in terms of the questions it raises. Are we to accept the poet's gloss of the meaning of the pentangle at face value, or is it ironic in that five is more frequently associated with its "in malo" association with the senses, as in the portrait of the Wife of Bath? Like the Green Knight, is the pentangle a Christian symbol, a pagan symbol, or a pagan symbol made over into a Christian one? Obviously this decision affects one's reading of the poem, and all the choices are defensible. Does the presence of the Virgin on the inside and the presence of the pentangle on the outside of his shield represent Gawain's resorting to magic to combat the fairy knight and hence indicate a weakness of Gawain's faith in the Virgin? Does his later acceptance of the green girdle indicate that he is still not certain of their joint power? In this regard, it is important to note that Gawain gets his wish for shelter only after resorting to a prayer to the Virgin and that the pentangle does not seem all that helpful.

(g) On his journey to Hautdesert, Gawain encounters many wild beasts. Should the beasts be considered symbolic, or are they just the generalized foes that one traditionally encounters on such a journey? Does Gawain's journey into the marches represent his translation into the displaced world of romance? Is it the first stage of the tripartite structure of separation, initiation, and return found in archetypal journeys? Most importantly, why does he go on the journey in the first place? He's clearly been tricked; why doesn't he simply forget the whole matter? Does he honor his pledge simply because he is a knight, or does he do so out of obligation to himself, his king, or his society? Is his compliance rooted in his pride and/or his honor? Why couldn't Gawain's lesson be learned at home?

(h) Bertilak's court is presented, first, as a type of libidinous playground, a testing ground of *wylle*, and, second, in terms of the contrasts it presents to that of Arthur. While Arthur's court is served double portions, Bertilak tells Gawain that his court, while royally fed, "fasts" by eating fish. There is only one reference to mass at Arthur's court, and that is to the company's bursting forth from the sacrament in order to continue the revels. In contrast, mass is said frequently—some five times—at Bertilak's court. Also emphasized is the problematic figure of Morgan. What is her status at this court? Is she the mistress of revels at a pagan court or an example of the folk convention of the "loathly lady"? Is her appearance an indication of his moral status, or is it a blind designed to lead astray those who rely solely on appearances? Should Gawain know who is in charge here? What is the difference in greetings afforded by Gawain to Morgan and his host's wife? Does the difference reflect Gawain's preoccupation with the surface? Invariably students find the difference in greetings humorous but entirely understandable. In short, Gawain does exactly what they would have done. Is our identification with Gawain modern or medieval or both?

(i) The exchange contracts are compared to the earlier contract made between Gawain and the Green Knight. Should Gawain note the resemblance, or is he still only concentrating on the surface? This same literalism is seen in the first exchange when Gawain refuses to name the person from whom he won his day's "spoils" by noting that such a revelation was not literally called for in their contract. This literalism is also apparent in Gawain's initial reaction to receiving his "nick" from the Green Knight Gawain believes himself to be clever by invoking the letter or literal meaning of the law. Is Gawain's cleverness typical of that of heroes such as Odysseus in dealing with Polyphemous, or is it self-deceptive? How does Gawain's behavior in the third exchange differ from that of the first two? Finally, should the kisses be taken at face value as typical courtly gifts, or should they be considered exegetically as suggestive of betrayal? In the same fashion, is the crowing of the cock with which each hunt begins a bit of realistic detail or another instance of biblical iconography?

(j) In treating the temptation and hunt scenes, I tend to place the weight on the temptations. Clearly there is a relation between Gawain and the hunted animals. Are we to understand these as general correspondences (Gawain is timid like the deer, defensive like the cornered boar, sly like the fox), or are we to make more elaborate exegetical correspondences? The temptations provide excellent examples of courtly wordplay and are a good place to introduce the idea of *amour cortois*. Should these scenes be read as a moral allegory or lesson about temptation to sin, or are they intended as comic relief with the traditionally comic figure of the aggressive lady and the passive knight? Are the two readings mutually exclusive? Is the poet saying that piety or knightly virtue is antithetical to the virtues of the lover or the courtier? Why does Gawain accept the girdle? How does that acceptance look in the light of his previously stated reasons for rejecting it? Were those reasons just talk, or has he violated the courtly code?

(k) Gawain's subsequent confession is, of course, another rich topic for discussion. Is the confession valid? The narrator seems to say it is, yet Gawain confesses while intending to break his pledge made "bi God" to his host. Does the intent to sin in the future invalidate the confession? Is Gawain riding out the next day with a mortal sin on his head? How is the second confession different from the first? How is Gawain's behavior after the second confession different from his behavior after the first?

(l) What is the function of Gawain's rejection of his guide's advice to flee? Does his response partially redeem him in our eyes, and is such redemption necessary if the reader is to sympathize with the protagonist after observing his continued folly at the court of Bertilak?

(m) In regard to Gawain's receiving of the return blow, how does the Green Knight's mockery of Gawain parallel the earlier mockery of Arthur as well as the temptress's mockery of Gawain? How are Arthur's and Gawain's responses similar? Is Gawain, then, an exceptional individual or a representative of the court?

(n) Gawain's recognition of his own failure—the seriousness of which is, again, problematical—is best treated in stages. First, there is the Green Knight's explanation of the meaning of the three feints along with his assessment of why Gawain has failed. Most first-time readers of the poem have not already guessed the identity of Bertilak. Should they have done so? At this point, what is the distance between reader and character? Is Gawain an exemplum or a fellow human being liable to the same more or less excusable faults to which we are all heir? Does the latter view mitigate a judgment that the poet wants us to make? Those with critical fish to fry might well wander into the displaced world of reader-response criticism. At some point in the process, even the best students are likely to despair over the amount of material that they have missed as they have gone through a poem whose action and issues seem so clear at first glance. One response is to note that, in this respect, we are much like Gawain, who habitually fails to notice the many clues scattered throughout the poem, and that the poem demonstrates in the reader what it demonstrates in its central character.

(o) Next, there is Gawain's acceptance of his failure along with his attempt to place himself in the tradition of men who were deceived and brought to their downfalls by women. Gawain lists four examples and implies that he is the fifth. The second part of Gawain's emendation comes when the Green Knight, in response to Gawain's "antifeminism," states that it was Morgan le Fay who has brought about the events. Does this confirm Gawain's assessment, or does the Green Knight here offer a corrective by noting that Gawain has been bettered, not done in, by these events? Is the fifth man to be done in by a woman Arthur rather than Gawain? Can we assume that the poet knew the full history of Arthur, including the betrayal of Arthur by Guinevere? Does the phrase "first age" in the initial description of the court indicate that the events of the poem took place in a period of innocence before the queen's infidelity? How fair is it to read the poem in the light of material outside the boundaries of the text?

(p) Clearly a central question is our judgment of Morgan. Does she bring about good or evil, consciously or unconsciously? If she brings about good, does the poem then challenge our ideas about medieval antifeminism?

(q) Finally, there is the problem of evaluating the court's response to Gawain's tale of his own failure. Is the court's adoption of the green girdle a reduction of a serious lesson to a frivolous matter of fashion, or is it a sincere recognition of its own shortcomings? Is it a kindly act designed at minimizing Gawain's exaggerated sense of his own sin? Is it a fair token of a not really serious fault that has been taken too seriously by critics?

At this point, the richness of the poem, with its seemingly endless possibilities, begins to overwhelm the reader. Yet the lesson is that all the seemingly contradictory answers that these questions evoke can be defended. The poem remains both highly suggestive and highly elusive in its meaning. Simple answers and sweeping generalities work no better for the reader of the poem than they do for its protagonist. Even more important, the seemingly limitless possibilities are a source of pleasure, not consternation. Fortunately, however, some order does arise out of the chaos, and, vigorously pursued, the answers to such questions eventually begin to coalesce into several separate readings of the poem as a whole:

(1) The poem may be a handbook or lesson about chivalry and may be a part of the induction into or celebration of the Order of the Garter—hence the placement of the order's motto at the poem's conclusion. The poem touches on such knightly virtues as loyalty, chastity, fortitude, hospitality, courage, and *trawþe*. It shows the necessity of protecting and nurturing these virtues since even the best of knights sometimes fail. Unfortunately, *trawþe* does not fare well in translation. Like many terms for chivalric virtues, *trawþe* has a number of different, although related, meanings in Middle English that are not apparent in translation. However, discussing the poem in terms of chivalric knighthood places the emphasis on the broad outlines of situation and action and, hence, minimizes the loss of linguistic subtleties. The speech in which Gawain asks to relieve Arthur of the challenge is an excellent example of courtly diction, as are his speeches to his temptress. One of the poet's strengths is his ability to create different dictions for Gawain's alternating chivalric roles as courtier, champion, and lover, and although some of the subtleties are lost in translation, much remains.

(2) The poem may be a holiday tale, written primarily for the entertainment of the court as part of a Yuletide celebration. The emphasis is on the poet's considerable ability to entertain and delight rather than on the religious elements that are the foundations of other readings. We see the opulence of the initial Christmas celebration as an idealized model of contemporary fashions in celebrating the season rather than as an indication of worldliness and excess. All these elements seem accessible in translation.

(3) The Green Knight may be a pre-Christian fertility god. The poem demonstrates the pre-Christian roots of much Arthurian material. The poem does seem to be a welding of two Celtic themes: beheading and temptation. Possibly pagan elements such as the knight's greenness could have been incorporated into the poem without the poet's knowledge of their pre-Christian meanings or origins. Or the poet could have consciously set up a contrast between the pagan intruder and the Christian court. Whether consciously or unconsciously applied, the Green Man is in Celtic folklore a figure who must be slain in order to effect his own and nature's rejuvenation. Moreover, Bertilak and Gawain have been linked to sun gods. Each morning, Bertilak, like the sun, goes out to run his daily course, only to return at the end of the day. Passages that support these mythic readings—the descriptions of the passing of the seasons, the Green Knight, Morgan, and the barrow-chapel—are readily accessible in translation.

(4) The poem presents Gawain as a type of Everyman who learns about his own spiritual imperfection and provides a warning to its audience about sin and/or a lesson about God and the sacraments. However, all such readings must inevitably rest on the reader's identifying the virtuous and the sinful—a problem that may be the central ambiguity of the poem. One must decide

whether the Green Knight is the devil, as Gawain suspects. Or is Arthur's court guilty of excessive worldliness and pride, and is the green intruder a prophetic messenger of its doom who harrows out the single virtuous man (an important theme of the apocalyptic *Purity*)? Although such judgments rest on the subtleties of the poet's language, there is, even in translation, ample evidence of the Arthurian court's haughtiness, pride, and bickering.

Such "patristic" readings of the poem offer the most variety in terms of interpretation, but they also offer some serious pedagogical difficulties, including the formidable demand of a specialized knowledge of both theology and iconography on the part of the student. More serious is the problem that patristic readings frequently tempt one to deal with parts of the poem to the exclusion of the whole. An exegetical reading of the pentangle, no matter how splendid, makes for confusion in the classroom if such an explication is made without reference to the rest of the poem. Moreover, patristic readings of the poem in translation have two other minor drawbacks. First, they require more frequent consulation with the original text for specialized meanings that non–patristically minded translators do not render. For example, the term "sourquydrye" (311, 2457) is a special type of pride that is mortal rather than venial, a distinction not usually rendered in translation. Loaded terms such as *wylle* are usually rendered so as to make consultation with the original text a necessity. Secondly, patristic readings frequently require allusion to the other poems usually ascribed to the same poet. These three works not only serve as a source of the poet's "theology" but also aid in matters of translation and interpretation. For example, the term "glaum" (46) used to describe the "din" in Camelot is ambiguous since the term has both positive and pejorative connotations within the works of the poet, including its use in *Purity* to describe both the speech of God's angels (830) and the clamor of the Sodomites who pound on the door of Lot's compound (849). Similarly, the binary structure juxtaposing two courts in *Purity* is almost identical to that of *Gawain*. However, the objection most frequently voiced to patristic readings is that such readings "take the joy out of the poem." To be sure, while some patristically based readings of the poem do concentrate on the maintenance, testing, and even development of virtues, such as *trawpe*, the majority in fact concentrate on what might be termed the protagonist's shortcomings, if not sins—especially pride, an important theme expressed in terms of the sacraments (i.e., Gawain's two confessions) and doctrine (the themes of *felix culpa* and original sin as well as fourteenth-century apocalypticism). Despite the prominence of the themes of sin and even apocalyptic destruction, this fear of overseriousness seems unfounded. Surely the difference between the greetings afforded the loathly lady and the beautiful temptress at Bertilak's court is both morally instructive and gently amusing, as we recognize our own foibles in the actions of the knight. The poem, like the tale told by Chaucer's Nun's Priest, represents the best of medieval literature: the ability to be didactic, even morally instructive, without being dreary, the ability to combine what Harry Bailly calls "sentance" *and* "solas." In that sense, the poem teaches a valuable lesson about the difference between modern and medieval aesthetics.

A number of seemingly mutually exclusive readings, then, arise naturally out of the preoccupations that we as readers bring to the task of interpretation. That lesson, itself, may help to correct the very reductiveness of which Cervantes warns in his analogy of the tapestry by reviving the joyous ambiguity that the translator must sacrifice in order to render the multiplicity of meanings in one idiom in favor of a single meaning in another. In the end, what lurks behind the arras described by Cervantes may, indeed, be only the broad outline of the poem, a Polonius "full of high sentence but a bit obtuse." But if what we find there is caricature rather than character, it is still, in the words of Prufrock, a caricature fit to "swell a progress, start a scene or two," and perhaps even a semester's study of medieval literature.

LOWER-DIVISION
UNDERGRADUATE COURSES

Freshman Composition: Epic and Romance

John M. Fyler

I first read *Sir Gawain and the Green Knight* in graduate school—as part of a seminar in Middle English—and deeply regretted coming to the poem so late; ever since, I have taught it to undergraduates as often as possible, in Middle English or Modern. Like many others, I have in fact taught *Sir Gawain* much more frequently in translation—especially as part of a sophomore survey of English literature, using the *Norton Anthology*; as a result, Marie Borroff's admirable translation is by now at least as familiar to me as its original. Certainly my teaching of the poem to freshmen and sophomores develops from her choices in translating, as at the one point I can think of where she embellishes the *Gawain* poet's meaning, however slightly. When the lord takes off his hood to launch a Christmas game (983), he vows: "And I schal fonde, bi my fayth, to fylter wyth þe best / Er me wont þe wede, with help of my frendez" (986-87). Borroff's translation—"And I shall try for it, trust me—contend with the best, / Ere I go without my headgear by grace of my friends!"—rightly gives increased prominence to the undercurrent of beheading jokes, a series of indelicate reminders to Gawain of what awaits him at the Green Chapel: the rolling head in fitt 1; the probable allusion in the name Holy Head (despite Norman Davis's skepticism [Tolkien and Gordon 97–98, nn. 691ff.]) to the decapitation of Saint Winifred; and

119

the brandished boar's head in part 3. For those unable to read Middle English, her translation is the best possible substitute, because it conveys so successfully the poet's subtleties of meaning and tone, as well as the metrical effects of the alliterative line and the bob and wheel.

I have often taught the poem in freshman seminars, with such works as *Hamlet* and *Great Expectations*, as part of an introduction to literature. But I have also used it several times in a seminar with a narrower focus, called Epic and Romance. This seminar, like most freshman composition classes, runs as a discussion group; there are six or seven five-page expository essays required (one of them on *Gawain*), and no final examination. The center of the course is Tolkien's trilogy, *The Lord of the Rings*, which, because of its length, takes up the first half of the semester. The other works claim about two weeks—that is, six fifty-minute classes—apiece: they are, in order, Robert Fitzgerald's translation of the *Odyssey;* either Malory's *Morte Darthur*, in the abridged edition by Derek Brewer, or Tennyson's *Idylls of the King;* and *Gawain*.

The seminar has been successful, for several reasons beyond the inherent delights of the reading list. Since most students in the class have read Tolkien previously, we advance rapidly past the bane of freshman literature courses: the assumption that plot summary is the chief goal of literary study. And proceeding from Tolkien to the other works on the list encourages the development of what seems the hardest thing for beginning undergraduates to master: the ability to think analogically, to move among literary works, abstracting structural and generic patterns from their narrative surfaces. To encourage such ways of thinking, I occasionally introduce epigrammatic versions of conventional romance themes—indeed, I begin the course with Tolkien's story *Farmer Giles of Ham*, which wittily rehearses a good many of them. Such themes are often the more sharply etched for students when they appear outside the bounds of romance, isolated in different poetic contexts. Accordingly, I use Robert Lowell's "For the Union Dead" to discuss heroism and our relation to a more heroic past, and I talk about the declining world and our responses to time's passing as they are described by Tennyson's "The Epic" and by Robert Frost's "Spring Pools," "The Oven Bird," and "Directive." I usually leave paper topics open, though I make some suggestions, and many others emerge from class discussion. Teaching *Gawain* last is particularly apposite in the fall semester, as the Christmas holiday approaches, but the romance is a suitable conclusion to the course in either semester because it so powerfully recapitulates familiar thematic patterns and encourages students to think about the generic qualities of romance.

There are, indeed, many such patterns to be discussed, in part because *Gawain* was much on Tolkien's mind when he was writing the trilogy. The most comprehensive is the movement of time, both in the annual cycle of the seasons and in the larger sequences of history. All the works on the list have the usual romance nostalgia for a more heroic past, the pervasive sense that the world is declining and that better things irrevocably lead to worse. As the *Gawain* poet says, "Hit were now gret nye to neuen / So hardy a here on hille" (58–59). (Tennyson's "The Epic," his original frame for "Morte d'Arthur," proclaims such nostalgia in especially vivid and comically lively fashion, and in *Farmer Giles of Ham* Tolkien jokes, "There was more time then, and folk were fewer, so that most men were distinguished.") But in the trilogy and *Gawain*, this view of history is complicated and enriched by a thoroughgoing sense of cyclical pattern. The hobbits progressively discover that they are recapitulating, sometimes with a remarkable similarity of detail, the heroic struggles of an earlier, more magnificent age. In the opening of *Gawain, translatio imperii*, the alternation of "blysse and blunder" (18), and the unending cycle of the changing year provide a larger, chastening context for the poet's subject, a story from the "first age" (54) of Arthur's court. And both works encourage their audiences to read and understand events from a historical perspective that is unavailable to, or at best slowly earned by, the characters themselves.

In both works, too, heroic achievement has its price: the heroes find when they return home that they are now set apart, to some degree at least, from the societies whose values they have defended. Though Arthur's court is obviously a very different place, in its glittering sophistication, from the provincial Shire, they seem to share an inability to understand things beyond their immediate purview: the laughter of Gawain's friends has its counterpart in the more obviously uncomprehending reactions of the hobbits. Tolkien's hero in fact discovers that he cannot go home again: unlike Sam Gamgee, Frodo is not able to regain contentment in a circumscribed life, and his malaise is akin to that of Ulysses in Tennyson's poem and in canto 26 of the *Inferno*.

The most startling point of comparison, perhaps, is the position assigned the audience, developing from our detached, retrospective view on the heroic events of the past. Both Tolkien and the *Gawain* poet are careful to implicate us, first by revealing that a strong sense of place ties the distant past to the present. Gawain's sudden appearance on the north coast of Wales, in a carefully detailed segment of his journey, puts him near his readers, though centuries before; Tolkien, correspondingly, insists that Middle Earth is no fantasy world but our own in an earlier form—what was then the Shire is now England, and Farmer Giles the dragon tamer lived near Oxford. Moreover, the *Gawain* poet and Tolkien, like Malory and Tennyson, emphasize our modern puniness by playing on our sympathy with some unheroic responses to heroic endeavor. In *Gawain*, one thinks of the rolling head, "Þat fele hit foyned wyth her fete, þere hit forth roled" (428) and of the court's complaint that Gawain should have been kept from leaving on his foolish quest (674–83). In both works, such responses—from impulses that we recognize, with some humor, as our own—are involved in the larger matter of redefining heroism and its elements. For Gawain, the important thing is not the quickly dispatched fighting of worms and giants (720–23) but passive endurance—of the lady's courtship and the Green Knight's promised ax blow. For Tolkien, as John C. Pope has characterized Tolkien's essay on *The Battle of Maldon*, the central concern is an "abiding sympathy for the heroism of the little man" (*Seven* 73): the hobbits are, at first glance, the unlikeliest of heroes. And, finally, in both works the crucial acts of redemption are to be found, surprisingly, at the periphery of things: in the distant, unregarded Shire or a provincial castle off somewhere in the north, where Bertilak's men welcome Gawain as a sort of traveling Emily Post, the "fyne fader of nurture" who can instruct them in "þe teccheles termes of talkyng noble" (917–19).

This seminar has occasionally served to recruit students for a more advanced course in Middle English, and I am careful to remind the class that Borroff's poem is a translation by playing either the Borroff-Bessinger recording or the tape made by Paul Piehler and some graduate students at Berkeley, which is somewhat less polished but more exuberant (see "Aids to Teaching" in the "Materials" section). But even for those students whose experience with English, let alone Middle English, is limited to the two required freshman courses, reading *Gawain* in translation is a lot better than not reading *Gawain* at all. No one, certainly, has ever complained that it was boring, and that gives it a rare distinction among freshman texts.

Involving Students in *Sir Gawain and the Green Knight*: An Introductory Survey Course for Nonmajors and Non–Liberal Arts Majors

Rosemary Ascherl

The course is a required survey of English literature, and the students are majoring in various engineering technologies at Hartford State Technical College. While they are bright, most of them are not particularly interested in literature. One problem is their tendency to read *Sir Gawain and the Green Knight* sketchily for the main events of the story and not to notice its use of rich detail and symbolism. Another problem is that they often have a passive attitude about the work, being only too willing to go along with what the teacher says without examining the evidence and seeing its patterns for themselves. Class discussions, papers, and essay questions in the past have reflected this lack of personal involvement.

I found a solution to both problems recently that pleased both the students and me. It pleased them because they were doing something new and demanding and the results were surprising to them; it pleased me because it gave the students a chance to take part in class discussions of the story as creative scholars, with a personal interest in pointing out how the story worked, and because the papers resulting were the best I had ever received from these classes. The procedure involved having each student trace a different element through the story. I have used the procedure twice, with even better results the second time as a result of slight changes.

In order to teach the story in this way, the instructor should make up a list of details that appear in the story more than once, sometimes many times. Each student will be responsible for a single detail in class discussion, and that material will become the topic for a short paper to follow. In the list, distributed by the teacher, the words "references to" should precede each topic so that students realize that a comprehensive listing of all references to the material is required. Some topics I used were as follows: written and oral accounts; guilt; religious holy days; the devil; youth; sexual behavior; the Trojans; wonders and marvels; gifts; embroidery and weaving; gems and jewelry; fairyland, things of fairies and fays; fear; churches, kirks, chapels, chancels, and oratories; birds; saints; wild places; animals; silk; shields and armor; music; masses and matins; green; cutting tools and cutting; knots; red and blood; heads; cold and winter; white; old age; Bible stories; food and meals; family relationships; agreements, covenants, and bargains; the dark; and the seasons. (The exact wording of the topics should be adjusted to the wording of the translation used.)

The first time I used this approach, I let each student choose a topic from the list. The result was not ideal, since some students chose topics that were not particularly suited to their abilities, such as those requiring recognition of rather subtle patterns. The second time, therefore, I distributed copies of the list of topics with a student's name beside each topic. By that time in the course, I had observed the students' perceptions in class discussions of other works, and I was able to assign the more difficult symbolic topics to the more capable students, the topics requiring careful notation of many occurrences to the extremely diligent ones, the most mundane topics to the weaker students, and the more religious to those with traditional religious backgrounds or with an interest in religion. There were no complaints about my assignments. While I was pleased with the results, another instructor in another class situation might prefer to give the students freedom of choice to follow their interests.

The first time, the students chose their topics before reading the story. This method did not work out so well, because they either looked too hard for their elements in the story and missed important parts of the whole romance or read for the story and overlooked instances of the elements that they were supposed to be tracing. The second time, the students heard nothing about their topics until they had finished reading the story.

Before assigning this first reading of the story, I told them that the story was strange and would keep them reading but that the very beginning was difficult to understand, even with the footnotes provided. I went over this first part with them in class, telling them about the Trojan War and Aeneas and about the legendary material here connecting Britain with the Trojans. After I had explained this material and read it aloud, they read the rest of the story in two reading assignments for the next two class hours. The George K. Anderson prose translation seems to work best for these students.

In these two class sessions of going over the story as a whole, I first said a few things about the unknown author and the area where the poem was written, and I made sure they understood that though their translation was in prose, the original is a poem. By way of Socratic questioning on my part, we then discussed the story, taking the material in its order of appearance. The students remembered that the Green Knight resembled the jolly green giant of the vegetable advertisements and that holly is evergreen; they noticed, or were made to notice, the contrasts of castles and wilderness areas and of the hunting going on inside and outside the castle; they discovered reasons for Sir Gawain's actions and for his guilt; they found that the Green Knight's explanation of the events raised more questions than it answered.

The students were then given their specific topics and an assignment sheet explaining what they were to do. It read:

Read the whole story again carefully, looking for the references assigned to you, and marking each reference (in the margin or with a highlighter, perhaps).

Then try to answer these questions to your own satisfaction:
How many references are there?
Why are there so many, or so few?
In what parts of the story do these references occur?
Why did the author include them?
Are there discernible patterns in their use?
Is there any special meaning connected with the detail you have been tracing?
Is it used realistically or symbolically?
What would the story be like without these references?

While they did this work at home, other short works were read in class and discussed during the next two class sessions.

The students then discussed the story again from the point of view of its details, taking up each topic on the list in turn. This class discussion, which ran two sessions of an hour each, was lively and often humorous. Students shared what they had noticed about their own topics, and they added to, agreed with, or disagreed with the comments of the others as well. It seemed that close attention to one topic had carried over into interest in the role of the other details. I had much less to say than usual. Everyone had a specialty. The students saw the tapestried quality of the story, the play of many threads, as they would not otherwise have seen it.

The required papers that followed were reports in miniature on these motifs, with each student's topic serving as a title. Since many details can be difficult to organize in a paper, and since I wanted very short papers of one and a half to two pages handwritten or handlettered, less if typed, I required a strong structure, with the main point in a single-sentence first paragraph that incorporated a listing of some kind. The items listed in the main point were to be taken up in turn in the succeeding paragraphs, one item to a paragraph. I provided them with a format sheet and grading guidelines for this paper and encouraged them to get help from me in formulating their main points, organizing their material, and dealing with specific problems they had on their rough drafts, such as whether there should be a comma at a certain point. The paper was due a week from the day that it was assigned.

Students sought help eagerly, but they had their own ideas about content, and most of them were certainly not looking for content from me. They generally needed help in organizing their ideas into a strong and concise main point. Only a few were puzzled about the significance of their references. In talking to them about the material, I tried to avoid giving them the answers they were looking for as I saw them and tried instead to ask them questions that they would answer themselves. For example, the student writing on churches was puzzled about the mention of the chancel. He told me with respect to the context that the beautiful lady in the castle is first seen coming out of the chancel in the castle. I asked, "Does she seem to belong there?" The student lit up with the irony of it and wanted to be off to write the paper.

The students discovered all kinds of things. For example, the student writing on bird references noticed birds as ornaments on articles of clothing of both Sir Gawain and the Green Knight, and he also found that birds appeared as indicators of the season. Another student wrote about the cutting of the ox and the head-cutting of the principal figures. The student studying gifts said that some gifts in the story were material but that many were abstract, such as thoughtfulness and kindness, hospitality, and the gift of life itself. The writer of a paper on family ties cited the mention of Aeneas's family, the Round Table as a brotherhood, the sister's son relationship of Sir Gawain to King Arthur, and Morgan's being the half sister of the king. A writer about cold and winter associated those references with anger, evil, or barrenness.

This approach has been a fruitful way to teach the story to nonmajors, particularly non–liberal arts majors, because it makes them read the story carefully and do the kind of detective work that results in imaginative involvement and personal conviction. Another happy result is that it seems to develop an eye for detail that is helpful in reading many other works.

Course Outline

Week	
1	Old English; *Beowulf*
2–3	Middle English; Chaucer, *Canterbury Tales*
4	Arthurian literature; *Sir Gawain and the Green Knight*: discussion of poem (2 meetings); medieval lyrics; medieval drama
5	*Sir Gawain and the Green Knight*: presentation of special-topic reports (2 meetings); introduction to Renaissance and the new astronomy
6	Shakespeare, *King Lear*
7	Sonnets of Spenser and Shakespeare; Donne
8	Milton, *Paradise Lost*; Age of Reason; Pope, *Essay on Man*; Swift, *Gulliver's Travels*
9	Romantic period: Blake, Wordsworth, Coleridge, Keats
10	Victorian period: Tennyson, *Idylls of the King, In Memoriam*; Browning
11	Modern age: Yeats, Eliot, Joyce

"A ȝere ȝernes ful ȝerne": Teaching *Sir Gawain and the Green Knight* in the Survey for Majors

Sherron E. Knopp

Students become English majors because they like to read. They usually have definite ideas about what they like, and for the most part our curriculum at Williams College leaves them free to select courses accordingly, but at some point in the sophomore or junior years they must submit their predilections to the test of English 301 and 302, English Literature from the Middle Ages to the Early Twentieth Century. I start with the fact that they like to read and that whatever it is they like in particular (novels, poems, individual authors), the character of their favorites, like the character of a person one loves, is the culmination of a variety of developments and relations. As lovers of literature they should be as curious to know about all of that as one is to know everything about someone one loves. The survey provides an aerial view—to borrow an image from Ernst Curtius's *European Literature and the Latin Middle Ages*—as opposed to the kind of exhaustive, close inspection of specific works they undertake in English 101, Introduction to Literary Analysis. To many the pace is frustrating and intimidating. In the first weeks, when students often moan that they do not have enough background to keep their bearings, it is satisfying to be able to assure them that the survey *is* the background. I also emphasize that they can learn things from an aerial view that they cannot learn standing on the ground examining minute details under a magnifying glass. The goal of the survey is not to cover the Middle Ages or the Renaissance comprehensively but to read enough of the best and most representative works of each period to acquire a good sense of its major genres, styles, themes, and authors. They will not emerge as experts in medieval romance, for example, but they will know enough about one romance—*Sir Gawain and the Green Knight*—to know what to expect when they see a course in the catalog called Medieval Romance. And they will know what makes *Gawain* distinctively medieval, in contrast to the Renaissance use of romance in a work like *The Faerie Queene*. Most students discover new favorites in literature they initially assume is remote from their interests, but even if they do not, the knowledge they acquire in the survey should give them a wiser and deeper love for their own favorite works.

The Middle Ages in particular is a distant and alien period for many students. Without denying its remoteness, I want to show them how intellectually interesting the literature is on its own terms and, simultaneously, how it speaks to the gut—their guts—in direct, powerful, and timeless ways.

If *Beowulf* sometimes leaves them unconvinced, *Gawain* is a cinch. In the course I teach, *Gawain* comes immediately after *Beowulf* and just before selections from the *Canterbury Tales*. For all three works I want my students to have a glimpse behind the cold, impersonal pages of modern print in the *Norton Anthology* (ed. Abrams) to the unique individuality of medieval manuscripts. Before beginning discussion of the poem, therefore, I pass around Gollancz's EETS facsimile of Cotton Nero A.x, drawing attention to its miniatures and commenting on its stanzaic form (they have already looked at the facsimile of the *Beowulf* manuscript and will look later at reproductions from the *Ellesmere Chaucer*). I also pass around Tolkien and Gordon's standard edition of the poem, identifying it as the text they would use if they were going to read the poem in Middle English and pointing out the notes as a rich source of information. Since *Lord of the Rings* fans have usually heard rumors about Tolkien the scholar and are always delighted to have the rumors confirmed, our sessions on *Beowulf* end with excerpts from his landmark essay "The Monsters and the Critics"; his edition of *Gawain* provides an occasion to read the opening stanza of the poem in Middle English and to talk briefly about its relation to the passage of Old English they looked at earlier.

In the spirit of the medieval rhetoricians, to capture the good will of my students and arouse their curiosity about an area of study some of them might want to pursue, I also introduce the original into their discussions of the poem's meaning on two occasions that I hope will make the Middle English concrete and memorable for them. The first comes when they are discussing the Green Knight's appearance and have noticed the details that make him at once chivalric lord, half-giant challenger, and supernatural wonder. I like to point out that the poet's medieval audience would have been alerted to his problematic nature by the poet's first designation of him—not "unknown rider," as the *Norton*'s translation reads, but "aghlich mayster" (136). Most of them are quick to guess that "mayster" comes from Old French and have no trouble surmising its connotations of culture and authority. They also quickly guess that "aghlich" comes from Old English and are intrigued to learn that *aglæca* means "wretch," "monster," "demon," "fierce enemy"—a word more appropriate for Grendel than for a chivalric *mayster*. Thus they become aware that the ambiguities of the poem are imbedded in its very language and that the poem does have a language of its own that is not the translator's. (If there is time it can also be fun and instructive to compare other translations of the phrase). My second opportunity to make students aware of the original comes in our discussion of the seduction scenes, with Lady Bertilak's "ȝe ar welcum to my cors." Here the translation is excellent: "My body is here at hand, / Your each wish to fulfill" (1237–38). Nevertheless, when students see the Middle English they are rewardingly impressed by the boldness of the come-on and are consequently more alive to the vivid raciness of these scenes.

At this point, however, I do not want to overwhelm my students with linguistic details. We will talk more about Old and Middle English when they are reading the language of the *Canterbury Tales* for themselves. For the present I have only two fifty-minute periods to spend on *Gawain*, and I want at least two-thirds of both to be devoted to discussion. Focusing on the Green Knight's appearance in court and on his challenge, the first day begins with a fairly conventional transition from the Old English heroic world of *Beowulf* to the courtly romance world represented by *Gawain*: if epics exalt the qualities of a national hero fighting against great odds (and in the case of *Beowulf* against great monsters) to preserve civilization, what kind of challenge does the Green Knight pose? Since students tend to accept the Green Knight's greenness with the same equanimity they accept information in the *Norton* headnotes, they are often surprisingly slow to appreciate that he is as fantastic a spectacle—even by the standards of medieval romance— as anything from the most far-flung galaxy of *Star Wars* and as comical in his impact on Arthur's court as E.T. in suburban California. To help them see how much fun the poet has with his characters, I like to ask what they knew about Arthur and his knights before reading the poem. Even if their impressions have been shaped by popular novels and Hollywood, they will know enough about Arthurian conventions to perceive that the characters in this poem are trying as hard as they can to live normal romance lives in a situation that simply defies normal romance rules. From this topic we move on to the implications of the Green Knight's challenge: is Gawain brave or foolish to play his game? Idealistic members of the class insist that if Gawain lives up to the values of his pentangle and trusts in God, he will obviously pass the test and prove his bravery. Pragmatists point out that neither the pentangle nor his trust in God will keep his head on his shoulders if the Green Knight strikes a blow under the conditions specified: faith will save his soul, not his life. Debate on this issue is almost always intense, and it is easy to keep it so by playing devil's advocate. I try to end the class at a moment when the ambiguity of the challenge and of its consequences is felt most keenly and, accordingly, when suspense about the poem's meaning is high.

The second day of discussion is devoted to the temptation scenes, the significance of the girdle as opposed to the pentangle, and the ending. Since the poem deliberately manipulates emotions and expectations, I am always curious to know if and when my students realized that Bertilak is the Green Knight and how they felt when they got to the end only to find out that the real test took place when no one was expecting it: when Gawain (and most readers) were passing time, waiting for the real adventure to continue. In the seduction scenes themselves, I want them to see how Lady Bertilak, like her husband, pushes Gawain to the wall, skillfully and humorously blurring issues for him, inviting him to one thing (dalliance) by labeling it something else (courtesy). Gradually moral questions become more pressing, even sinister, in conjunction with the hunts and the references to confession and judgment, and the debate of the preceding day resumes as we try to pinpoint what Gawain does wrong and when. The simplest answer—he takes the girdle—quickly involves the class in further problems. Those who argue that Gawain replaces his faith in God with faith in magic must take into consideration that fighting magic with magic is the very stuff of romance. Given the terms of the beheading game and the obviously superhuman nature of the challenger, taking the girdle makes eminent sense, not re-placing but supplementing other values. Those who contend that Gawain's fault lies rather in breaking faith with his host to keep the girdle for his own benefit must consider what the garment represents. As a token of sexual intimacy and in conjunction with Gawain's impressive daily harvest of kisses, it is hardly an item to be dangled in a husband's face. To avoid insulting his host and compromising his host's wife, actions both dangerous and irre-sponsible, Gawain chooses to ignore the agreement made with Bertilak in idle sport over wine.

When the class is thoroughly immersed in these competing moral per-spectives, we turn to the ending of the poem and the interpretations offered by the characters themselves. The court's view, that Gawain has trium-phantly returned from a marvelous adventure, makes the poem sheer en-tertaining romance. Gawain's view, that he has utterly betrayed his chivalric and religious ideals, makes the poem a quasi-allegorical morality play about a hero who confronts his own sinfulness (real and potential) as he journeys through life to death and judgment. Finally, the Green Knight's view, that despite minor fumbling Gawain has proven himself a "pearl among peas," makes the poem a comedy, both chivalric and moral, about the tensions between idealism and reality, about striving for perfection while coping with imperfection.

Each of these views can be related to the dimensions of the Green Knight's character discussed on the first day and to different interpretations of his green color. For budding symbol hunters especially, the conflicting signif-icances of the color provide a valuable lesson in caution. As collateral reading for the occasion I assign "Thomas Rhymer" and "The Wife of Usher's Well" (both in *Norton*). In accord with the court's view, the Green Knight's color, like the green clothing in "Thomas Rhymer," reveals an association with the Celtic otherworld. Neither bad nor good, just other, his greenness makes him a quintessential example of the marvelous and, consequently, an ideal romance adventure. In support of Gawain's view, green is the color worn in medieval folklore by that formidable hunter of souls, the devil (as, for example, in Chaucer's Friar's Tale), and the Green Knight's red eyes, his Green Chapel (where "the devil himself [might] be seen / Saying matins at black midnight" [2187–88]), and—in the character of Bertilak—his red hair and beard and penchant for hunting suggest a diabolic tempter who shakes Gawain to the core, with good reason. When not specifically associated with the devil, green can also be a token of death, as in "The Wife of Usher's Well" when the sons appear to their mother wearing hats of birch. But this poem is not as relevant to *Gawain* as are the other examples I have given, and I want my students to see that too. Finally, green is the color of life and nature, and the green knight with his elegant green accoutrements, carrying as an emblem of his vitality the evergreen holly, is the perfect lord to challenge the artificial idealism of Arthur's court with a healthy dose of reality. Indeed it takes the entire poem for Gawain to say what should have been blatantly obvious to him from the beginning: "But if my head falls to the floor / There is no mending me!" (2282–83).

My view of the poem and emphases in teaching it are obviously indebted to the works of A. C. Spearing (Gawain-*Poet*) and Larry Benson (*Art and Tradition*), and I am inclined to agree with Spearing in favoring the Green Knight's view of the adventure. However, it is important for students to see the simultaneous validity of all three perspectives, for this multilayered resonance is something they will encounter again in the *Canterbury Tales*. For most students the amusing humanity of the characters and the subtle complexity of the moral vision in these works are an exciting revelation. Gawain's determination to meet the Green Knight with faith in God and in his pentangle ennobles him. No one wants him to protest at the beginning of the poem that he cannot put his head back on if the Green Knight cuts it off, and there is no honorable way he could raise the objection anyway. The poet takes seriously the Christian mandate to strive for perfection. But ideals are perfect, simple, and abstract, while the reality to which they must be applied is complex and unpredictable. In his refusal to take that reality seriously—and it includes his own human fallibility—Gawain sets himself on a collision course with humiliation and flirts with *contemptus mundi* before he is able or willing to accept any weakness in himself. Because failure is natural and unavoidable, the poet finds his dogged zealousness more than a little comical. And it is this attitude that makes the poem, as the *Norton* introduction says, "profoundly Christian."

The Christian doctrine of salvation is at the heart of every narrative we read after *Beowulf*, from *Gawain* to the *Canterbury Tales* to *The Faerie Queene* to *Paradise Lost*. Students need to recognize and understand the theology involved, and a play like *Everyman* presents it simply and clearly for those who are unfamiliar with it. But the great poets are sensitive to the

realities of human imperfection and failure as well. In the literature of the
Renaissance, students will see how an increasing awareness of human psychology and the allure of evil makes the moral choices of characters like
Faustus, Redcross Knight, and Satan increasingly problematic and threatening. But for the literature of the Middle Ages—and for the Christian moral
vision of *Gawain* and the *Canterbury Tales* in particular—I want them to
come away with vivid memories of laughter and compassion.

Sir Gawain and the Green Knight as a Masterpiece of World Literature

Katharina M. Wilson

The comparative literature department at the University of Georgia offers two courses on masterpieces of world literature as one set of sophomore literature classes designed to satisfy the humanities requirement for under-graduate students. The first course (CML 121) covers the period from Greek antiquity to the Renaissance, and the second (CML 122) the era from the seventeenth century to the present. The unit on *Sir Gawain and the Green Knight* that I describe is part of CML 121 and its honors equivalent CML 125H. The usual fixtures of the syllabus include one of the Homeric epics, three or four Greek plays, the *Aeneid*, the *Inferno*, the *Decameron*, the *Canterbury Tales*, *Gawain*, *Gargantua and Pantagruel*, a Shakespeare play, and some of Montaigne's essays.

As a comparatist, I teach these works in their relations to each other and to the larger patterns of literary development (generic, thematic, etc.), en-couraging students to explore literature as both the product and reflection—however distorted—of a complex cultural matrix. My major focus during the course is the evolution of the heroic ideal—or rather a particular culture's perception of the heroic and what that perception reveals about the culture's philosophic and ideological presuppositions. To emphasize the multifaceted and not only cultural, social, generic, and periodic but also sexual diversity of the ideal, I have added some women writers (Marie de France, selections from the *troubairitz*, Margarite de Navarre) and the anonymous *Aucassin and Nicolette* to the canon. The inclusion of two of Marie de France's lais (*Yonec, Lanval*) proves especially interesting in the context of the courtly ideal, because her texts provide genuine alternatives to the depictions of the courtly knight and his usually ornamental appendix, the courtly lady. Moreover, *Aucassin and Nicolette*, with its ambiguous tone and narrative perspective, provides an excellent standard of comparison and evaluation for *Gawain* because it prepares students for the startling discovery that relativism and the loss of a clear narrative perspective are not the exclusive domain of modern literature.

In the belief that to make a literary text compelling and memorable one must make it accessible as well as comprehensible, I have adopted a twofold approach—attempting both to involve students in the exploration of the text and of its relevance to their own interests and aspirations and to provide tenable tools and necessary background information for tackling the texts.

Student Involvement

I encourage students to specialize in a particular aspect of intellectual inquiry, an aspect that they can proudly claim as their own and on which they become "authorities" as the course progresses. At the beginning of the course I compile a list of twenty-five or thirty topics (see my course outline, below), and I let each student select one topic that is of special interest. For the rest of the course, the students are responsible for looking carefully at each text from the point of view of their chosen topic. In this manner their analytic skills as well as their talent for close and careful reading are sharpened, as is their perception of literature as the exploration of perennial human problems, concerns, and desires. Having a clear focus that, even initially, reflects their own interest, students have an immediate entrance to the text, an opening that widens by constant accretion as they apply what they learned from one text to what they find in a new one.

Since great literature is perennially relevant because it deals with the fundamentals of human experience, I urge students to bridge the chronological gap between the period we are discussing and the 1980s by finding that relevance themselves. In addition to contributing to class discussion as the authorities on their chosen topic, students bring to class newspaper clippings or pictures that in some way bear on the text we are studying. This assignment accomplishes two goals: first, before students can look for a modern manifestation of the theme, they have to arrive at a clear conception of some major issues raised by the text; second, finding a contemporary version makes them appreciate both the universality of the theme and the uniqueness of its treatment.

Background

Since what was common knowledge to a literate medieval audience is certainly not common knowledge to the average sophomore, I begin my unit on the Middle Ages with lectures on Catholicism, monasticism, and the rise and fall of feudalism and chivalry, supplemented with slides on Romanesque and Gothic architecture, handouts of Andreas Capellanus's rules of courtly love, John of Salisbury's and Diaz de Gamez's description of the ideal knight, and one or two legends from the *Legenda aurea*. After spending one and a half weeks on Dante's *Inferno*, one week on Marie de France and the *troubairitz*, two to three days on *Aucassin and Nicolette*, and one week on selections from the *Decameron*, we are ready to tackle *Gawain*. By then students are somewhat familiar with the traditions of shorter romances, particularly the elements of courtesy, *fin amour*, love of fame, the frequent occurrence of marvels, notions of loyalty, service, courtesy, bravery, chance, and *trawþe*. Following a fine medieval tradition—that is, the conviction that aesthetic pleasure and full literary appreciation result from knowing the antecedents of a particular work and recognizing literary allusions—we begin our discussion of *Gawain* by drawing parallels between the prologue, with its allusions to the past, and what we have already studied: the reference to the fall of Troy (with its clear implications of breaking the obligations to one's host in the Paris-Helen story, as well as the initial mythical reason for the war in the competition of three goddesses who use human beings as their helpless puppets of revenge) lends itself not only to a vague awareness of impending disaster at Arthur's splendid court but also to a discussion of parallels between Sir Gawain's and Paris's temptations and between the machinations of Morgan Le Fay and those of the Homeric goddesses. We also relate the initial authentication of *Gawain* to those of the other romances.

I then provide some literary background on both the beheading game and the temptation theme from Larry D. Benson's excellent *Art and Tradition in* Sir Gawain and the Green Knight. Discussing Arthur's court, famous for its chivalry, and Sir Gawain as the representative of that court's values, we explore Sir Gawain's character as that of a model knight, renowned for his courtesy, in the context of the description of his shield—a symbolic object that, ever present, dominates the reader's assessment of Sir Gawain's behavior. Since we are looking at *Gawain* in view of what we read before, the question inevitably arises whether the Green Knight is "real" or a figment of Arthur's or Gawain's imagination. As in *Lanval* and *Yonec*, where the protagonists' inmost wishes materialize in the form of a person so in *Gawain* the entry of the churlish Green Knight is prepared by Arthur's wish for some "adventure." We compare the court in *Gawain* to those in the lais of Marie de France, and we observe the predominance of references to "play" and "game" at Arthur's court—terms that, as Leyerle ("Game") argues, constitute the poetic nucleus of *Gawain*. The challenge of the Green Knight, the court's response, and Gawain's brave acceptance prompt comparisons with the heroism of Marie's knights and also occasion the observation that in her instances of life-risking heroism, neither the impetus nor the event is ever referred to as a "game."

Progressing to Gawain's temptations in Lord Bertilak's castle, we note the symmetry of the details of the two "hunts" and Gawain's success in preserving his continence as well as his courtesy—but not fully his promise to his host. We note the similarity between the dual temptations (chastity, courtesy) of Sir Gawain and of Marie's Lanval and the protagonists' different reactions to them—a contrast that reinforces Gawain's overwhelming preoccupation with courtesy. We compare Lady Bertilak to the ladies of other romances, delineating her conventional and unconventional, romance and nonromance characteristics. The discussion of Gawain's temptation by the guide, which shows him at his best—loyal, brave, and honest—and his encounter with Sir Bertilak at the Green Chapel, which for an instant reveals the "uncourtly" side of his character, prompts a discussion of the careful symmetry of the poem. We use the board to map out the many interlocking sets of variations of the three events that govern the structure of *Gawain*.

We conclude our discussion of *Gawain* by attempting to place the text in the romance tradition. In doing so, we note the ambiguity of narrative attitude toward Sir Gawain, Lord and Lady Bertilak, and, therefore, the chivalric ideal. When comparing *Gawain* to *Aucassin and Nicolette*, we find that the antiromance elements in *Gawain* are far fewer but much more strategically located than in *Aucassin and Nicolette*. We evaluate *Gawain*'s anti-romance elements and its ambiguities in the context of what Wittig calls a functional relation of a genre to the culture that produced it, a relation reflected in the structure of romance and that she defines as a "problem-solving pattern which enables the community to mediate important contradictions within its social, economic and mythic structures" (189). Since *Gawain* contains both romance and antiromance, traditional and antitraditional elements and lacks a clear, unambiguous narrative attitude toward the mask of Sir Gawain's heroism, *Gawain* superbly reflects the philosophic presuppositions of late fourteenth-century society, for which the values of chivalry and of romance were no longer unquestioned absolutes.

Our general discussion is followed by individual reports by students, and the unit concludes with a creative assignment on *Gawain*. The topics for this exercise include assigning all characters of *Gawain* to their appropriate place in Dante's *Inferno*; composing a parody of *Gawain*; discussing the work as if all the noncourtly, nonromance details were eliminated; tracing all references to game or to love throughout the text; and comparing the ladies of *Gawain* to those in Marie de France's lais, *Aucassin and Nicolette*, and the *Decameron* in terms of their roles as actor/reactor, initiator/follower, lover/beloved, inspired/inspiration, and giver/receiver.

In the Renaissance segment of the course we return to *Gawain* in the context of our discussion of Castiglione's perfect courtier—a hero much more multifaceted than Sir Gawain but equally intense in his preoccupation with moral and physical excellence and equally reflective of the values and presuppositions of the society that produced him.

Course Outline

Text:

Maynard Mack, gen. ed., *The Norton Anthology of World Masterpieces*, vol. 1

Week

1–2	Introduction to Greek Culture; Homer *Iliad*
3–4	Aristotle, *Poetics*; Aeschylus, *Oresteia*; Sophocles, *Antigone* Euripides, *Hippolytus*; Aristophanes, *Lysistrata*
5	Vergil, *Aeneid*; Lucretius, *On the Nature of Things*
6	Introduction to Middle Ages; *Aucassin and Nicolette*; Marie de France, *Lanval, Yonec*
7	Dante, *Divine Comedy*
8	Boccaccio, *Decameron*; Chaucer, *Canterbury Tales*
9	*Sir Gawain and the Green Knight*
10	Rabelais, *Gargantua and Pantagruel*; Montaigne, *Essays*; Machiavelli, *Prince*; Castiglione, *Courtier*; Erasmus, *Praise of Folly*

Choice of Topics for Specialization

filial and parental relationships

attitude toward wealth (land, money)

class consciousness

psychological and physical attributes of aristocratic ladies

psychological and physical attributes of aristocratic men

psychological and physical attributes of members of the lower classes

perceptions of right and wrong

paradigms of excellence

sense of decorum

recreation

intended audience

metaphoric language

attitudes toward murder and war

attitudes toward love and lust

attitudes toward poverty and charity

clues for recognizing a villain

clues for recognizing the hero

symbolic objects and their function

authentication of the text

persona

humor

history

law (canon and civic)

orthodoxy and heterodoxy

marriage

chance, fate, fortune

God and his miracles, divine intervention

the devil and his weapons

civility and barbarism

UPPER-DIVISION UNDERGRADUATE COURSES (*GAWAIN* IN TRANSLATION)

Gawain and the Middle Ages: Teaching History, Teaching Genre

Peggy A. Knapp

Its particular textural richness and balanced equivocation make *Sir Gawain and the Green Knight* an ideal exemplary text for teaching the arts and skills of interpretation. In one text, it tells two quite different stories—one about a great knight, recounted in the genre of romance, the other about a penitent Christian, recounted in the genre of exemplum or moral fable. Which story readers see depends on which set of details they bring to the foreground and how they link those details together. A series of class discussions can make student readers aware of both stories simultaneously. How each alternative is described depends on the aims of the course and the other texts it includes. If historical understanding of a period of the Middle Ages is a major objective, the instructor can call one reading of *Gawain* nationalistic, the other penitential; if a major emphasis is literary creation in the medieval period, the two stories may be called chivalric romance and exemplum. No matter how the course is organized, Gawain's situation as young man meeting (or perhaps exceeding) the requirements of his society engages students directly. They become caught up in the problem he faces when he returns to the court—who is right about his story, and what is implied about an accommodation to the adult world?

I have read *Sir Gawain and the Green Knight* with students in several different kinds of courses, always keeping these emphases in mind but assigning different levels of priority to them. I will describe two of the courses here: the Medieval Semester, a highly experimental program in which the same twenty-five students took five courses in the Middle Ages concurrently, and a more conventional course called Medieval Literature, taught in translation. The Medieval Semester was offered in its fullest form in 1972; twice since then colleagues and I have taught variations of it, both times waiving the requirement that each student take all five courses. In the first arrangement, all of us adopted roles in a medieval court: the court at Salisbury during the building of the cathedral. One of the five courses, Patterns of Medieval Consciousness, helped students research their social, religious, and personal situations and identities. In the others, they studied philosophy, history, Anglo-Saxon literature, and later English and Continental works. Here is part of the announcement of the semester plan

- Patterns of medieval consciousness: an attempt to discover the Middle Ages by examining some of its multifaceted patterns, which operate in styles of dressing, painting, speaking, cooking, hunting, singing, etc., as well as in literary form.
- Epic and prose before 1300: a study of medieval poetry and prose from the swamp-stompers and marsh-haunters of *Beowulf* to the heraldic world of *Roland*.
- Romance, mysticism, and drama before 1500: a study of the great courtly poems—*Erec, Tristan, Troilus, Gawain,* and *Lancelot*; of mystical and devotional literature; and of the beginnings of drama, through our own productions.
- Problems in medieval history: a study of the environmental cradle for medieval visions of the world and the passionate confrontations that those visions provoked (e.g., dissent, reform, heresy, the Jew).
- Medieval philosophy: a study of medieval philosophy from its beginnings in late classical thought (Stoicism, Epicureanism, Platonism) through Augustine, the church fathers, the encyclopaedists, the mystics, and finally the scholastics.

Our court cook and her assistants prepared our noon meal every Friday and got up several substantial feasts. We decorated our room with stained glass and tapestries, swore fealty, exorcised demons, sat as a love court, looked on at armed combat, and finally held an inquisitorial trial, involving everyone as accusor, accused, or judge. The intensity of the involvements we enacted—some warm, some tense—are still vividly present to my mind. Although the experiment was remarkably successful (at a high price in exhaustion), we could never repeat it because we never found another group of students who could afford to spend a whole semester on the Middle Ages. The more ordinary course I have offered since has benefited from that experiment, both in the knowledge it made available and in the pedagogical lessons it suggested. Among those lessons is the advantage of concentration on a historical moment, and it is the historical reading of *Gawain* I will treat here first.

It is always chastening to remember that everything we have that constitutes evidence about medieval life comes to us already mediated. A romance presents somebody's image of life, molded according to the demands of a conventional generic form; so does a sermon or a chronicle. Neither the "sober document" nor the "fanciful poem" may be taken as absolutely prior. My scheme for making medieval life and thought available to students is to move back and forth from documentary to literary texts, using each to inform and modify the others. When Gawain returns to Arthur's court at the end of *Sir Gawain and the Green Knight*, we feel torn between, on the one hand, believing in and understanding Gawain's deeply felt (and perhaps excessive) repentance for his lapse of trust in God, and, on the other, believing in and understanding the court's festive (and perhaps blind) celebration of his successful chivalric adventure. Gawain the penitent represents an "aroused and serious Christianity" (Bloomfield, "*Sir Gawain*" 11) abroad in England and available to us through many penitential manuals and private memoirs from the period. We have evidence of the fourteenth-century Church's concerted plan to inculcate the penitential spirit and of the contrite response of laypeople to that campaign. The *Livre* of Henry of Lancaster is an especially apt example of the latter, because Henry was a knight of the "new round table" (Order of the Garter) instituted by Edward III in 1348.

Edward's "round table" brings into focus a political dimension of the other story *Gawain* is telling, the story of high and subtle adventure that dignifies the heroic circle of Arthur's legendary court as a way of arousing England's national pride. The direct effect of this ploy was felt, of course, by the aristocracy, but even peasants set aside their various dissatisfactions with Edward's regime and enlisted voluntarily in his armies (McKisack 251–58). Treating the poem as a serious work about a serious conflict in values locates it as an image of a particular, but not static, historical moment (Knapp). The poem also presents in little those social and religious forces that inform the *Canterbury Tales*—also a work about penitence and nationalism, God's demands and society's. Using *Gawain* as a frame for other fourteenth-century works allows the class to freeze the flow of historical information for closer inspection and concentrate on the way such an era might have seen itself, forestalling that uncomfortable sense of continual movement that survey courses often invite.

In Medieval Literature, I like to stress the importance of genres. Here is a brief outline of the course:

- The visible world of the Middle Ages: slide show
- The unseen world: selections from Augustine's *On Christian Doctrine* and Boethius's *Consolation of Philosophy*
- *Beowulf*, "The Wanderer," "Deor's Lament," and *The Dream of the Rood*
- Chrétien's *Lancelot*
- Dante's *Inferno*
- *Sir Gawain and the Green Knight*
- Chaucer's *Canterbury Tales*: General Prologue, Miller, Nun's Priest, Wife of Bath, Franklin, Pardoner
- Malory's *Morte Darthur*
- Drama: *Second Shepherds' Play, Everyman*

Having moved through several stark contrasts already, we are prepared to see the two alternative readings of *Gawain* as two different generic shapes, which indeed they are. We define the shape of moral fable by attending to the following sequence of details:

- In the midst of a splendid Christmas celebration at Arthur's renowned court, a confrontation with death, imaged as single combat with an axe, intrudes (fitt 1).
- The seasons (natural history, the life of a man) are shown in their inevitable passing, the turning year (fitt 2, st. 12–13).
- On his way to meet a seemingly certain death, the hero is offered the temptations of comfort and pleasure, which he does not allow to deter him, and a magic token of unknown warrant, which he does, briefly, trust (fitt 3).
- A climactic struggle, again presented as combat, leads the hero to penance, confession, and resolve to amend his life (fitt 4).
- The resulting stern wisdom is brought back to the original court and rejected (fitt 4, st. 101).

In this light the fresh, intricate, surprising plot of *Gawain* is seen as the familiar story of the protagonist's salvation and as a warning to court and reader.

The romance shape emerges from these details:

- A specific, evocative treatment is given of court life, emphasizing its vitality, elegance, manners, and customs (fitt 1, st. 1–7).
- The appearance of the intruder is presented as the answer to Arthur's wish for a marvel, resulting in an invitation to adventure (fitt 1, st. 5).
- The detail and richness of the hunting and attempted seduction scenes reveal courtly pursuits and outline a secular dilemma—conflicting promises to Bertilak and his wife (fitt 3).
- The hero's courage and forthrightness vindicate Arthur's court and provide it with a model of knightly perfection (fitt 4, st. 99).
- The final scene suggests the reintegration of the court in the adoption of the girdle and the entry of Gawain's adventure in "Romance's rarest book" (fitt 4, st. 101).

The approach through genre discloses the same array of interpretive problems as does the historical approach, and, like it, clarifies the reader's role in providing closure, since no textually decisive clue dictates a choice between the two endings provided. Some students argue for one reading or another; some look for a way to mediate between the available conclusions. Both arguments rest on the interpretation of both specific passages and the poem's structural design.

The same equivocation in the text troubles students' more direct reactions to *Gawain*. They see Gawain pulled two ways—toward personal moral awareness and toward courtly excellence—at a time when their own youthful idealism collides with their own flawed society's invitation to compromise. The ending raises acutely the problem of whether a penitent like Gawain *can* be taken back into the court on his own terms, whether his clear vision of human frailty can be blended with the court's genial laughter. If the answer is yes, Gawain is a prototypical survivor of a rite of passage, ready for a leader's role in a functioning culture. If the answer is no, the ending of *Sir Gawain and the Green Knight* marks the beginning of Gawain's role as the prophet to a doomed people.

Such a classroom treatment of *Gawain* introduces historical knowledge, pursues close textual analysis, and argues interpretive strategy. Gawain's quest is a moment in Europe's history, a tightly woven fabric of words, and an evocation of a problem pressing in on students' own lives.

The Literature of King Arthur and Camelot

Victoria L. Weiss

An upper-level English course in Arthurian romance attracts a diverse group of students—not the usual clan of English majors. Most of them have read—indeed, have been weaned on—tales of Merlin, King Arthur, Sir Lancelot, and all the rest. They have read and reread *The Once and Future King*, starred in—or at least seen—Lerner and Loewe's *Camelot*, and sat through countless viewings of John Boorman's *Excalibur*. There is not one who has not seen *Monty Python and the Holy Grail*. But chances are none of them has read Malory, Chrétien de Troyes, Wace, Layamon, or *Sir Gawain and the Green Knight*.

When I first encountered this group of fantasy lovers, I sought a way to capitalize on their fanciful interest in things Arthurian and at the same time to inspire interest in the origins of these fantasies, the early works that first gave rise to the legend of King Arthur and his knights. One way I hit on to connect these writings to the works with which these students were familiar was to interest them in the whole idea of the growth of legends—how they start and how they develop. What gives rise to them, and what assures them of continued life?

My course, The Literature of King Arthur and Camelot, meets twenty-eight times during the semester. After a day of introduction, we look at the earliest mentions of Arthur. For these references, I use Richard L. Brengle's *Arthur King of Britain* part 1 (on reserve in the library), which includes the brief mentions of Arthur in works by Gildas, Bede, Nennius, William of Malmesbury, Giraldus Cambrensis, and Ralph Higden. (We spend one class period discussing these.) We devote two class periods to the chronicle tradition represented by Geoffrey of Monmouth's *Historia* (excerpts in Brengle), Wace's *Roman de Brut*, and Layamon's *Brut*. Next we consider the romance tradition, spending five classes on Chrétien de Troyes's *Erec et Enide*, *Cligés*, *Yvain*, and *Le chevalier de la charrette*, followed by two class periods on the Welsh romances "Culhwch and Olwen," "The Dream of Rhonabwy," and "The Lady of the Fountain" in *The Mabinogion*; two classes on *Sir Gawain and the Green Knight*; and one class period on the alliterative *Morte Arthure* (excerpt in Brengle). We complete the medieval section of the course with approximately six classes on Malory's *Morte Darthur*. In Vinaver's *Malory: Works*, we read all of book 1 ("The Tale of King Arthur"); book 2 ("The Tale of Noble King Arthur That Was Emperor Himself . . ."); parts 1, 4, 7, 14, and 15 of book 5 ("The Book of Sir Tristram de Lyones"); and all of books 6, 7, and 8 ("The Sank Greal," "Sir Lancelot and Queen Guinevere," and "The Death of Arthur"). This roughly chronological approach is continued after a four-hundred-year gap with approximately three classes devoted to Victorian interest in Arthurian literature. We read William Morris's "Defence of Guenevere" and the prelude to Algernon Swinburne's "Tristram of Lyonesse" (both in Buckley and Woods's edition of *Poetry of the Victorian Period*, which I put on library reserve), and as much of Alfred Tennyson's *Idylls of the King* as we have time for—at least "Lancelot and Elaine," "The Holy Grail," and "The Passing of Arthur." The course concludes with approximately four classes on T. H. White's *The Once and Future King*. (The system outlined here allows for one catch-up day.)

In keeping with the stated focus of the course (the growth of the legend), each student in the class is assigned two fifteen-minute reports to present orally. (See the detailed list of report topics at the end of this article.) The topics focus mostly on origins. They are designed to provoke discussion of questions such as the following: What concerns may have given rise to the notion of the Round Table? At what point do we notice the fighting man suddenly becoming courtly? When does love between man and woman enter the picture? How did the Holy Grail become attached to the Arthurian legend? In addition to providing a summary of scholarly findings about the topic, the students are asked to take special note of issues about which the scholars disagree and to cite those scholars. Since most report topics are critical cruxes in Arthurian scholarship and therefore have much written about them, students are urged (warned?) to complete their research well in advance of their report date so that they will have time for sorting out and organizing their material. I also urge students to prepare a handout or outline containing their most important or most complicated points, which I then xerox for distribution to the class.

This emphasis in the reports on origins and subsequent development is intended to make the students careful readers, attentive to new developments in familiar motifs and new accretions to familiar devices and characters. It is useful not only in better understanding the medieval works that make up the first part of the course but also in sharpening the focus, later in the course, on how modern writers of Arthuriana have changed their medieval sources. Why is a new personality assigned to a character familiar to us from previous versions of the story? Why is an entirely new knight (such as Lancelot) added to the cast of the Round Table? What effect does his introduction to the cast have on the stature and personality of the other familiar knights—the famous ones already associated with the legend?

When we begin to consider *Gawain* in the course, our reports focus on questions concerning character—both Gawain's and the Green Knight's—and exploration of the knightly code as an ideal. In keeping with the course's focus on origins and development, our first report examines Gawain's portrayal in *Gawain* as the supreme romance hero with a reputation for courtesy and prowess. French had been the language of romance since the days of

Chrétien. When English romance appears in the fourteenth century, the French hero par excellence, Lancelot, has been supplanted by a courtly Gawain whose reputation seems firmly in place. This view of the hero is so at odds with earlier accounts—where he is often a testy fellow, quick to succumb to the charms of a beautiful maiden or turn his back on a friend—that one wonders why the poet chose him here as the knightly exemplar of Arthur's Round Table. Have we come back to an old, essentially English view of Gawain, or does this characterization seem entirely new? What and where are Gawain's origins? What did the French do to his character? What view of his character emerges in *Gawain*?

A second report concerns the relation between duty and love—in broader terms, between the ideals of the knightly code and the human frailty of its practitioners. The conflict between duty and love is at the heart of the earliest treatments of the Arthurian story, and Chrétien de Troyes gives it considerable attention in works like *Erec et Enide*. In *Gawain*, the hero's duty to appear before the Green Knight unarmed confronts head-on his love for his own life. The ending of the poem, where Gawain despairs over his own failings while the Green Knight and the members of the Round Table view him as the paragon of virtue, suggests some chinks in the armor of the knightly code itself, a sense that the code demands a selflessness of which no man is capable. Or does it? The poem may suggest that the desire for fame and honor led Gawain to strike a death blow at the Green Knight rather than the simple tap the Green Knight himself gives Gawain at the end. A close look at the actual language of the challenge reveals that the Green Knight calls merely for a stroke—not for a decapitation.

Another report focuses on the alliterative form as a vehicle for romance. The use of this form suggests a reaffirmation of indigenous English values, perhaps a move away from the ideal, even fanciful conditions of French romance—and its often sprawling, formless nature—to a well-formed, less fanciful, more realistic literary work. It may represent also the resurgence of English pride in things distinctly English, appearing as it did during the period of England's Hundred Years' War with France. But, curiously, *Gawain*, along with many other English alliterative works of the same period, is not quite the affirmation of English knightly values that we might expect. The important point here is that poets of the fourteenth century seized the alliterative long line as a vehicle well suited to political and moral satire. The poet's artistic use of the alliterative long line is certainly beautiful. Is the beauty all we are meant to see in the poet's choice of this form as the vehicle for his romance? Does the use of the alliterative form point to a satiric message in the poem?

A final topic asks the students to consider the various interpretations of the Green Knight. He is a special type of opponent to the Round Table. What is his significance? Why is he completely green? Is he a good guy or a bad guy? What do his abilities to transform himself tell us about him? Here our discussion of the origin and appeal of legends explores the mythic dimension of the Arthurian story, the way in which elements of myth—such as the Holy Grail and Gawain's green opponent—provide details that not only appeal to us but pull on our unconscious, speak to the mysterious in life itself, to those forces both inside and outside of ourselves that we find difficult to classify or pigeonhole.

So goes the part of the course that requires research from the students. Their major paper does require outside reading, but for this project they put the experts aside. Instead, they read on their own a contemporary treatment of the Arthurian legend (exclusive of *The Once and Future King*, which we read and consider in class). We begin our look at modern adaptations by noting the large number of contemporary treatments of Arthurian stories. I try to bring together as many modern versions as I can from the library, bookstores, and my own collection. As a class, we attempt possible explanations for the contemporary popularity of these stories. This discussion forms a basis for the students' independent work on a modern version of the legend. Each student writes a paper that focuses on two points: the author's use of medieval materials and the work's own artistic merit. After providing a brief plot summary of the modern work and identifying the particular medieval sources (often identified in a preface or endnote), students are asked to consider whether the modern writer reaches a different conclusion or provides a different outlook on the characters than do the medieval sources. What does the modern writer gain by altering the medieval story or by including Arthurian elements in the story he or she has decided to tell? Finally, the students give the theme of the modern work as they see it. Is the author's use of Arthurian material appropriate to the point he or she wishes to make? How?

While many modern Arthurian stories deal with rites de passage of the sort Gawain experiences in *Gawain* and with dangerous challenges put to a knight by unknown or superhuman opponents, a number of the works include episodes featuring Gawain specifically as the hero. Students are quick to recognize the quick-tempered, impulsive Gawain of Malory in John Steinbeck's *The Acts of King Arthur and His Noble Knights*. Even better for comparison with *Gawain* is Thomas Berger's *Arthur Rex*, which includes the author's own version of *Gawain*, a version considerably different from the original romance. Berger's novel retells several other romance stories involving Gawain, Tristram, Lancelot, and other knights of the Round Table. Also of interest to students of Gawain is the way this novel combines the two personalities assigned at various times to Gawain—the English conception of Gawain as the paragon of prowess and fair play and the French conception of him as the lecherous conqueror of women.

In addition, a number of recent works are distinct and deliberate retellings of *Gawain* alone. The best is Vera Chapman's *The Green Knight*, a novel that arose from the writer's sense that "the story told in the romance seems on the face of it unfinished." Other retellings include several children's books—in fact, a surprising number of them, given the sophistication of the bedroom scenes in the romance. At any rate, most of these pale in comparison to the original poem but are nonetheless useful for students to examine, since a writer of children's books will often be concerned with not only simplifying the story but also clarifying the motives of characters.

Often this procedure involves eliminating the troublesome episodes of the original. For example, both Constance Hieatt's prose retelling, *Sir Gawain and the Green Knight*, and Ian Serraillier's poetic version, *The Challenge of the Green Knight*, eliminate all mention of Gawain's confession to a priest after he has accepted the green girdle from his host's wife, and Hieatt's Lady Bertilak focuses her attention much more single-mindedly on the giving and receiving of material objects during her three visits to Gawain's room than does her counterpart in the original romance. Other children's versions include *Sir Gawain and the Green Knight* by Selina Hastings, aimed at readers between the ages of eight and eleven, and Y. R. Ponsor's *Gawain and the Green Knight*, also aimed at young readers. Students who opt to do their papers on these children's versions are asked to read at least two and to compare them, while also addressing the specific questions asked of all students.

Another work worth mentioning, though it does not deal specifically with *Gawain*, is a prize-winning novel by Gillian Bradshaw, *Hawk of May*. This is fertile ground for analysis of the character of Gawain, since "Gwalchmei" is the novel's first-person narrator.[1]

I hear rumors of an animated version of *Gawain*, often available to cable-television subscribers, and of a filmed version with real actors, which is just going into production, as well as a commissioned opera based on the romance. The recent flurry of activity in producing modern versions of *Gawain* points to the timeless appeal of this story of a good man who winds up in a tight spot when he sets out to do what he thinks is right. Undergraduates find it easy to relate to this hero—a fellow who faces a situation where, no matter what he does, he just cannot win. And I invite the students to recognize that good motives and no-win situations like Gawain's are unique to neither the poet's time nor our own. The result of our discussions is a greater appreciation for this carefully crafted fourteenth-century romance and its extraordinary ability to speak to us six hundred years later.

NOTE

[1] I am indebted to Robert H. Boyer (St. Norbert Coll., De Pere, WI) for his assistance in locating modern versions.

Sample Report Topics

Wace, *Roman de Brut*
  Merlin the magician
  Wace's contribution to the story of Arthur:
    the Round Table

Wace, *Roman de Brut*; Layamon, *Brut*
  The legend of the return of Arthur
  The origin and significance of the isle of Avalon

Chrétien de Troyes, *Erec et Enide*
  Chrétien and romance as a genre

Andreas Capellanus, *The Art of Courtly Love*
  How serious was Andreas Capellanus? The meaning of courtly love

Chrétien de Troyes, *Cligés*
  Chrétien's concept of a knight

Chrétien de Troyes, *Yvain*; *The Mabinogion*, "The Lady of the Fountain"
  Chrétien's Yvain and the Welsh "Lady of the Fountain" relation

Chrétien de Troyes, *Lancelot* or *Le chevalier de la charrette*
  Origins of Lancelot and Chrétien's presentation of him as the Knight of the Cart
  Chrétien and courtly love

Sir Gawain and the Green Knight
  The origin and development of Gawain: the English and the French views of his character
  The knightly code: What's happening to it in *Gawain?*
  The Alliterative Revival of the fourteenth century
  The significance of the Green Knight

The alliterative *Morte Arthure*
  The medieval wheel of fortune

Malory, *Morte Darthur*, book 1
  Who was Sir Thomas Malory?

Malory, book 6
  Theories of Grail origin
  Malory's attitude toward the Grail

Malory, books 6–7
  The function of the Grail quest in the *Morte*
  Malory and *amour courtois*

Victorian poetry: Morris, Swinburne, Tennyson
  Victorian interest in medievalism
  What Tennyson did to Malory's final book

White, *The Once and Future King*, book 2: *The Queen of Air and Darkness*
  The hunt of the unicorn
  The origin of Morgause

White, *The Once and Future King*, book 3: *The Ill-Made Knight*
   White's view of Lancelot in view of medieval conceptions of his character

White, *The Once and Future King*, book 4: *The Candle in the Wind*
   White's treatment of the dissolution of Arthur's kingdom

Term Papers

The major written project in this course will be a paper (approximately ten pages, due at the end of the semester) on a modern treatment of the Arthurian legend, which you will read in addition to the assigned reading material. In this paper you are asked to consider two points: the author's use of Arthurian sources and the work's artistic merit. In other words, you should consider how the writer makes use of medieval materials related to Arthur and his knights and then determine whether or not the author has written an effective story or work of art. In writing this paper, be sure to consider the following:

1. Can you identify the particular medieval source the author has used? (Often the author will identify his or her source in a foreward or preface to the work.)
2. Does the writer reach a different conclusion or provide a different outlook on the character(s) than does his or her medieval source?
3. How does the writer's source differ from the medieval sources? What does the author gain by altering his or her medieval source or including Arthurian materials in the story?
4. What seems to be the theme of the modern work? Is the author's use of Arthurian materials appropriate to the point he or she wishes to make? Why?

Selected List of Modern Arthurian Adaptations

Berger, Thomas. *Arthur Rex*
Bradley, Marion Zimmer. *The Mists of Avalon*
Bradshaw. Gillian. *Hawk of May*
———. *Kingdom of Summer*
———. *In Winter's Shadow*
Canning, Victor. *The Crimson Chalice*
Carmichael, Douglas. *Pendragon*
Chapman, Vera. *The King's Damosel*
———. *The Green Knight*
Christian, Catherine. *The Pendragon*
Cooper, Susan. *The Dark Is Rising*
Drake, David. *The Dragon Lord*
Godwin, Parke. *Firelord*
Green, Roger Lancelyn. *King Arthur and His Knights of the Round Table*

Hastings, Selina. *Sir Gawain and the Green Knight*
Hieatt, Constance B. *The Castle of Ladies*
——. *The Joy of the Court*
——. *Sir Gawain and the Green Knight*
Kane, Gil, and John Jakes. *Excalibur!*
Lerner, Alan Jay. *Camelot*
Lewis, C. S. *That Hideous Strength*
Malamud, Bernard. *The Natural*
Mayne, William. *Earthfasts*
McDermott, Gerald. *The Knight of the Lion*
Monaco, Richard. *The Final Quest*
——. *The Grail War*
——. *Parsival*
Monty Python's Flying Circus. *Monty Python and the Holy Grail* (screen play)
Munn, H. Warner. *Merlin's Ring*
——. *Merlin's Godson*
Newell, William. *King Arthur and the Table Round*
Newman, Sharan. *The Chessboard Queen*
——. *Guinevere*
Norman, Diana. *A Sword for a King*
Ponsor, Y. R. *Gawain and the Green Knight*
Pyle, Howard. *The Story of King Arthur and His Knights*
——. *The Story of the Champions of the Round Table*
Rosen, Winifred. *Three Romances: Love Stories from Camelot Retold*
Serraillier, Ian. *The Challenge of the Green Knight*
Seton, Anya. *Avalon*
Steinbeck, John. *The Acts of King Arthur and His Noble Knights*
Stewart, Mary. *The Crystal Cave*
——. *The Hollow Hills*
——. *The Last Enchantment*
——. *The Wicked Day*
Sutcliff, Rosemary. *Sword at Sunset*
——. *The Sword and the Circle*
Turton, Godfrey Edmund. *The Emperor Arthur*
Twain, Mark. *A Connecticut Yankee in King Arthur's Court*
White, T. H. *The Book of Merlyn*
Williams, Charles. *Taliessen through Logres*
——. *The Region of the Summer Stars*
——. *War in Heaven*

Tolkien and His Sources

Jane Chance

A course such as J. R. R. Tolkien or Tolkien and His Sources, which involves a work of modern creative and fantastic imagination indebted to medieval authority, may appeal to those instructors interested in teaching a unit on *Sir Gawain and the Green Knight* in a course with a modern base. That Tolkien knew and loved Old and Middle English literature is clear to the student and scholar of the Middle Ages because of his seminal *Beowulf* essay, his editions of *Sir Gawain and the Green Knight* and the *Ancrene Riwle*, and his translations of *Sir Gawain and the Green Knight*, *Pearl*, and *Sir Orfeo*, perhaps the best known of his many scholarly works. That these scholarly interests may have influenced the creation of literary works like *The Hobbit* and *The Lord of the Rings* becomes clear to undergraduate students only when their attention is focused on various minor creative works of Tolkien taught in tandem with those medieval works that Tolkien knew best.

Tolkien parodied various medieval poems explicitly in several of his minor works—*The Battle of Maldon* in *The Homecoming of Beorhtnoth Beorhthelm's Son*; "The Voyage of Saint Brendan" in "Imram"; the Breton lay in "The Lay of Aotru and Itroun"; and *Beowulf*, *Sir Gawain and the Green Knight*, and Chaucer's *Canterbury Tales* in *Farmer Giles of Ham*. The last, a mock romance, parodies lines from *Sir Gawain and the Green Knight*; transforms Gawain as the exemplar of chivalry and courtesy into a vulgar farmer, Giles, and his honorable uncle Arthur into a violent and miserly king; inverts and exaggerates the theme of manners and courtesy (the knights, for example, become more interested in discussing the fashion in hats than in defending their king's honor by combat, and the king himself is rude); and replaces the time and setting of the opening Christmas feast with a highly ironic ending on the day of the Feast of Epiphany (6 January or Twelfth Night, the traditional celebration of the appearance of the Christ child to the Magi), on which Giles is revealed as a true hero and knight in his confrontation with the dragon. Thus Tolkien's interest in medieval literature, especially *Gawain*, provides the materials for an upper-level undergraduate course that will allow modern students to examine the medieval sources of a popular writer.

In the Tolkien course I have taught at Rice, the fifteen weeks are divided into three segments concerning Tolkien as medieval critic and scholar, as fairy-story writer, and as epic writer. The course takes its focus from his pronouncements on Old and Middle English literature, which appear chiefly in his essay "*Beowulf*: The Monsters and the Critics" and in comments entitled "Ofermod" appended to his verse drama *The Homecoming of Beorhtnoth Beorhthelm's Son* (19–24; in *Tolkien Reader*). The latter contains his view of *Sir Gawain and the Green Knight* and what he regards as its cultural relation with *Beowulf*. For this reason *Beowulf*, Tolkien's *Beowulf* essay, his verse drama, and *Sir Gawain and the Green Knight* are all assigned in the first two weeks of the Tolkien course.

Tolkien's verse drama was created as a sequel to the Old English poem *The Battle of Maldon*, which dramatizes the fall of the Lord Byrthnoth and his men in 991. For Tolkien this date is significant: it marks the transition from the heroic Old English period to the chivalric Middle English period. The Norman Conquest of 1066 is normally used to distinguish the two periods, and the late tenth-century date of the Battle of Maldon, for Tolkien, accentuates the demise of Anglo-Saxon (heroic) values and the birth of Norman French (chivalric) practices. In the appended section "Ofermod," Tolkien compares the Anglo-Saxon lords Beowulf and Byrhtnoth with the King Arthur depicted in *Sir Gawain and the Green Knight*. Beowulf, at the end of the poem, sacrifices himself needlessly in battle with the dragon, an adversary in fact killed by his subordinate Wiglaf, while Byrhtnoth needlessly sacrifices his men in the Battle of Maldon. Similarly, in *Sir Gawain and the Green Knight*, Gawain as one of King Arthur's knights accepts the challenge of the Green Knight in order to protect his lord's name and reputation as head of the Round Table, which King Arthur readily allows his subordinate to do. The difference between Old English heroic and Norman French chivalric values remains clear to Tolkien: according to the latter, the king views his knights as extensions of himself, pledged to serve him and to glorify his name through acts of prowess in combat. For Tolkien this attitude illustrates a pejorative pride (*ofermod*).

In the first week of the course, students read and discuss *Beowulf* and Tolkien's interpretation of it in his essay on the poem; in the second week, they read the verse drama, "Ofermod," and then *Sir Gawain and the Green Knight*. During the first day on *The Homecoming* I look at differences between the two characters Torhthelm and Tidwald (they represent two value systems: the minstrel's young son stands for the idealization of the Germanic heroic tradition; the old practical farmer, common sense tinged by Christian morality). I also ask them to identify the third voice breaking in at the end of the verse drama, which speaks not in alliterative (English) verse but in rhyming (French) verse. (The voice may belong to the Danish king Canute, who preceded the Normans in their conquest of England and whom Tolkien notes in his prefatory remarks [*The Homecoming* 3–5, in *Tolkien Reader*] as having rowed past the monks of Ely, according to the *Historia Eliensis*.) If time remains on this first day, I then ask them how Tolkien interprets *The Battle of Maldon* in "Ofermod" (as a criticism of the chief Byrhtnoth and as praise for the bold retainer Beorhtwald). What does Tolkien mean when he states (23) that consideration of the work of one of three poets—the authors of *Beowulf, The Battle of Maldon,* and *Sir Gawain and the Green Knight*— leads to consideration of the works of the other two? Finally, what is the cultural significance of Tolkien's interpretation of the three poems?

On the second and third days, we discuss *Sir Gawain and the Green Knight* in the light of Tolkien's interpretation. After a brief introduction in which I define chivalric romance and alliterative verse, I ask whether the students agree with Tolkien's major thesis, that "*Sir Gawain* . . . is in plain intention a criticism or valuation of a whole code of sentiment and conduct, in which heroic courage is only a part, with different loyalties to serve" (23). In proceeding, we then focus on three aspects of the poem: Tolkien's definition of chivalry, Arthur as king, and Gawain as knight. For the discussion of Arthur we use as a touchstone Tolkien's statement that "This element of pride, in the form of the desire for honour and glory, in life and after death, tends to grow, to become a chief motive, driving a man beyond the bleak heroic necessity to excess—to chivalry" (20). Does this statement apply to Arthur? Where and how? (Tolkien believes that it does: "It is no accident that in this poem, as in *Maldon* and in *Beowulf,* we have criticism of the lord, of the owner of the allegiance" [23].) Students may need some help: they might note the Green Knight's challenge to Arthur and the kind of challenge it is; they might also note that Arthur is "a little boyish" (Borroff's translation, line 86) and views the challenge as chiefly physical. And how is this a test of the court?

About Gawain, Tolkien remarks that "Sir Gawain, as the exemplar of chivalry, is of course shown to be deeply concerned for his own honour, and though the things considered honorable may have shifted or been enlarged, loyalty to work and to allegiance, and unflinching courage remain" (23). But it is important to ask the students whether Gawain *is* an exemplar. How so (here the description of the shield is important [lines 648–65])? Is he not criticized? How many of his various tests does he pass (the first, testing his allegiance to his lord Arthur, in the challenge of the Green Knight; the second, testing his chastity and courtesy, in the temptations of the lady; and the third and fourth, testing his faith in God, in the temptation of the guide and the meeting with the Green Knight)? Students may conclude, when Gawain seems a churl and the Green Knight courteous and charitable, that Tolkien is right in his remarks only in that Arthur sets the tone for his court.

After finishing this segment of the course—on Tolkien as medieval critic and scholar—we analyze him as fairy-story writer in the next three and a half weeks. We first look at his essay "On Fairy-Stories" (*Tree and Leaf* 3–84, in *Tolkien Reader*) and then apply his aesthetic to his fairy stories "Leaf by Niggle," *Farmer Giles of Ham, The Hobbit,* and *Smith of Wootton Major.*

The students discover that these stories reveal the same morality and medievalism as do the essays on *Beowulf* and *Sir Gawain and the Green Knight*, and indeed that *Farmer Giles of Ham* in many ways parodies the latter work. Finally, in the remaining eight weeks of the course we examine Tolkien as epic writer in *The Lord of the Rings* by devoting two and a half weeks to each of its three volumes.

Requirements for the course include a midterm and a final examination (50% of the grade), plus an oral report and two papers, one short (5–8 pp.) and one long (10–15 pp.) (50% of the grade). The first paper must center on one of Tolkien's minor works (i.e., other than *The Lord of the Rings* or *The Silmarillion*), the second on *The Lord of the Rings*. The oral report may be used as a base for one of the papers. Among the topics from which students may choose are Tolkien's life; a history of critical responses to Tolkien's works; Tolkien and children's literature; Tolkien and the Inklings; H. Rider Haggard's influence on Tolkien; *The Lord of the Rings* as epic, as romance, as satire, as fantasy; and finally various topics concerning Tolkien's sources in *The Lord of the Rings* and *The Silmarillion*.

A more advanced course, entitled Tolkien and His Sources, would be suitable for students already familiar with Tolkien's major works. This course (which I have taught only as an independent reading survey) focuses on Tolkien's minor works and on the medieval English and European sources for the major works. Divided into three sections, it begins with a brief introduction to Tolkien's life, during which students read either Humphrey Carpenter's biography or Tolkien's *Letters* to perceive the connection between his creative and scholarly interests. The second (Old and Middle English) section invites students in five to six weeks to read first *Beowulf* and Tolkien's *The Homecoming of Beorhtnoth Beorhthelm's Son*, then *Sir Gawain and the Green Knight*, selections from Malory's *Morte Darthur*, and *Farmer Giles of Ham*. This segment concludes with the *Ancrene Riwle* (which Tolkien himself edited), Tolkien's fairy stories, and his essay defining their aesthetic. In the last seven to eight weeks of the course students read other European medieval sources used especially in the creation of Tolkien's major works. Here students might look at Tolkien's *Unfinished Tales*, if they have not previously. The sources that they read might include the Welsh *Mabinogion* (Gantz translation), the Scandinavian *Elder* and *Prose Eddas* and *Volsunga Saga* (Morris's translation), and the French *Song of Roland* and German *Nibelungenlied* (in *Medieval Epics*). Supplementary works might begin with Joseph Campbell's *Hero with a Thousand Faces*; for the independent reading I also list my book *Tolkien's Art: "A Mythology for England"* (Nitzsche). The requirement for this course consists of a long paper on Tolkien and his sources.

In both courses students uncover iconoclastic ideas that shatter the rigid assumptions they have been taught about literature and its cultural and artistic values. First, they are pleased to discover that the twentieth century is not as divorced from the Middle Ages as they may once have thought; so-called cultural differences between works like *Sir Gawain and the Green Knight* and *The Lord of the Rings* are less important than their essentially similar Christian-heroic values. Second, students realize that the pedantic distinction commonly made in classifying these two works as literature—that is, between the "popular" (entertaining) and "great" (difficult, artistically complex)—collapses. Not only do they find *Sir Gawain and the Green Knight* as enjoyable to read as *The Lord of the Rings*, they also find the three-decker novel as aesthetically rich and rewarding to analyze, in a different way, as the medieval poem—or, I might add, for those undergraduate majors more familiar with modern literature, as the modern novels of Joyce, Woolf, and Faulkner. Thus, in the process of learning a little about two periods, students also gain a new respect for the mimetic artistry of Tolkien in particular and the twentieth-century novelist in general.

Sir Gawain and the Green Knight and a Course in Literary Criticism

John M. Ganim

Though it has a disturbing tendency to subvert such contexts, *Sir Gawain and the Green Knight* is a poem frequently assigned in courses on romance, on Arthurian legend, and on medieval literature. What I want to describe here is how it can be used in a course on literary criticism. Few medieval poems lend themselves as well to formal explication and stylistic analysis as *Gawain* does, but in addition, it can be profitably used to illustrate methods and approaches other than those we refer to as "practical criticism."

For a number of years I have used *Sir Gawain and the Green Knight* in just such a course at the University of California at Riverside. Students are generally upper-division English majors, all of whom would have had a one-quarter course introducing them to the methods of practical criticism. The approaches I discuss include myth criticism, psychoanalytic criticism, and various forms of reader-response criticism, although I also use the poem to debate some difficult but important recent critical theories, including varieties of structuralism and poststructuralism, particularly important issues for those students intending to pursue graduate study. The chief project of students in this course is to explore critical positions on a work other than *Gawain*, which we use for illustration and discussion.

The first week of the course offers a general overview of major critical questions. Reading for this week consists of a handout containing critical statements from Plato to Arnold. Obviously this overview does not pretend to be a history of literary criticism, but since students will have come across a few of these thinkers and writers in other courses, it serves to draw them into discussions by supplementing the brief fragments we are reading. This discussion moves into the second week, and I end it by lecturing on some presuppositions of the New Criticism, which students will have been familiar with from their course in practical criticism.

Students will have been reading the Borroff translation of *Gawain* during these two introductory weeks, and in the third week we engage in a close reading of the poem. At this point, I outline some problems of interpretation, and students are asked to read some important overviews of criticism (Bloomfield, "*Sir Gawain*"; Howard, "Structure and Symmetry" and "*Sir Gawain*"; Hanning; and Hanna, "Unlocking").

The fourth week begins our examination of criticism of *Gawain* with an introduction to myth criticism. The novice reader of the poem, particularly when reading it in translation, is almost overwhelmed by the mythic dimensions of the work and the more obvious, if not the more important, workings of the plot. Indeed, after its initial appeal to social and historical constructs, the poem seems to beg for the sort of readings that we lump together as myth, ritual, and archetypal criticism. We usually read the essay by Manning; I supplement this with my own presentation of John Speirs's well-known argument. Out of fashion with medievalists and critics in general, these readings, however, address directly the initial response of students. For an antidote, C. S. Lewis's "The Anthropological Approach" may be assigned, although I usually take the time at this point to give a general presentation on Jungian interpretation.

The fifth week of the course is devoted to psychoanalytic criticism, with selections from Freud's own writings as our chief texts. While many examinations of criticism place psychoanalytic criticism first for historical reasons, there are good pedagogical reasons to deal with Freud at this point, not least of which is that students have a tendency to regard Jung as an answer to problems created by criticism inspired by Freud—such enthusiasm often smacks of avoidance. There is an excellent, if surprising, chapter in Derek Brewer's *Symbolic Stories* (72–92) worth assigning in conjunction with selections from *The Interpretation of Dreams*. The troubling question of whether family life in the Middle Ages has the same dynamics that Freud perceived in his patients might be addressed through discussion of Moller's essay, which ascribes a quasi-oedipal origin to the "courtly-love complex." (Of course, courtly love has recently become as controversial as psychoanalytic theory.) In fact, Brewer's dependence on certain psychoanalytic theorists gives his essay a suspiciously Jungian tone, something students will actually recognize. The really troubling issue is how to move from a traditional version of psychoanalytic criticism to current positions deeply influenced by structuralism. At this point, I briefly introduce some of Lacan's notions, which we touch on later in our discussion of Hawkes. If time permits, I recommend assigning the chapter on the Wife of Bath's Tale from Norman Holland's *The Dynamics of Literary Response*. Aside from its intrinsic interest and its application of a "modern" approach to a premodern text (one of the points, I assume, of choosing *Sir Gawain and the Green Knight*), the chapter introduces some contemporary theories of reader-response criticism, which I deal with in the sixth week of the course.

Although the bibliography surrounding reader-response criticism and reception theory has grown over the past few years, the ability of students to use it wisely has not. In fact, the danger of introducing reader-response criticism to undergraduates, like that of introducing myth criticism, is its ease of application and the possibilities of misuse or of definition so broad as to render the rigor of criticism meaningless. For its polemic value, as well as its suggestiveness, then, I assign the preface to Stanley Fish's *Self-Con-*

suming Artifacts. Despite its more eclectic origins, I sometimes recommend my own chapter on *Sir Gawain and the Green Knight* for a reading at least partly indebted to some current theories of reader-oriented criticism (Ganim 57–78). I also summarize some notions of Jauss and Iser at this point (Tompkins; Suleiman and Crosman). But from the point of view of literary theory, a consideration of reception and response, even in an undergraduate class, leads to a crucial question. What if the text before us is not as unique as we think it is?

Such a question, of course, always lay behind the traditions of source study and at least implicitly fueled the critique of New Criticism on the part of historical critics. But the question derives new theoretical force from its formulation in structuralist theory, of which I attempt a bare introduction in the seventh week of the course. There is, unfortunately, no ready-made high structuralist interpretation of *Sir Gawain and the Green Knight*, though there are many studies of the poem's structure and Wittig is a helpful model. Hence, some improvisation is necessary. Students may be assigned Hawkes's *Structuralism and Semiotics.* In addition, Benson's *Art and Tradition* may be mined, perhaps unfairly, for the sort of information we would need. The various versions, sources, and analogues of the plot that Benson presents (esp. 3–109) can be remapped along the lines of Lévi-Strauss's famous description of the Oedipus legend. Students can take part in this exercise, using Leach's helpful introduction to structuralist analysis in his *Claude Lévi-Strauss.* While students might recognize the similarities between structuralist and myth or genre criticism, it may be important not to confuse the issues.

It is perhaps equally important not to confuse the varieties of structuralist and poststructuralist theories that have been, admittedly, subject to syncretism, particularly in America. The instructor may here suggest some ways in which the poem bears a complex relation to the signs of its own culture, not just to its literary analogues. In so doing, I assume that the seams and contradictions of that culture will be revealed, something medievalists will recognize as one of the constants of *Gawain* criticism. As with Chaucer, the uncanny analogue between the self-reflexiveness of the text and the operations of some recent styles of reading indebted to poststructuralism can be unsettling as well as seductive. How do we finally map the limits of the poet's irony?

At this point in the course, students are asked to present their own reports, which examine criticism surrounding texts other than *Sir Gawain and the Green Knight* so that students may see the importance of the questions we have been dealing with outside the immediate context of one work. I have devoted as long as three weeks to reports without losing the direction of the course.

It will have been noticed that I have said very little so far about deconstruction, feminist criticism, or neo-Marxist criticism, though I ensure that
some student reports will address feminist revisions of literary history and
interpretation steeped in social history. But the real power of these new
critical modes is that they are not merely critical approaches and that they
are based in large part on a radical critique of previous formulations. Instead
of presenting ready-made interpretations based on the critical developments
of the past two decades (in the United States, the past decade), it seems to
me more in the spirit of both the poem and most poststructuralist criticism
to use this criticism to encourage students to think about both poem and
traditional criticism in a new light.

One way of doing so is to present a model of deconstruction from Culler's
relatively clear *On Deconstruction* and to play with the possibilities of dealing
with certain passages of *Gawain* in this manner. There is danger here, which
I alluded to in my question about mapping the limits of the poet's irony, of
ascribing all ironic and contradictory effects to the poet—something common
in apparently deconstructive readings of other authors. Another way of setting students on to the procedures of this kind of thinking is to direct them
to the description of Macherey's method in Eagleton (esp. 18–19, 34–36,
51). What are the "silences" in the poem? What does it leave out or leave
unaddressed? Perhaps the most intriguing of such silences is that of sexuality—and certainly both Gawain's outburst in fitt 4 and the fact that we
never quite get to hear Lady Bertilak's side of things lead to some chief
questions of feminist literary theory. The tradition of antifeminist discourse
so prominently featured in the Wife of Bath's performance needs to be
recalled here as a counterpoint.

Fredric Jameson's essay on romance, "Magical Narratives," seeks to appropriate genre criticism to a Marxist historiography. What place, one may
ask, does *Gawain* play in the development of the genre? Is there any relation
between its elements of "antiromance" and the crisis of the fourteenth century? Is the idealism so prominently featured in the poem in contrast to the
apparent development of bastard feudalism? Is the old Hulbert thesis—that
alliterative verse represents a "baronial" reaction against Ricardian cosmo-
politanism—still viable? Must we revise the mechanistic assumption that
the increasing power of the middle classes and the military obsolescence of
the knight render futile the values of romance? That is, does the notion of
cultural hegemony so prominently featured in the writings of Gramsci (see
Joll for an overview) and increasingly important in Marxist theory today offer
a more satisfying explanation for "the Indian summer of English chivalry"?
None of these questions alone necessarily requires a Marxist framework for
its answer, but all are more easily integrated within that framework.

I have phrased these issues as questions because it seems to me that the metacritical dimension of much recent theory—especially, but not only, Marxist theory—is its most crucial direction. Why do we ask the kinds of questions we do? I usually assign Eagleton's *Marxism and Literary Criticism* in conjunction with Jameson's essay "Metacommentary" as reading during the last three weeks of the course. I refer to these readings and to Hawkes's book frequently in my comments on student reports. Instead of directing the discussion toward details of interpretation, appropriate in another kind of course, I attempt to point the class to similar cruxes in *Sir Gawain and the Green Knight* and to suggest how specific problems or disagreements may be indicative of larger theoretical issues that call into consideration the possibilities and limitations of interpretation itself. My reason for doing so is that students, particularly after a sea of reports and a menu of approaches, either embrace an indiscriminate eclecticism or question the validity of interpretation altogether. Hence, I seek to end with a position that addresses this apparently naive response as a serious issue. Such a position is consistent, I think, with that of a poet who, as Hanning points out, is as concerned as we are with "the perils of interpretation" (23). *Sir Gawain and the Green Knight* can teach us as much about literary criticism as literary criticism can teach us about *Sir Gawain and the Green Knight*.

DUAL-LEVEL (UNDERGRADUATE-GRADUATE) AND GRADUATE COURSES (*GAWAIN* IN THE ORIGINAL)

Introduction to Medieval Culture

Julia Bolton Holloway

The University of Colorado at Boulder offers a course, Introduction to Medieval Culture, that is cross-listed in medieval studies, humanities, and comparative literature and given simultaneously at the graduate and undergraduate levels. Edward Nolan and I reorganized the course three years ago to stress the fourteenth century and its cultural backgrounds, dividing the course into sections centered on field and town, monastery and friary, cathedral and university, court and castle, pope and emperor, pilgrimage and crusade, time and eternity. In 1984 the course stressed the medieval Mediterranean (Judaism, Christendom, Islam) but still included *Gawain*. The literary texts that we study are usually Dante's *Commedia*, Chaucer's *Canterbury Tales*, Langland's *Piers Plowman*, and the works of the *Gawain* poet. We discuss *St. Erkenwald* at length in the section on cathedral and university, placing that poem in the context of Erwin Panofsky's discussion of the use of Romanesque to represent oldness, Gothic for newness (*Painting* 133–49). The students read the historical passages that relate to *St. Erkenwald* in Bede (217–18) and Geoffrey of Monmouth (Thorpe translation, 89–

100). I use *Sir Gawain and the Green Knight* for the section on court and castle. The course concludes with the *Pearl* poem in the section on time and eternity. For texts we use John Gardner's translation, the *Complete Works of the* Gawain-*Poet*, as it contains all three *Gawain* poet's works that we assign (*Sir Gawain and the Green Knight, St. Erkenwald*, and *Pearl*), while I expect the graduate students to use the Gollancz EETS text of *Gawain*.

Medieval poetry frequently relies on allegory, but at the same time it is intensely aware of its literal and historical reality. Therefore the course begins with visual representations of fourteenth-century society—the Siena Town Hall frescoes of Good and Bad Government and the Pisan Campo Santo Triumph of Death, the *Très riches heures* miniatures for the duc de Berry and the miniatures of the *Luttrell Psalter*—as background to the allegorical poetry. The frescoes combine allegory and reality as does Dante's *Commedia*. In teaching *Sir Gawain and the Green Knight* I return to the depictions of court and castle in the *Très riches heures* and to Gaston Phoebus du Foix's *Book of Hunting*. I also draw on my knowledge of British castles and folklore, gained in childhood. In 1982 Phillip Damon gave a guest lecture on the political context of *Gawain*, in which he discussed the tension between the household of John of Gaunt in the north and the household of Richard II in the south and suggested that the poem was a gentle satire against the immature, "sum-quat child-gered" (line 86) Richard. (In connection with this argument, see also Burrow, *Ricardian Poetry*; Savage, *The* Gawain-*Poet*, who equates Gawain with the hero of Tuchman's *Distant Mirror*, Enguerrand de Coucy, once a son-in-law of Edward III and a Knight of the Garter; and Terry Jones, *Chaucer's Knight*.) Both Coucy and Gaunt had estates in the *Gawain* poet's linguistic region. I side, however, with the Gaunt rather than the Coucy connection. We discuss how Ricardian history saw itself as replicating Arthurian mythology. Froissart (65–66, 194–96, 211–30, 317, 404–08, 418, 428, 440, 463–66, 470) and Geoffrey of Monmouth are especially useful for *Gawain* and Chaucer, and Robertson, *Chaucer's London* (3), notes the parallel in contemporary documents between Troy and London, Troilus and Richard II. Brandt, *The Shape of Medieval History*, notes two modes of perception: stance for the nobility, causality for the clerical world. Both modes coexist in *Gawain*. All this material, which is useful background to the poem, I present as the interplay of fact and fiction, allegory and history.

I place the poem in the context of medieval dialectic. I show how *Sir Gawain and the Green Knight* and Chaucer's *Troilus and Criseyde* are oxymorons, deliberately yoking oppositions such as the profane and the sacred, the Christian and the pagan, body and soul. I see the nineteenth century as having taken courtly love too seriously and romantically and feel that this excess, in turn, distorts our perceptions—and those of our students—of

medieval texts. In the Middle Ages courtly love was a game that, if taken
seriously, in "ernest," led to painful consequences (Newman). To explain
my viewpoint I discuss *Inferno* 5, where Paolo and Francesca reenact the
sin and adultery of Lancelot and Guinevere and the sin and fall of Adam
and Eve, which is then imitated in turn by Dante, who "falls as a dead body
falls" ("e caddi como corpo morto cade" [line 142]). The fate of Francesca
and Paolo would be expected of adulterers of their social status at that time,
though the world of literary texts might lead one to believe otherwise. I
suggest that *Troilus*, *Gawain*, and *Inferno* 5 can be read pornographically
(Rousseau's "books read with one hand") and could thus cause their readers'
fall in a domino effect, but this would be a false, literal, carnal, serious,
tragic reading rather than a true, comic one I argue that the "ernest," wrong
reading would only embrace death; the comic one, in "game," would par-
adoxically include both pornography and life. *Inferno* 5 presents its readers
with a lesson in reading and misreading. I point out to the students that
sacred medieval books similarly often contain bawdy marginalia and that
monastic choir stalls can have vaudeville scenes sculpted on their miseri-
cords, which parody the sacred dialectically. I speak of Bakhtin's "two worlds"
(1–58, 437–74), of Latin and celibacy, of the vernacular and sexuality, the
two coexisting as they do in the Middle English and Latin lyric "Sing cuccu."
I speak of Dante's discussion of Arthurian texts as the "ambages pulcerrimae"
("the most beautiful ambiguities" [*De vulgari eloquentia* 1.10]) and note that
ambages ("doublenesses") is the word used also for the Cretan labyrinth and
the Sybilline riddles in Vergil's *Aeneid* 6.29 and 99.

A graduate student, Katyayani Khree, wrote a splendid paper for me on
the poetic craft of *Gawain* as being itself a kind of magic, its poet therefore
a magician. The poet in *Gawain* plays a similar role as does his Sir Bertilak;
Chaucer mirrors himself mischievously in Pandarus in *Troilus and Criseyde*;
and Dante likewise is himself the Galeotto of *Inferno* 5: "Galeotto fu il libro,
e chi lo scrisse" ("A go-between was the book, and he who wrote it" [137]).
These poets, both outside and within their poems, are trickster-saviors,
leading their readers to both damnation and salvation, both bliss and blunder.
They manipulate and mock the code of courtly love and wear both tragic
and comic masks.

I say the *Gawain* tale is about not only love but also death (like Chaucer's
"Pardoner's Tale," Tolstoy's "Death of Ivan Ilych"), but I state that on the
other side of that coin is life, exemplified in the pagan fertility rites and
games enacted in courtly fashion within the poem. I place the *Gawain* story
and its green lace brought back to Camelot parallel not only to Welsh and
Irish myths but also to Edgar Allan Poe's "Masque of the Red Death" and
suggest that Gawain's fall is a miniaturization of Adam's (just as Francesca's
is of Eve's); one brings corruption to Camelot, the other death to humankind.

I plunge into unscholarly Celtic mists and note that the Wife of Bath in Chaucer and the lady of the castle in *Gawain* could be manifestations of the pagan Magna Mater, "Morgne þe goddes" (2452), who had an important shrine at Bath and was capable of shape-changing into maiden, bride, or crone (Sharkey, *Celtic Mysteries*; Graves, *White Goddess*). I argue that Camelot is the world of youth and innocence, "bot berdleʒ chylder" (280), where there is yet no dying, but that the northern castle contains the old crone as well as the young wife and represents the world of experience, aging, and death (941–69, 1315–18), as in Blake's *Songs of Innocence and of Experience.* The triad of virgin, bride, and crone of the Magna Mater exists in the poem as the Virgin within Gawain's shield, the Green Knight's wife, and the elderly crone, Morgan. In Celtic myths the hero meets with the three who warn him of his dying.

I discuss the significance of games in the poem and describe the English ones of my childhood, such as "Oranges and Lemons," whose last lines "Here is the candle to light you to bed, / And here is the chopper to chip-chop-chip-chop off your head" subject each and every child to a mock beheading, and "Ring around the Rosey, / Pocket full of Posey, / Atichoo, atichoo, All fall down," which mimics the black death's symptomology and prevention as a magic charm against it. American children at Halloween similarly dress up as ghosts and skeletons, in order to ward off death through playing at being the dead. It is worthwhile pointing out that the original game of football was played with a human head (*Gawain* 428). Games are frequently about death; only in play can we afford to confront the most terrifying aspects of life. At this point I refer to Huizinga's *Homo ludens*, Hugo Rahner's *Man at Play*, Hermann Hesse's *Magister ludi*, Eric Berne's *Games People Play*, and R. D. Laing's *Knots*. I observe that the violence lurking beneath the courtliness of Camelot can be seen in the great similarity between *Gawain* and *Beowulf*, the same motifs of the uninvited guest, the direful quest, and the feminine and unexpected terror at the center—Grendel's dam and the Green Knight's wife. (I take pains in my teaching not to say that Sir Bertilak and the Green Knight are one and the same man until my students have read in the text that far; I use that same device when teaching *The Winter's Tale*, concealing the truth about Hermione until the ending.) I observe how Irish myths play with the beheading motif (a favorite one that comes from John Fleming of Princeton is of the Irish saint who was martyred by being beheaded and who then picked up his head in his teeth and swam across the Boyne with it). These Celtic myths are documented in Mabel Day's introduction to Gollancz's EETS edition. But I also speak of the castration fear in the Hebraic and Christian festival of Circumcision, which this poem celebrates (44). All the games in the text involve transactions of reciprocity (64–70, 981–90, 1372–96, 1635–47, 1823, 1936–46), "forfeits" having to be paid for any error. Gawain initially breaks this pattern of equivalencies by returning not with the original ax for the beheading but with his sword (288–93), the Green Knight needing to substitute a new, Danish ax in its place (2223).

I like to note that the beheading game is really just a game in the first instance, though potentially "ernest" and deadly in the second and that the Green Knight has something odd about his appearance; everything is in perfect proportion except for his neck and head, which are larger, taller than they ought to be (138–46, 181–86, 332–33). He is a carnival figure. Then the fake head is chopped off, bright blood gushing forth (429). That trick was well known in the Middle Ages. At Canterbury a gruesome play of the martyrdom of Thomas Becket was acted on a pageant wagon in the streets of the cathedral city for the benefit of pilgrims (Finucane 194). Bladders of pig's blood were used to make the seeming execution realistic. I then like to tell the story of the holy sinner, Saint Julian, patron of hospitality, who by error slit his parents' throats, thinking they were his wife and her lover (shades of *Inferno* 5 and *Monty Python and the Holy Grail!*). Saints Julian (774), Giles (1644), and Eustace are all associated in their legends with a deer hunt (Voragine, *Golden Legend* 130–01, 515–19, 555–61 and the Pisanello *St. Eustace* in the London National Gallery). My colleague and co-teacher of the medieval Mediterranean course, Fred Denny, tells me this motif is also Arabic, as is that of the Green Man. One can discuss *Inferno* 28.121 and 135–38, where Bertrand de Born carries his head in the Green Knight's manner, for having incited a young English king's rebellion against his father.

A major theme is betrayal: therefore Peter is mentioned (813) and the thrice-crowing cock (1412). Another is of the left-hand, sinister direction of the devil (422, 2146, 2487), which we observe also in Dante's *Inferno*. North is the biblical direction of the devil. One comic consequence of betrayal, I suggest, would be the act that Gawain would have had to perform with his host (an act against which the Host of the *Canterbury Tales* rebels at performing with the Pardoner) if he had fallen to the wiles of the wife, the act of sodomy, connected in medieval thought with devil worship and the Knights Templar. I note that the Green Knight plays a role similar to that of the Devil in Job and in Chaucer's Friar's Tale (where he is likewise in green and northern), in each case being God's agent in testing and trying men. Goethe is to do the same with Mephistopheles in *Faust*.

Goethe's Faust similarly relies on the magical emblem of the pentangle or pentagram for protection. I especially discuss Richard Hamilton Green's "Gawain's Shield and the Quest for Perfection," noting how the Middle English text praises the pentangle, though in medieval culture it was generally associated with magic, especially with Solomon (625) and the Knights

Templar. Here I often show the Chartres stained-glass window depicting King David and King Solomon—the first wise, white-haired, fingering a harp, the instrument in the Middle Ages conceived as closest to the harmony of the spheres (Holloway), and the second simpering, effeminate, fingering a magic ring that was still being shown to Jerusalem pilgrims in the Middle Ages. I note that in Macrobius the body is *demas* ("knot") with its five senses—and relate this term as well to Melibee's daughter in Chaucer's Canterbury tale, wounded in five places and left for dead, and to Christ's five bodily wounds at the Crucifixion. Dante in the *Convivio* (4.7, discussed in Mazzotta) speaks of the pentangle as symbolizing the human condition in being sundered from the perception of God. It is important to note that medieval authors themselves, Christine de Pisan among them, felt it quite within bounds to use "antiphrasis," to say one thing but mean the opposite (7). This is what I believe the *Gawain* poet does with his trickster-savior praise—rather than blame—of the pentangle. His medieval audience would have known of his joke.

Concerning the red and gold (*gules* and *or*) shield, I argue that its representation of the pentangle on the outside symbolizes the flesh and that the blue-clad Virgin and her child on its inside symbolize Gawain's soul. The shield is thus a metonymy for Gawain himself—and for Everyman. The crux of the poem is whether to choose the "cros-kryst" of the Virgin (762) or the knot of the Magna Mater. In appearance they are deceptively similar. Knots, in *Gawain*, are embroidered on clothing (188–95, 217–20, 612), painted on the shield as the endless knot of the pentangle (627–30, 656–65), and tied into the lace that the lady gives Gawain, and from there they extend out to all the baldric-wearing courtiers at Camelot, ensnaring them likewise. They even extend beyond the bounds of the poem to the courtiers of Edward III and Richard II, given the *ambages*, the riddle "HONY SOYT QUI MAL PENCE" ("Shame to him who evil thinks"), motto of the blue (rather than green) knot of the Order of the Garter quoted at the end of the unique *Gawain* manuscript. That knotted motto had just been preceded by the concluding knot of the poem, the bob and wheel that spoke of the knotted crown of thorns. For this discussion on knots I like to show the scene from Gaston Phoebus du Foix's *Book of Hunting* of the count's green-clad huntsmen all busily knotting snares with which to catch their prey. A relation has been suggested between the "endless knot" of the shield and the morris sword dance. I show my students photographs I took of morris dancers in Sussex weaving their swords in and out, culminating in the star or knot of swords held aloft, then unwoven again in the hypnotic steps of that labyrinthine dance. I likewise speak of the interlace design of the Books of Kells and Durham and of discussions of labyrinths, mazes, and tangled threads as representing the game of Troy of *Aeneid* 5.588–603, and their associations with the Magna Mater (Knight, *Cumaean Gates*; W. H. Matthews, *Mazes and Labyrinths*; Graves, *White Goddess* 89).

The structure of the poem is chiastic in the manner of classical, medieval, and Renaissance poetry and is written in a mode alien to modern linearity. The poem begins with Troy, then Camelot, then Wales; a series that could be represented in letters as ABC. Gawain reaches the northern castle and enters it; the next morning the lord of the castle hunts outside while Gawain lies in bed. This pattern is repeated three times, the seduction scenes always enveloped by the hunting scenes (the medieval pun on venery as both loving and hunting). Then Gawain goes to the Green Chapel, leaving this supposed haven. The pattern of being outside, then inside, then outside the castle is this: DEDEDEDEDEDED. F is for the Green Chapel. Then the poem returns to Camelot, then Troy: BA. Its careful symmetry is disordered only by the Welsh wanderings with monsters and the Green Chapel execution scene: ABCDEDEDEDEDEDEDEDFBA. The poet thus shapes his linear narrative to circular time and space. The poem's centering on Gawain in bed three times over reminds one of Scipio in bed in Carthage in the *Somnium Scipionis*, of Boethius on his prison bed chained to the whores of the theater in the *Consolation of Philosophy*, and of Mankind in the *Castle of Perseverance*. I make use of *Gawain*, *Consolation*, and *Somnium* manuscript illuminations and the *Castle of Perseverance* acting diagram, observing from the latter Gawain's similar subjection in turn to the World, the Flesh, and the Devil, the South, the West and the North, in the God game of the poem.

I argue that Gawain is an antihero, that he is a failure. My students chivalrously leap to his defense, and a lively debate ensues as to what constitutes a hero. They counter my condemnation by stating that his slight blemish should be overlooked. We note together that that imperfection makes him ourselves, human, acceptable, whereas a perfect hero would be less attractive to us. The class has thus unwittingly participated in a medieval *demaunde*: "Is Gawain Hero or Villain?" Together our answer becomes that he is both. He is Everyman. I note the parallel between the baldric-wearing courtiers, with their frivolous world of stance, and Gawain's "aȝenbite of inwyt," his bitter knowledge of causality and consequence, to that between the chorus of *Oedipus Rex* and its hero. In Christian doctrine, Gawain, Christ's knight, should have been willing to lose his life to save it. He should have made restitution of the lace to his host, having confessed its possession to the priest. Instead he is a less than perfect pearl (2364–68) in loving his bodily life more than his spiritual soul, in choosing the knot rather than the cross, pagan magic rather than Christian faith.

Though Gawain is himself a failure to a slight degree, the poem is consummate artistry, its movement a playful yet serious pilgrimage through paganism to Christianity. Some Moslem carpets, which are mentioned in the northern castle and which also adorned Christian churches, to be perfect had to be imperfect: their makers marred them with a cut, which was then sewn up, as only God could create perfection. The poem presents the dialectic of the old fertility ritual of time and life and death and the vegetation god, the "Jolly Green Giant" (of *blunder*land) whose chapel is an earth barrow, a grave mound (from which came the destruction of *Beowulf*'s world), and the new liturgical ritual of Christ's mass (of *blysse*). Even the disparaged ax, a pagan weapon in contradistinction to the cross-hilted sword that Gawain takes on his quest, parallels the magical pentangle in contradistinction to Gawain's muttered "cros-kryst" (762) on seeing the Virgin on the inside of his shield and the concluding bob and wheel of the poem. Sir Bertilak and Morgan le Fay in her aspect as the young wife are most noble and admirable adversaries who can shame the stance of the knights and courtiers of both Arthur's Camelot and Richard's London. The criticism is done with courtesy. "HONY SOYT QUI MAL PENCE."

St. Erkenwald is similar to *Gawain* in its juxtaposition of pagan and Christian material, the just judge and the Christian bishop, the old and the new, as integral parts of a whole. Moreover, *Gawain* and *Pearl* are presented as a dialectic to each other—the one green (pagan, demonic, and the color of fertility; the Green Giant swears "bi Gog" the giant rather than by God in line 390 and will not touch running water), the other white (the color of eternity); the one about knots, symbolizing the body, the other about pearls, symbolizing the soul. *Sir Gawain and the Green Knight* is neither elegy nor epithalamium, though it is centered on death and sex. *Pearl* is, in contradiction to logic, both elegy and epithalamium. I note that Edmund Spenser's sonnets, the *Amoretti*, centering on Narcissus, and his *Epithalamion*, centering on Echo, achieve a *concors discordia* in marrying the male poet to his female bride in their verses in a manner similar to that employed in the juxtaposition of *Gawain* and *Pearl*. I mention the statement made by Aristotle's physician, Alcmeon, that "Men die because they cannot join the beginning and the end" (Kermode, *Sense of an Ending* 4), and I relate it to these two poems and to the *Commedia* and *Finnegans Wake*, whose structures are similarly endless and circular. I use Isak Dinesen's statement, "And pearls are like poets' tales: disease turned into loveliness . . ." ("The Diver," *Anecdotes of Destiny* 12).

Kermode in *The Sense of an Ending* discusses the ends of literary works as miniature apocalypses. I describe the final examination in a course that way to my students. It is also, of course, a medieval "trial by ordeal." Thus in my presentation of *Sir Gawain and the Green Knight* I combine the playful and the serious, the text and its cultural context, playing each off against the other in a manner that can both delight and teach. I consciously match my teaching to the ludic and serious aspects of the medieval world—Chaucer's "The word moot nede accorde with the dede" (ManT 9.208). I have not yet had a class interrupted by an impersonation of *Beowulf*'s Grendel, but I have had a lecture on *Gawain* suddenly erupt into laughter—rather than fear—when some of my students entered the lecture hall, two garbed as a pantomime green stallion, the third as a Green Knight. I often set "Discuss pearls and knots in *Pearl* and *Sir Gawain*" as a final examination question and expect the students to answer it by discussing not only the times these artifacts appear within these works but also how the works themselves resemble these artifacts in their dialectical structuring, how the alliterating ("with lel letteres loken" [34]) *Gawain* and *Pearl* end as they begin: an endless knot, of the body in time, and a circular pearl, of the eternal soul, opposed and wedded to each other.

Course Outline

Week
1–3   Introduction
       I. Field and Town
       Texts: *Piers Plowman*, Visio; *Canterbury Tales*, General Prologue *Commedia*, *Inferno* 15, 21, 22, 24, *Purgatorio* 6, 8, 27
       Paradiso 31 similes; Sienese frescoes, Good and Bad Government; Pisan Campo Santo frescoes; miniatures, *Luttrell Psalter*, *Très riches heures*. Black Death.
4–5   II. Monastery and Friary
       Desert Fathers. *Jerome, Saints Anthony and Paul (photocopy). Rule of St. Benedict. *Regularis Concordia*. "Dream of the Rood." Liturgical drama, *Resuscitatio Lazari* from Orléans 201 (photocopy). Peter the Venerable. *St. Bernard "To the Abbot William" (photocopy). Plan of St. Gall. Christina of Markyate. Franciscan, Dominican materials. *Paradiso* XI–XII. Leclercq, *Love of Learning*. Bede. *Inferno*
6–7   III. Cathedral and University
       *St. Erkenwald. *Letters of Abelard and Eloise. Carmina Burana. Mâle, *Gothic Image*. Panofsky, *Early Netherlandish Painting*. *Piers Plowman* 101–40.
8–9   IV. Court and Castle
       Mabinogion, selections. *Geoffrey of Monmouth, *History of the Kings of Britain*, selections. *Inferno* V. *Sir Gawain and the Green Knight*. *Chaucer, Franklin's Tale. *Troilus and Criseyde*. *Book of the Duchess. Les très riches heures. The Book of Hunting*. Historiography, Matters of Rome, France, Britain. Froissart, *Chronicles*. Castles.

10   Midterm
       V. Pope and Emperor
       *Dante, *De monarchia*. *Piers Plowman* 11–12, 19–20. *Purgatorio* 10. *Golden
       Legend*, Gregory and Trajan. Spanish Chapel frescoes. Matilda of Tuscany.
       St. Catherine of Siena. St. Birgitta of Sweden.
11–12 VI. Pilgrimage and Crusade 13–17.
       Purgatorio. *Piers Plowman* 13–17, *Chaucer, *Canterbury Tales*, Knight,
       Wife of Bath, Pardoner, Shipman. Julian of Norwich and Margery Kempe.
       Runciman, *History of the Crusades*. Military Orders. Folda. *Crusader Man-
       uscript Illuminations*. Joinville, *Chronicle*.
13–15 VII. Time and Eternity
       *Cicero, *Somnium Scipionis*. *Augustine, *Confessions*. *Boethius, *Conso-
       lation*. *Julian, *Revelations*. *Paradiso*. *Piers Plowman*. *Canterbury Tales*.
       Pearl.
*required reading (others handled with seminar reports.)

1.   Ne no pysan ne no plate þat pented to armes
          a   a   /   a   x
2.   Ne no schafte ne no schelde to schwue ne to smyte
          a   a   /   a   x
3.   þat is grattest in grene when greuez ar bare
          a   a   /   a   x
4.   And an ax in his oþer, a hoge and vnmete
          a   a   / a   x
5.   þat watz wounden wyth yrn to þe wandez ende
       (a)   a   (a)   b /   a   b

Late Medieval Literature: Ricardian Poetry

Penelope B. R. Doob

Few periods in any country's literary history could be as dazzling as the English Ricardian Age (1377–99), conveniently so titled by J A. Burrow in 1971. Chaucer, Gower, Langland, the *Gawain* poet—each in his own way a fourteenth-century humanist deeply and sympathetically aware of the complexities of daily life, of the need for and ironies of human aspirations, and each a humorous, philosophical, inventive master of the craft of poetry: what more could anyone except Matthew Arnold, with his misguided comments on Chaucer's lack of high seriousness, ever want? It was with this conviction that, in 1975, I first taught a graduate course in Ricardian poetry, followed shortly by undergraduate and dual-level courses accommodating both graduate students and honors undergraduates with some knowledge of medieval literature. These courses have two major aims: first, to discover what is particularly characteristic of an author (his style; preoccupations; favorite themes, genres, and narrative structures; and so on); second, to discover how each author shares certain assumptions about the arts of life and of poetry with his fellow Ricardians. I found no problems at all handling students from different levels in the same course (in fact, the carefully screened undergraduates were often more able than the graduates) or in focusing intensively on the works of three major poets (Gower, alas, soon dropped out of sight except for some discussion of the frame and certain tales in the *Confessio amantis*). We still read Boethius's *Consolation of Philosophy*, *The Romance of the Rose*, selected fabliaux, parts of Brewer's *From Cuchulainn to Gawain*, and other background primary texts. What students lack in breadth, they gain in depth, emerging with a thorough familiarity with much of Chaucer's work, *Piers Plowman*, and, usually, all four poems by the *Gawain* poet. This careful knowledge, I think, is far more valuable than the smatterings of information about *The Owl and the Nightingale*, medieval drama, *Sir Orfeo*, Henryson, and so on acquired in the medieval survey course I had previously taught: when students come to love medieval poetry because they've read the masters, they often proceed to less immediately appealing material on their own, and they are well equipped to handle it.

But there were some problems. Perhaps the greatest difficulty in teaching any medieval work is the terrifying distance—linguistic, philosophical, religious, cultural—between modern students and medieval texts. I can and do try to cope with the distance in the usual fashion: by assigning primary and secondary readings that initiate the students into medieval habits of mind; by giving formal lectures and impromptu digressions as needed on background topics; by spending a lot of seminar time reading, translating,

171

and commenting on the poetry; by showing slides, playing music, and staging a banquet to give students some sense of the magnificent richness and complexity of medieval culture. None of this, however, solves the problem that annually reduces students to sheer terror: how can they possibly know enough about this splendid but alien culture (and if they don't find it alien, they're in *real* trouble) to say or write anything valid about its literature? And how, then, do I have the gall to tell them that they will not receive more than a B unless they do original work? A related problem is ensuring that the students, immersed in the particularities of the texts in the original dialects, achieve some mastery of the spirit of the literature, that they see the forest and a path through it instead of clutching random twigs and leaves from a few trees.

These problems of distance and of the need for an overview are put in a useful perspective by Robert Scholes:

> The process of interpretation is not complete until the student has produced an interpretive text of his or her own. . . . Specifically, the text we produce is ours in a deeper and more essential way than any text we receive from outside. When we read we do not possess the text we read in any permanent way. But when we make an interpretation we do add to our store of knowledge. . . . Without this productivity, in fact, the process of humanistic education is incomplete. (4–5)

I found quickly that traditional essays, exams, and seminar reports were not necessarily sufficient to stimulate students to produce their own interpretations of Ricardian poetry as a whole, or even of the *Gawain* poet's works. Nor was reading Burrow's *Ricardian Poetry* sufficient, marvellously suggestive as that book is. But, inspired by Burrow, I evolved a strategy that solved a number of related problems for students at all levels: it gave students confidence to approach medieval texts freshly and perceptively; it gave them a way to see the forest as well as the trees; it allowed them to use their own favorite approaches (stylistics, formal analysis, history of ideas, and so on) to create their interpretations—and, incidentally, it freed me from the need to give exams by demanding that they demonstrate complete familiarity with everything we had studied.

This strategy is simple: each year, every student must present a series of five "unity theories," statements of some major common feature that, for the student, unifies a work or a group of works. Based on a careful reading of the poems but inevitably augmented by any other experience the student has had of medieval literature and history, these reports, which constitute roughly half of the final grade, must be short, provocative, original, and, naturally, adequately documented by reference to the text.

At the start of the course, my students are apprehensive about this requirement: they are used to summarizing critical studies, to writing on assigned topics, or at least to developing their topics in close consultation with instructors. They are generally more comfortable with narrow than with creative scholarship, and they do not really understand what a unity theory is until they try one, even though I give them general guidelines, including the following:

1. Do not go to critical works to develop your unity theory: go to the texts and to your own informed perception of them.
2. Your principle of unity can be anything: a narrative device, a poetic technique, a recurrent image, a common theme, a philosophical attitude—whatever you think important and appropriate.
3. Remember that your theory must, on one hand, provide a way into the literature; on the other hand, it must be derived from the literature rather than imposed on it.
4. Creating your theory involves a characteristically medieval operation: finding a unity within multiplicity. Nevertheless, you should remember to make any necessary distinctions among authors and works even as you describe a common feature that makes all Chaucer's work Chaucerian or all Ricardian poetry Ricardian.
5. There are no right or wrong theories; what matters is that your theory be reasonably well supported by the texts and that it be illuminating.

The task is invariably daunting, so we move into it slowly. The course begins with Chaucer's *House of Fame* and *Parliament of Fowls*, followed by *The Romance of the Rose* and Boethius's *Consolation*; during this period, most students write an optional diagnostic essay that, not so incidentally, develops the skills needed for the unity theories. Suggested topics—a comparison of the narrators of two works, a discussion of some aspect of the dream-vision genre, a look at the influence of Boethius, to name a few—involve the basic "compare and contrast" approach. We then move to the *Canterbury Tales* (ed. Robinson), and the first unity theory is due after we finish the Man of Law's Tale, by which time I have already pointed out some major similarities in plot, character, theme, and so on in the opening group, so that students are prepared to develop their own theories fairly easily. Later unity theories cover all of Chaucer's works assigned, all of *Piers Plowman* (we generally read the *Visio* in the B-text original [ed. Schmidt], the rest in Goodridge's Penguin translation), the works of the *Gawain* poet (*Gawain* and *Pearl* are read in Andrew and Waldron's Middle English text, *Patience* and *Cleanness* in Stone's translation), and, finally, Ricardian poetry in general.

Depending on the size of the class, the individual reports range from three minutes (for the first theory) to eight or ten, so that the presentation of theories and their discussion throughout the year can take up to fifteen hours of class time, admittedly a substantial proportion, but well worth it. Larger classes might offer some theories in writing, but then the sense of group discovery is lost: the advantages of the oral presentation are the excited discussion and mutual respect engendered. More jaded instructors than I might well suspect that not every report will be worth hearing, but in fact I have yet to hear one that does not contain at least a good idea easily salvaged in discussion if the student has not managed to develop it adequately. In general, the sophistication and intelligence shown in the unity theories seem to surpass what is found in more traditional seminar reports, and I have, rather surprisingly, never had duplicate theories in the same class.

Of course, not every theory is completely new and startling. There are, for example, independent rediscoveries of the *Gawain* poet's interest in cleanness and patience as virtues, his love of structural complexity, his fascination with the superhuman tester and with the problem of reconciling earthly and heavenly values, his habitual understatement. But these rediscoveries are at least new and intriguing to the students; moreover, they are invariably developed along rather different lines from those followed by, say, Burrow or Spearing. They are each student's own creative interpretation of the assigned texts, not only employing the student's particular literary sensibility and background knowledge but also inspiring essays that often rival much published criticism. For instructors, of course, unity theories are a boon, a guarantee that they too will make discoveries in texts they thought they had explored quite fully. For instance, recently one of my best students provided a unity theory for the Ricardian poets based on their use of debate tactics. In the process, she went through several poems by each author using Gilman's terminology of vertical and horizontal debate: in vertical debate, an authoritative person instructs an inferior intelligence; in horizontal debate, more or less equal parties discuss a subject, with or without resolution (159–60). As she talked, I suddenly realized that much of the comedy in Ricardian poetry arises when an obtuse character debates with a superior as if they were equals—that is, when a horizontal debate is superimposed on what should be a purely vertical one. The implications of this technique, which we proceeded to discuss, led us all to some fascinating insights into the debate between Gawain and Lady Bertilak. This new perspective on works familiar to everyone in the class is exactly what unity theories are all about.

When paired with general coverage of medieval backgrounds (to forestall thoroughly absurd unity theories) and intensive study of particular texts (to ensure that they are perceived in their brilliant specificity), unity theories allow for the individual creativity and the fruitful collective brainstorming that my students and I alike find thoroughly invigorating. These assignments enforce the fusion of detail and generalization and encourage students to trust their own judgment, to do their own thinking, to decide for themselves what is important instead of having my predilections forced on them. Unity theories enrich the class's and my own sense of what characterizes this author, this period. Naturally, they also involve a great deal of work: another student told me this year that she had never spent so much time on any essay as she had on each oral report but that she considered the experience more valuable than anything she had ever done before—not least because the stringent time limits taught her how to edit herself. My own rewards are even more valuable: I love the feeling of participating in collective discovery, and, needless to say, I am constantly surprised and never bored.

BIBLIOGRAPHIC NOTE

Recommended primary readings include Boccaccio, *Decameron*; Gower, *Confessio amantis*; and the *Lais* of Marie de France (no particular editions).

For political, social, and cultural backgrounds I suggest Du Boulay; Huizinga, *Waning*; Keen, *England*; Mathew; McKisack; Tuchman; and Ziegler.

Works that provide literary background and criticism for Ricardian literature include Ackerman, *Backgrounds*; Derek Brewer, *Chaucer and His World*; Burrow, *Medieval Writers* and *Ricardian Poetry*; Richard F. Green, *Poets and Princepleasers*; Krochalis and Peters; Lewis, *Discarded Image*; Jill Mann; Miller; Muscatine; Olson; and Spearing, *Gawain-Poet* and *Medieval Dream Poetry*.

Course Outline

Week
1   Introduction to the fourteenth century
2   Dream vision: Chaucer's *House of Fame*
3   Dream vision: backgrounds—*The Romance of the Rose* and Boethius's *Consolation of Philosophy*
4   Dream vision: Chaucer's *Parliament of Fowls*
5   Chaucerian satire: General Prologue to the *Canterbury Tales* and the Nun's Priest's Tale
6   Chaucerian romance: the Knight's Tale
7   Chaucerian romance: the Squire's Tale and the Franklin's Tale
8   Chaucer's fabliaux: the Miller's Tale and the Reeve's Tale
     (background reading: Hellman and O'Gorman 1–26, 51–66, 81–96, 105–22, 145–58, 167–79; the Friar's Tale; the Summoner's Tale)
9   Chaucer's women: the Wife of Bath's Tale, the Clerk's Tale, the Prioress's Tale, and the Man of Law's Tale
10   Unity theories: tales of day one (Knight, Miller, Reeve, Cook, Man of Law)

The Celtic Heritage of *Sir Gawain and the Green Knight*

Jeffrey F. Huntsman

Sir Gawain and the Green Knight is the masterpiece of the Arthurian tradition in English and, arguably, in any language. It balances the heroic but somewhat vainglorious trappings of Arthur's court with vivid details of the North Wales countryside; it presents both moral philosophy and human drama without pretense or pandering; and it chronicles the triumph of the human spirit in a parlous world. But by approaching this poem only as a masterwork of English literature we obscure *Gawain*'s position in an intellectual culture that transcends linguistic boundaries. Nor will it do to search for a particular lost French original (an enterprise typical of some earlier approaches to the Arthurian material), because *Gawain* is at base a Celtic monument, even though by the fourteenth century the body of Arthurian legend had become the common property of many linguistic cultures—Welsh, Cornish, and Icelandic, as well as German, French, and English.

The intricate beauties of the poem have been discussed many times, and there is little distinctively English among them. More striking and unusual is its incomparably rich prosodic structure, for whose origins we must look only to Celtic lands. The prosodies of those Greater British cultures north and west of London are the most elaborately structured in the Indo-European linguistic community, far outstripping in complexity and texture any to be found in the better-known languages of medieval Europe. This prosodic tradition is an ancient one, and only recently have Irish poets ceased to use the archaic accentual meters inherited from Proto-Indo-European and attested in the oldest texts in Slavic, Greek, and Vedic Sanskrit (Watkins; Carney).

Gawain is, of course, only one poem of the so-called Alliterative Revival of fourteenth-century England. This flourishing of alliterative verse is usually described as a revitalization of the prosodic practices of the Old English period, and the poets of eastern England seem indeed to continue the familiar Anglo-Saxon patterns. Yet scholars have long noted that the poets of the West Midlands, and, to a lesser extent, the Northwest, are remarkable for using alliteration with special skill, subtlety and complexity. Nonetheless, even when the craft of Western poets is acknowledged, critics usually assume that their husbandry nourished only Germanic stock. For example, Charles Dunn and Edward Byrnes, in their text *Middle English Literature*, note that for the West a more accurate term than the Alliterative Revival might be "the Alliterative Survival, since the tradition was unbroken" (29). But matters are rather more complicated than Dunn and Byrnes (by default) suggest. *Gawain* is marked not just by a richer pattern of alliteration than the paltry two- or three-element structure allowed by Old English prosody but by a complex pattern of alliteration concatenated with a number of other poetic features—rhyme, assonance, consonance, and several types of binding repetition of words and phrases—features for which our English prosody lacks even names. Presenting the Celtic heritage of *Gawain* in the classroom requires some knowledge of both the technical details of its complex prosody and the general cultural and historical background of later medieval England, but you do not have to be a full-fledged Celticist to be successful. The few paragraphs that follow here provide a bare sketch of the central issues.

The constraints of space prohibit a discussion here of the languages and cultures of the Celtic marches (for details, see, e.g., Huntsman; Rees; Richards; and cf. Wrenn). But conclusive evidence does exist that, for many generations surrounding the floruit of the *Gawain* poet, the border lands harbored what Melville Richards characterized as a "state of real bilingualism along the Border [in which] Welshmen were bilingual Welsh and English and . . . Englishmen were bilingual English and Welsh" (91). Furthermore, we know that many educated Welshmen of the day spoke English, Welsh, and French; Dafydd ap Gwilym's poetry, for example, abounds with French and English loans and with bilingual puns that would only have been intelligible to bilingual audiences. How far this influence extended is difficult to say, but it is easy to demonstrate that the alliterative poets of the West Midlands wrote within a prosodic convention that replicated, as far as the English language would allow, an ancient Celtic pattern.

Celtic rhyme and alliteration was not based on the actual pronunciation of the words but on the underlying value of the sounds of the language (in technical terms, on subphonemic distinctive features). For example, Germanic /d/ would alliterate only with /d/, /t/ only with /t/, and so on. Irish and Welsh alliteration would allow /d/ to be matched with /d/, /b/, and /g/ (i.e., reciprocally within the entire class of voiced stops). Furthermore, the alliteration worked on a word's basic (or underlying) form, ignoring any changes that might take place in the pronunciation as a result of the famous Celtic initial consonant mutation. Thus a lenited /t/ (phonetically [Θ]) would alliterate both with an unmutated /t/ (phonetically [t]) and with a nasalized /t/ (phonetically [d]), as well as with a mutated or unmutated /p/ or /k/. Similarly, the converse of this restriction of alliteration to underlying forms means that the nasalized form of /t/ (phonetically [d]) would not alliterate with an unmutated /d/ (also phonetically [d]) or with the two other members of the /d/ alliterative class, /b/ or /g/. In a congruent manner, the subphonemic features of the vowels were used to determine rhyme, of which there were many kinds. In so basing their prosody on the underlying abstract structure of their spoken language, the Celts were unique among their neighbors.

(For the details of this prosody, see Murphy; Williams; Williams and Jones; and cf. A. T. E. Matonis.)

Since the English language lacks initial consonantal mutation, poets could not readily translate this prosodic practice. Yet the *Gawain* poet could approach it with one sound, that beginning the hero's name. The orthographic character most frequently written as a simple ⟨g⟩ in fact represents a complex sound, [g^w] (in technical terms, a voiced labialized velar fricative). Tellingly, this sound alliterates either with the subphonemic features characterizing a simple /g/ or with those characterizing the labialization, that is, /w/. Thus we find *grayþed, Gawayn, graythely* as well as *worthe, Wawen, wende,* and similar patterns are found for Arthur's queen: *gode, Gawan, grayþed, Gwenore* and *wener, Wenore, wyȝe.* This evidence is not subtle, but it occurs infrequently and thus may have been simply overlooked by commentators or considered insignificant. In other elements of the prosody, however, there is ample and obvious evidence of the influence of Celtic practices on the shape of *Sir Gawain and the Green Knight,* as well as on poems like several of the Harley lyrics (see A. T. E. Matonis), "Summer Sunday" from ms. Laud 108, the *Pearl, Wynnere ana Wastoure,* and the *Parlement of the Thre Ages.* The prosodic complexity of these poems cannot reflect a spontaneous reinvention of a system that had taken the Celts many centuries to refine; instead it proves that their English-speaking creators knew, at least secondhand, the poetic traditions of their Welsh neighbors.

Among the other major features of Celtic prosody that occur in West Midlands poetry are—to use terms from both Welsh and Irish sources— *cynghanedd* (alliterative binding of lines and stanzas to each other); *trebad* 'weaving,' *aicil, breccad* 'speckling'and *fidrad freccomail* 'letters of joining' (all types of internal and linking rime); and *dúnad* 'closing' (a word or phrase from the beginning of a poem that is repeated at the end). Limits of space preclude many examples, but two from Gollancz's edition of *Sir Gawain and the Green Knight,* of *cynghanedd* and *dúnad,* will illustrate the point. (Even more striking examples can be found in *Pearl* and other West Midland poems.)

cynghanned:	þise were diȝt on þe des, and derworþy serued,
	And siþen mony siker segge at þe sidbordeȝ (113–14)
dúnad:	Siþen þe sege and þe assaut watȝ sesed at Troye (1)
	After þe segge and þe assaute watȝ sessed at Troye (2525)

Even the famous bob-and-wheel structure that ends each stanza is apparently an adaptation of the Welsh *englyn gadwynog*, a four-line stanza of seven syllables, rhyming *baba*, to which the poet has prefaced the two-syllable, *a*-rhyming bob that echoes the excrescent one-, two-, or three-syllable line fragment called in Welsh *gair cyrch*.

Nor are the Celtic elements in *Gawain* limited to the prosody. The poet is intimately familiar with the terrain that Gawain traverses as he heads toward North Wales, the direction of the British Otherworld. Gawain's journey is marked by streams that are thematically balanced with each other—the water obstacles with demons matching the stream that defines the Green Knight's glade—and such streams are traditional boundaries for the magical places at which this world and the Otherworld intersect. In fact, the "chapel" of the Green Knight is a pre-Celtic tumulus, a burial mound, thought to be an entrance to that Otherworld; tumuli are called "fairy mounds" even today in parts of Wales and Ireland. The Green Knight appears with holly, and Gawain travels through forests of oak, hazel, and hawthorne, all familiar elements of Celtic religious practice. Finally, while the motifs of ritual sacrifice, ritual combat, and ritual death (here in the form of a mock beheading) are common elements in many literatures, the only immediate counterparts of the *Gawain* story in the medieval British Isles are to be found in the literatures of the Britons and the Gaels (see Carney; O'Rahilly; and Rees and Rees).

Perhaps the most telling evidence that this is fundamentally a Celtic poem is the least obvious: the very name "Green Knight." The figure it labels is ambiguous, representing challenge and punishment, judgment and forgiveness. The aptness of the Christmas setting for the contest is initially questionable, for the religious framework of the poem, while undoubtedly Christian, is not particularly focused on the birth of Jesus. The key to the puzzle lies in the Welsh language. Celtic color terminology focuses principally on the saturation and intensity of the colors, not on shade and hue as does English terminology. "Green" in this instance is undoubtedly the counterpart of Welsh *glas*, a term used to describe colors ranging, in our terms, from gray-green to light blue. The objects that are *glas* are eyes, winter seas, frost, clouds, mist, the undersides of leaves, unripe wheat, streams, horses, silver, and the earliest light of morning. In compounds the term means "light." (The most accessible treatment of the Celtic color system is R. P. M. Lehmann's "Color Usage in Irish.")

And, in fact, the *dyn glas* 'grey-green man' is a familiar figure of Welsh folklore, the pivotal winter figure who represents simultaneously the dying of the old year and, in the promise of the slumbering earth, the birth of the new. While winter is the time of death, it is also the time of cleansing, of reflecting, of burnishing (just as Gawain burnished his rusty armor)—in other words, of the necessary process of cutting off and regeneration. The complex referents of this single word bring together many threads of *Gawain*: the setting of the poem at Christmas, the time that holds for Christians the promise of the ultimate regeneration; the association of the Green Knight with holly and oak, part of the sacred natural world of the Celts, both pre- and post-Christian; the almost magical but somehow almost realistic qualities of the Green Knight–Bertilak and his domain; and the cyclic pattern of the poem, with its careful balancing of element for element, action for action, and lesson for lesson.

The wealth of this magnificent poem is only touched on here, but an appreciation of its Celtic foundations may help students of a wholly English-language background to appreciate its riches more fully. Similar comments could be made about other literature from the Celtic borderlands, including the West Midland poetry already mentioned, Anglo-Irish literature (such as the Kildare lyrics), and the so-called Scottish Chaucerians. I have used *Gawain* with success in courses that encompass a variety of the non-Chaucerian literature of the late Middle Ages.

A typical arrangement begins with the better-known Scottish Chaucerians: King James's *Kingis Quhair*, "Christ's Kirk on the Grene," and selections from the works of Henryson, Dunbar, Douglas, and perhaps Lindsay. (A. M. Kinghorn's *The Middle Scots Poets* in the York Medieval Texts series provides a usable, if not entirely trustworthy, edition of much of this poetry.) The Celtic strains in these Middle Scots poems are sometimes tenuous, but their general similarity to the works of Chaucer and others provides a bridge to the more complex Celtic structures. Midway through the semester, Celtic poems in the original languages (with an accompanying translation) furnish a striking and challenging contrast with poetry in Scots, which looked to Romance-language prosody for its shape. (Such poems can be found in Gerard Murphy's *Early Irish Lyrics* and in Gwyn Williams's *Introduction to Welsh Poetry*.) If the course is not limited to poetry, *The Mabinogi* (in Patrick Ford's fine translation) followed by parts of Malory gives students an idea of the kind of sea changes true Celtic literature underwent in traversing the Channel to France and back. I usually end such a course with *Gawain*, even though it is temporally out of place, simply because it is the masterpiece, and the most complex, of the lot.

When the Celtic foundations of this "peripheral" literature are looked at, we better understand how truly international was the world of learned Britons. The evidence from historical accounts as well as from literature attests to the cosmopolitan nature of these cultures. We are not surprised by Chaucer's firsthand knowledge of France and Italy; why could not the *Gawain* poet be an intimate of another country even closer to hand?

A Graduate Seminar in the *Gawain* Poet and the Alliterative Revival: A Stylistic Approach to *Gawain*

Anne Howland Schotter

The dazzling style of alliterative poetry, at once elegant and exuberant, rhetorical and rooted in native tradition, is one of the most impressive qualities of *Sir Gawain and the Green Knight*. The extreme difficulty of West Midland dialect, however, makes this style all but inaccessible to undergraduates, who usually have to read the poem in translation. Thus, a great attraction of teaching a graduate seminar in the *Gawain* poet and alliterative poetry at Case Western Reserve University was to be able to explore the relation of the poem's rich and complex style to its meaning. While *Gawain* is most often compared with the other Ricardian works with which it has been canonized—Chaucer's and Gower's poetry, as well as *Piers Plowman* and the other three poems of the *Gawain* poet himself—I hoped to show students its similarities, in theme as well as in virtuosity of style, with the less well-known alliterative poems of the fourteenth century.

Although the class as a whole read only *Gawain*, *Pearl*, *Cleanness*, *Patience*, and Langland's *Piers Plowman* (ed. Pearsall), I had them introduce lesser poems of the Alliterative Revival through their seminar presentations, at points where these works would have the greatest generic relevance to the major poems. Thus, we discussed the *Morte Arthure* (ed. Krishna) and *Awntyrs off Arthure* (ed. Hanna) with *Gawain*, the biblical paraphrase *Susannah* (ed. Miskimin) and saint's legend *St. Erkenwald* (ed. Morse) with *Patience* and *Cleanness*, the dream visions *Parlement of the Thre Ages* (ed. Offord) and *Wynnere and Wastoure* (ed. Gollancz) with *Pearl*, and the satire *Pierce the Ploughmans Crede* (ed. Skeat) with *Piers Plowman*.

Since we read *Gawain* first, the students could compare it to these poems only in retrospect, but they got a preview of the similarities by reading general works on alliterative poetry. Thorlac Turville-Petre's *Alliterative Revival*, which places the revival in the context of the larger flowering of English poetry in the latter half of the fourteenth century, gives a good survey of alliterative genres, and A. C. Spearing's *The* Gawain-*Poet* gives an excellent, though brief, account of the revival. More extensive background can be found in David Lawton's recently edited collection *Middle English Alliterative Poetry and Its Literary Background*, whose contributors consistently argue that the poetry is literate and literary rather than oral in background. Finally, a collection of essays that focus on particular poems rather than on the revival as a whole is Levy and Szarmach's *Alliterative Tradition in the Fourteenth Century*.

From such reading the students saw that alliterative poetry had a recurrent theme: an admiration for the feudal values of youth, prowess, and material splendor qualified by an awareness of their moral limitation and transience. Such ambivalence is evident not only in the more overtly moralistic poems written in the plain style of the South Midlands (e.g., *Piers Plowman*), but also in the romances and allegories written in the high style of the North, which one would expect to be more positive about the values of prowess and luxury. Even the Arthurian romances, for instance, for all their celebration of the king, insist that his warfare is wasteful and his fall from fortune inevitable (Spearing, "*Awntyrs*"; William Matthews, *Tragedy* Benson, "Alliterative *Morte*"). Characters such as the ghost of Guinevere's mother in the *Awntyrs* and Sir Craddock in the *Morte Arthure* explicitly condemn blind faith in prosperity and urge attention to the needs of the poor. More obvious examples can be seen in the allegorical dream visions *The Parlement of the Thre Ages* and *Wynnere and Wastoure*, which are in fact debates on the legitimacy of feudal warfare and luxury. The former for instance, undercuts splendid descriptions of the dreamer's hunt and Youth's clothing with Old Age's criticisms of the frivolity of such things, while the latter balances the Black Prince's magnificent arming with Winner's condemnation of Waster's extravagance (see Kernan; Bestul 29–31, 73–80; Speirs, *Medieval* 263–301).

For all his love of luxury, the *Gawain* poet shares such a critical view of feudal values. For while, as Charles Muscatine points out, he does not confront the "age of crisis" in the obvious manner of Langland in *Piers Plowman*, neither does he simply retreat behind "style as defense" (14, 37, 69). His descriptions of such examples of material splendor as feasts, clothing, and buildings show an awareness of their triviality, since he gives an ironic context to the language that is traditionally used to praise them in alliterative poetry.

In order to see how stylistic aspects of *Gawain* contribute to its theme, one must understand some technicalities of alliterative style. The two aspects that I stressed were the use of specialized poetic diction and the highly formulaic nature of alliterative style. The first, as Marie Borroff (*Stylistic* 52–90) has shown, consists of "elevated" nouns for hero or warrior, such as *tulk* or *burn*, and "qualitative" adjectives imputing elegance or nobility, such as *riche* or *athel*. Less impressive is an often indiscriminate use of adjectives in the superlative degree to lend an elevated tone. As minimum background on these matters, I assigned the brief (and unfortunately unsympathetic) account of alliterative style that J. A. Burrow (*Ricardian Poetry* 23–28) gives in his chapter on Ricardian style.

The formulaic aspect of alliterative style is a more controversial question. Current thought holds that the poems (many of them translations from French and Latin) could not have been orally composed, though they may well have been orally performed. What is relevant to the criticism of style, however, is that from whatever source, they are undeniably built on verbal formulas. After recommending R. A. Waldron's "Oral-Formulaic Technique and Middle English Alliterative Poetry" and R. F. Lawrence's more accessible summary, "The Formulaic Theory and its Application to English Alliterative Poetry," I urged the students to read Larry Benson's chapter on style in *Art and Tradition in* Sir Gawain and the Green Knight for the aesthetic significance of formulas. I also stressed the larger narrative elements constructed from alliterative formulas—the recurrent themes (or topoi, in rhetorical terminology) such as battles, storms, hunts, feasts, buildings, clothing, and armor. Of these elements, John Finlayson ("Formulaic" and "Rhetorical") has analyzed formulaic descriptions of battles and landscapes, and Nicolas Jacobs descriptions of storms. As a summary particularly relevant to the *Gawain* poet, I assigned Spearing's account of formulas and themes and suggested that his definition of a formula as "an associative tendency among certain words to express a certain idea" (Gawain-*Poet* 21) is more useful to literary criticism than are Waldron's and Lawrence's, since it is semantic rather than syntactic. Spearing is particularly good in showing how the traditional associations of formulas and themes have been artfully exploited in *Gawain*.

The elevated poetic diction, formulas, and themes of alliterative style actually helped the poets express the ambivalence toward feudal luxury and violence discussed above. Originally, these features conveyed praise of such values and no doubt flattered the aristocratic audience that held them. But by the fourteenth century there had been a shift from an orally performed to a written—and often silently read—text, a shift that alienated the poem from both poet and audience and lent ironic overtones to this style (see Dennis H. Green). It thus became impossible to take the language of praise at face value any more—to accept, in the case of *Gawain*, the claim that Arthur's court was the best and bravest on earth.

In order to illustrate the interplay between style and theme in *Sir Gawain* on the first day of class, I passed out a photocopy of the first ninety-eight lines of the poem (Tolkien and Gordon's edition). The poet's ambivalence emerges from the beginning, as the opening praise of the British implied by the allusion to their Trojan ancestry is qualified by the reminder that treason at home was responsible for the fall of Troy. Stylistically, the praise implied by alliterative diction is similarly qualified: the reference to (most likely) Aeneas as "athel" and a "tulk" is undercut by the statement that he was "tried for his tricherie." In the same way, subsequent founders of cities among the ancestors of the British are tarnished in spite of the elevated language with which they are described. Romulus, though "riche," founded

Rome with pride ("bobbaunce" [8–9]), and Aeneas's grandson Brutus, though a "burn rych" ("noble warrior"), founded a Britain whose later fortunes were notably checkered (16–20). The reader has been warned that Arthur's court, now at the height of its fortunes, should fear a challenge to its pride.

When he brings his history up to Arthurian times, the poet's frequent use of superlatives conveys his ambivalence toward the aristocratic way of life. Arthur is "þe hendest" ("the most courteous" [26]), and his court made up of

> þe most kyd knyӡteӡ vnder Krystes seluen,
> And þe louelokkest ladies þat euer lif haden,
> and he þe comlokest kyng þat þe court haldes;
> For al watz þis fayre folk in her first age,
> > on sille,
> > þe hapnest vnder heuen,
> > Kyng hyӡest mon of wylle.   (51–57)

> The most famous knights under heaven,
> And the loveliest ladies that ever lived,
> And he was the noblest king that ever held court;
> For all this fair fellowship was in its first age,
> > in the hall,
> > The most fortunate under heaven,
> > The king the greatest man of will.   (trans. mine)

Similarly, the use of alliterative formulas and themes implies a celebration of courtly life, as in the evocations of Arthur's sumptuous feast ("With alle þe mete and þe mirþe þat men couþe avyse" 'with all the food and merriment that men could devise' [45] and "Alle þis mirþe þay maden to þe mete tyme" 'all this merriment they made until food was served' [71]) or in the description of the cloth adorning Guinevere's place on the dais:

> Smal sendal bisides, a selure hir ouer,
> Of tryed tolouse, of tars tapites innoghe,
> þat were enbrawded and beten wyth þe best gemmes
> þat myӡt be preued of pris wyth penyes to bye.   (76–79)

> Fine silk at the side, with a canopy over her,
> Of fine cloth of Toulouse, and many carpets of silk from the east,
> That were embroidered and set with the best gems
> That might be proved precious to buy.   (trans. mine)

But while the poet shares the fondness for courtly life that such language implies, he will ultimately underscore its limitations from a Christian perspective. Although his opening scene seems to promise an adventure that will prove the superiority of Arthur's court, in fact it prepares for the entry of the Green Knight, the moral challenger who will call mere chivalric superiority into question. The style of alliterative poetry thus proves a valuable resource for a poet trying to express ambivalence toward feudal values.

My purpose in the course was to explore *Gawain's* affinities not only with alliterative poems in general but also with the other three alliterative poems by the same poet in ms. Cotton Nero A.x. Parallels in theme and sensibility among the four poems—for instance, the presence of a fallible protagonist judged by an authority figure (whether God, the Pearl maiden, or the Green Knight) and the shared concern with courtesy (whether on a heavenly or an earthly plane)—have been pointed out by critics such as Spearing (*Gawain-Poet* 29–32) and Brewer ("Courtesy and the *Gawain*-Poet"). Many of these parallels, however, take on more meaning when viewed from the perspective of alliterative style. Does the similarity of the weather that afflicts Gawain as he seeks the Green Knight (726–32) to the storms that God uses to punish Old Testament sinners such as Jonah in *Patience* and the inhabitants of Sodom and Gomorrah in *Cleanness* suggest that the poet judges Gawain's "fall" severely? Or does his fault contrast with those of such characters? The descriptions of the hero's robes (862–70, 878–82, 1928–31) and Bertilak's castle in *Gawain* strongly resemble those of the maiden's heavenly robes and the New Jerusalem in *Pearl* (clothing and building themes respectively). Are the echoes unintentional, simply a consequence of formulaic composition, or is the poet implying a parallel or contrast? Critics taking the second view have argued both ways, either that Bertilak's and Arthur's courts are elevated through comparison to heaven (Spearing, *Gawain-Poet* 6–12) or that they are condemned as shallow and materialistic, devoted to earthly rather than heavenly treasure (Hughes). I think that the poet's view is more complex than either of these hypotheses and that he in fact relishes all the ambiguities. Regardless of one's conclusion, however, a recognition that other alliterative poets have used such descriptions to convey both praise and blame of courtly luxury is a starting place for answering these questions.

Before closing I ought to indicate how I dealt with the problem of Middle English, for today it is a problem, even in a graduate seminar. Since by no means all the students planned to be medievalists, it would have been unwise to assume that they had any background in the language. First I assigned the chapter on Middle English in Baugh and Cable's *History of the English Language*, drawing particular attention to the position of the West Midland dialect in the complex sociolinguistic situation of the fourteenth century. For help with *Gawain's* notoriously difficult vocabulary, I had them rely on the extensive (and often excessive) same-page glossing in the edition we used, Andrew and Waldron's *Poems of the* Pearl *Manuscript.* Finally, for the grammar of the poem, I supplemented the brief account in that edition with the more thorough one in Tolkien and Gordon (the edition I will use in the future).

Despite the students' uneven backgrounds, my fears that Middle English would bore them proved unfounded. Reading aloud (with the help of Bessinger and Borroff's recording of *Gawain* and *Pearl*) was not a chore but a delight: readings, in fact, had to be cut short to prevent them from usurping entire class periods. Although I am somewhat ambivalent about inspiring others to become professional students of medieval literature at a time when such a career choice requires heroism, I must note that two out of that group decided to do so, at least in part because of this course. Another, showing more *couardise* and *couetyse* than willingness to put his livelihood *in jopardé*, went to law school, but I understand that that prudent decision had been made beforehand.

BIBLIOGRAPHIC NOTE

For graduate-level courses I recommend the standard editions of the poems of the *Gawain* poet: Tolkien and Gordon, *Sir Gawain and the Green Knight*; Gordon, *Pearl*; Anderson, *Patience*; and Anderson, *Cleanness*. Those teaching the course on a lower level might find the following translations useful: Borroff, *Sir Gawain and the Green Knight: A New Verse Translation* and *Pearl: A New Verse Translation*; Stone, The Owl and the Nightingale, Cleanness, *and* St. Erkenwald *and Medieval English Verse* (for *Patience*); Goodridge, *Piers the Plowman*; Gardner, *The Alliterative* Morte Arthure, The Owl and the Nightingale, *and Five Other Middle English Poems* (also includes *The Parlement of the Thre Ages* and *Wynnere and Wastoure*); Loomis and Willard, *Medieval English Verse and Prose in Modernized Versions* (for selections from *Pierce the Ploughmans Crede*). Two helpful recent bibliographies are Andrew, *The* Gawain-Poet: An Annotated Bibliography, 1839–1977 and Colaianne, Piers Plowman: An Annotated Bibliography of Editions and Criticism, 1550–1977. Additional criticism on the alliterative revival as a whole can be found in Elliott, "Landscape and Rhetoric in Middle English Alliterative Poetry"; Oakden, *Alliterative Poetry in Middle English*; Salter, "Alliterative Modes and Affiliations in the Fourteenth Century" and "The Alliterative Revival"; and Shepherd, "The Nature of Alliterative Poetry in Late Medieval England." Helpful criticism on particular alliterative poems includes Göller, *The Alliterative* Morte Arthure: A Reassessment *of the Poem*; Lampe, "The Satiric Strategy in *Peres the Ploghmans Crede*" in Levy and Szarmach; Rowland, "The Three Ages in *The Parlement of the Thre Ages*"; and Stouck, "*Mournynge* and *Myrthe* in the Alliterative *St. Erkenwald.*"

Alliterative Literature

Edward B. Irving, Jr.

Sir Gawain and the Green Knight is bound to be the climax of a one-semester graduate course in the alliterative tradition in English literature. Such a course would work best if all members of the seminar had already studied some Old English, but such preparation is not often found. Teachers will give the course the slant they want: for instance, concentrating on details of technique and style peculiar to alliterative verse or encouraged by the form itself (such as wordplay), on literary history and evolution (examining the appropriateness of the term "alliterative revival"), or simply on the intrinsic literary qualities of the works read. What follows describes a hybrid of such interests.

A general survey of the field and its problems, such as that by Thorlac Turville-Petre, helps lay out boundaries and establish main concerns, as well as providing an ample list of relevant materials. The course begins with readings from short texts of the late Old English period, with translations and brief explanatory notes furnished where necessary. A sample consisting at least of *The Battle of Maldon* (dated some time after 991) and such late *Anglo-Saxon Chronicle* poems as *The Death of Edgar* (975) and *The Death of Alfred* (1036) furnishes a basis for discussing the traditional norms of Old English style, diction, and meter together with some late deviations from those norms (see Dobbie for texts and Whitelock for translations). Samples of Ælfric's homiletic prose are read as well, perhaps set in contrast with a heavily rhythmic but nonalliterating passage from a Vercelli homily. Pope's edition of Ælfric has an illuminating discussion of rhythmical prose, which he usually prints as verse. Szarmach offers a recent text of many Vercelli homilies. The common assumption that Old English heroic verse in the aristocratic tradition (though blocked from its normal course of development by the Norman Conquest) is the ultimate ancestor of "courtly" late West Midland poems like *Gawain* while alliterative sermon prose is the ancestor of didactic poems like *Piers Plowman* is certainly not demonstrable to everyone's satisfaction, but it makes a useful working model for teachers who want to point out the special poetic diction of the first kind and the loose rhythms, at once flexible and powerful, of the second. To some degree, of course, both these traditions are discernible in *Gawain*.

Next in the course we examine texts from the transitional interval between the periods conventionally labeled as Old English and Early Middle English, giving attention to what clues they may offer as to the directions that change is taking and as to any possible existence of a popular form of verse separate from the official "court" tradition. (Useful anthologies here are Dickins and

Wilson, Joseph Hall; see also Brook and Leslie, Clark.) In this group one
would include *Durham* (c. 1105; in Dobbie), *Worcester Fragment I, The
Grave*, samples of *The Peterborough Chronicle*, and some sizable parts of
Layamon's *Brut* (this last work a rich mine for surviving formulas and themes).
If time allows, specimens of the heavily alliterative prose of *Seinte Marharete*
of the Katherine group (see Frances M. Mack) might be read to show the
continuity of the Ælfrician homiletic tradition after the conquest.

But only about four weeks at most of a fourteen-week semester can be
devoted to all this early material if one intends to give major fourteenth-
century works adequate attention. Though I think that critics have often
exaggerated its literary merits, I move on to reading the alliterative *Morte
Arthure* (in Benson's or Krishna's edition) as an excellent introduction to the
heroic conventions of much Alliterative Revival verse: students can become
familiar with the peculiar lexicon, the metrical patterns, and the battering
rhetoric of such poetry. Another good choice is *Wynnere and Wastoure* (ed.
Gollancz), which also has intrinsic value and is highly typical, in this case
reflecting both courtly and didactic interests (if they are indeed separable).
Still useful for the period of the Alliterative Revival are the copious collections
of metrical and lexical material found in Oakden, though his approach is not
what we would use today. For general discussion of the period, see Pearsall,
Poetry (chs. 3, 6), and Levy and Szarmach's collection of essays.

Although sparing the time may be difficult, I think students should spend
at least two weeks sampling *Piers Plowman*. No Middle English poet can
match Langland at his occasional best, though it is true that his poem is out
of the mainstream that leads to *Gawain*. Langland is the best place to study
the superb microeffects of the alliterative style: the line, the cameo description, the cumulative paragraph, the rich possibilities for significant collocation (especially for ironic purposes) of alliterating words.

The works of the *Gawain* poet come next in the course, normally read in
the sequence *Patience, Cleanness, Pearl, Gawain*. Since full justice can
scarcely be done to *Pearl* in such brief time and since its style and structure
are unique, the teacher pressed for time and space might pass over it rapidly
or even omit it to allow a fuller study of the other poems.

At the end of such a course, students should be able to approach *Gawain*
with some special skills and interests. Certainly vocabulary idiom, and
syntax will present much less of a barrier to them than to most students—
those fresh from a course in Chaucer, for example. In fact, those in this
course should be ready to gain something from the kind of sophisticated
approach exemplified in Borroff's *Stylistic and Metrical Study*. They should
be capable of appreciating the wide range of styles mastered by the poet,
from stiffly splendid formal description to sinewy action sequences to quick
and witty repartee; of noticing meaningful juxtapositions of alliterating words;

of recognizing the characteristically complex blend of humor and moral earnestness evident in the other poems of the manuscript; and of examining the ways in which the alliterative style itself may "allude" to both romance and antiromance traditions.

This evolutionary way of arriving at the poem is assuredly only one way, and a narrow way. It should be clear that no time will be left to relate *Gawain* to myth and ritual, to older Celtic analogues, to the main Arthurian traditions, or to late medieval allegorizations of romance or moral judgments on it. What students may gain in compensation for these genuine losses will be close contact with a *style* that has survived many centuries, with good reason—a style both subtle and boisterous, laced into the delicate patterning of high conventions but still echoing the clash and stamp of ancient harp and Germanic meadhall.

SPECIFIC APPROACHES

Reading the Poem Aloud

Marie Borroff

In the play of its constantly varying rhythms and repeated sounds, *Sir Gawain and the Green Knight* is a delight to the ear as well as to the imagination, and if we neglect this dimension of the poem in our teaching, our students' experience will be sadly diminished. They should hear it read aloud, and they should be made to try reading passages of it themselves. Neither they nor we should refrain from reading the poem aloud for fear of mispronouncing the words or on the ground that "we cannot know for certain how the poet's spoken English sounded." *Gawain* was literally made to be performed, and any rendition, whether fully accurate philologically or not, gives it the life of the voice and moves its aural designs from the visible script into the domain of audible reality.

I began by speaking of "play": the description of the meter that I present below can be thought of simply as a set of rules, resembling those of a game. The value of any set of game rules is tested by the pleasure of playing the game, and the value of a set of metrical rules is tested in part by the pleasure of reading in accordance with them. I happen to believe that my rules also form a true description of the way the poet read his poem, but that is another—and a far more complicated—story.

My first two rules deal with syllable count. Once they have been applied, the metrical patterns of the wheels will be readily understood, and after presenting them I shall limit my discussion to the long alliterative line.[1]

Many students who read *Gawain* in the original will have read the *Canterbury Tales*, and Chaucer's verse in the *Tales* is a good place to start. Traditionally, the Chaucerian line has been analyzed as decasyllabic, except that it may have nine syllables when there is neither an unstressed syllable nor a trochaic reversed foot at the beginning of the line and eleven when an unstressed syllable is added to the normal ten-syllable sequence to make a feminine ending. The letter -*e* at the ends of words is frequently sounded to make up these sequences, and it is always sounded, where present, in rhyming words. But -*e* was already well on its way to becoming silent, as it is in modern English, in the Southeast Midland dialect of Chaucer's London, and philologists agree that this change to modern usage had occurred well before Chaucer's time in the Northwest Midland dialect area that was the home of the *Gawain* poet. The sounding of final -*e* in the verse of *Gawain* would therefore be an archaism, necessitated somehow by the metrical form. But the metrical form of the long alliterative line, whatever it is, is obviously quite different from that of Chaucer's decasyllabic line. It is my view that no rules for the sounding of -*e* can be deduced for that form as the *Gawain* poet used it, and therefore I propose that the long lines of *Gawain* should be read aloud without any sounding of -*e*.[2]

There are, however, two inflectional syllables of frequent occurrence that seem to have been sounded more often than not in the verse of *Gawain*, as also in Chaucer: the ending of the plurals of nouns and the third-person singular present indicative of verbs (spelled -*eʒ*, -*es*, or -*ez*, as the poem's scribe and its editors determine) and the ending of the past-tense forms and past participles of weak verbs (spelled -*ed*).

Here is a typical passage of Chaucerian verse, scanned in the traditional way. It contains examples of sounded -*e*, -*es*, and -*ed*.

> Whan Zephirus eek with his sweetë breeth
> Inspirëd hath in every holt and heeth
> The tendre croppës, and the yongë sonnë
> Hath in the Ram his halvë cours yronnë
> (Robinson, *Canterbury Tales* A5-8)

And here is a typical passage from *Gawain*, read in accordance with my proposed method of syllable count (silent final -*e*'s are italicized);

> After þe sesoun of somer wyth þe soft wyndëz
> Quen Zeferus syflez hymself on sedëz and erbëz,
> Wel*a* wynn*e* is þe wort þat waxes þerout*e*,
> When þe donkand*e* dew*e* dropëz of þe leuëz,
> To bide a blysful blusch of þe bryʒt sunn*e*.
> (Tolkien and Gordon 516-20)

It should be noted that *soft* and *bryƷt*, in similar phrases in Chaucerian verse, would be spelled and in all likelihood pronounced with final *-e*.

I suggest that the form of the long alliterative line—or rather the variety of its forms—should be studied in two separate stages, the alliterative patterns of the line being considered first, the metrical patterns thereafter.

In looking at the alliterative patterns, we must take into account the division of each long line into two half lines at some point of phrasal or clausal demarcation. We may call the half-line break a caesura if we wish, but it need not involve a pause calling for a punctuation mark. In the first line of the poem, "Siþen þe sege and þe assaut watz sesed at Troye," for instance, the dividing point comes between subject and predicate, and the line flows without interruption.

The basic alliterative pattern of the long line requires at least one alliterating syllable in each half line, linking the two together. Usually the first half line has two alliterating syllables, though there may be only one; the second half line rarely contains more than one, and this single alliteration does not as a rule fall on the last important word in the line. (The groups *sp*, *st*, and *sk* alliterate as if they were single consonants, and words beginning with vowels may alliterate with words beginning with other vowels and with *h*. The long line has a variant form containing two alliterating sounds: one word beginning with each sound will normally appear in each half line. In such lines, unlike those having single alliteration, the last important word will usually participate in the alliterative pattern.)

After explanation and discussion, students should familiarize themselves with the basic alliterative pattern of the long line, and some of its variants, by writing out in schematic form the patterns of a group of lines selected by the teacher. The point of division between half lines is indicated by a slash below the line. Alliterating sounds are marked *a* (or, where two sounds are present, *a* and *b*), and the initial sound of the last important word in the line, assuming that it does not alliterate, is marked *x*. I give a few examples, taking them, as I shall take all my examples from now on, from a single long-line sequence in *Gawain* (203-26):

1. Ne no pysan ne no plate þat pented to armes
        a   a   / a   x
2. Ne no schafte ne no schelde to schwue ne to smyte
        a   a   / a   x
3. þat is grattest in grene when greuez ar bare
        a   a   / a   x
4. And an ax in his oþer, a hoge and vnmete
        a   a   / a   x
5. þat watz wounden wyth yrn to þe wandez ende
     (a)   a   (a) b / a   b

In line 4, the alliteration falls on two different vowels and *h*. Given the possibility of vowel-*h* alliteration, line 5 must be analyzed as having two alliterating sounds. "Watz" and "wyth" in 5 have been marked (*a*) to indicate that their initial *w*'s are superfluous to the pattern. Their presence as alliterating words can be thought of as "accidental" in the same sense that they do not contribute to the lexical content of the line. Though its superfluous alliterating words are less conspicuous, line 4 presents the same problem.

Turning now to meter, as distinct from alliteration, in the long lines, I propose that the teacher begin by describing a basic pattern. Though I concede that what I call the basic pattern is at times honored more in the breach than in the observance, I believe that it is in fact the "basis," or point of departure, for the other metrical patterns found in the poem.

In lines conforming to the basic metrical pattern, there are four syllables— two in each half line—that clearly predominate in stress over syllables adjacent to them. I call them "chief syllables," and I call the other syllables in the line "intermediate." Readers and listeners familiar with the form will feel that the chief syllables of the basic line fall at temporally equivalent (though not *equal*) intervals of time. Whereas in Chaucer's decasyllabic verse stressed syllables are usually separated by single intermediate syllables, chief syllables in the long alliterative line may be separated by two, three, or, rarely, more than three intermediate syllables. And they may be juxtaposed; this happens more often in the second half line than in the first.

After the basic pattern has been described, students should write out in schematic form the patterns of a group of lines selected by the teacher as clearly having four predominant syllables and no more. Chief syllables should be marked *C*, above the line; as a review of syllable count, intermediate syllables in the first few examples should be marked *x*; and the alliterative pattern of each line should be shown.

Examples showing intermediate syllables:

```
       x  x  C x   x  x   C    x   C x   x C   x
1.  Ne no pysan ne no plate þat pented to armes
         a          a     /   a          x

       x  x   C    x  x   C    x   C    x  x   C
2.  Ne no schafte ne no schelde to schwue ne to smyte
         a           a      /  a           x
```

Examples showing chief syllables only:

```
          C          C           C         C
3.  þat is grattest in grene when greuez ar bare
          a          a      /    a        x
```

```
        C       C       C           C
4.   And an ax in his oþer, a hoge and vnmete
            a       a   /   a           x

            C           C       C   C
5.   þat watz wounden wyth yrn to þe wandez ende
            a           b   /   a       b
```

These examples show something of the range in the number of intermediate syllables found between chief syllables. In line 1, there are three between *pys-* and *plate* but only one between *plate* and *peat-*. If we were to divide the lines into metrical feet and call them by their traditional names, the most common foot by far would be the anapest, the next most common the iamb. In musical terms, triple time would seem to be the norm of the verse.

Lines like those above are self-explanatory, and rules for reading them would be superfluous. What is needed, rather, is a way of reading the entire sequences in which lines having the basic metrical pattern repeatedly appear. To this end, I have two rules to offer, and with them my account of the game of reading *Gawain* aloud will be complete. First, the metrical patterns of the lines, though linked with the alliterative patterns, are not wholly governed by them; the meter must be allowed to define itself. Second, in lines having heavy syllables above and beyond the basic four, there are nonetheless four syllables that predominate. I call these "major chief syllables." Heavy syllables within a line other than major chief I call "minor chief." I thus interpret the long line as a structure invariably containing four metrical units.

Evidence for the first rule is provided by lines in which the all-important single alliterating syllable in the second half line can be stressed only if we distort the natural patterns decreed by part-of-speech relations. For example, in line 987, "Er me wont þe wede, with help of my frendez," the alliterating sound is *w*, but the preposition "with" (the sole alliterating word in the second half line) must be accentually subordinate to the noun that follows it. Perhaps more important is the rhetorical emphasis that a dramatically expressive reading will allot, in the first half line, to "me." The lord is saying, "I'll compete with the best of them before *I'll* forego the prize!"

A trial reading of any sequence of long lines based on the assumption that there are no more than four major chief syllables to the line will find its biggest stumbling block in those lines that contain more than four syllables belonging to the major parts of speech: the nouns, the lexical adjectives, the verbs, and the lexical adverbs. This is true expecially when, as often happens, all of them alliterate. In lines 203–26, we can without distortion subordinate the conjunctive adverb "wheþer" in 203 and the preposition "in" and the colorless verb "hade" in 206. If we do so, we get a reading that conforms to the basic metrical pattern of the first six lines of the passage:

```
          C           C     C      C
   Wheþer hade he no helme ne hawbergh nauþer,
        a   (a)   a    /   a        x

          C           C     C    C
   Ne no pysan ne no plate þat pented to armes,
        a           a    /   a       x

          C             C       C       C
   Ne no schafte ne no schelde to schwue ne to smyte,
        a             a      /   a          x

          C  C              C   C
   Bot in his on honde he hade a holyn bobbe,
          a  a    /          a   x

          C       C         C      C
   þat is grattest in grene when greuez ar bare,
        a        a    /       a      x

          C      C     C        C
   And an ax in his oþer, a hoge and vnmete
        a      a    /   a          x
```

But now comes "A spetos sparþe to expoun in spelle, quoso myȝt," where a lexical adjective, the noun it modifies, and an infinitive all alliterate in the first half line.

In this phrase, and in many others in the long lines containing the sequence "adjectival modifier–noun," a reading with two major chief syllables finds its justification in the genius of the English language itself, which forbids the placement of primary stress on both components of such a sequence in a single phrase. Where adjective and noun are followed, as here, by an infinitive that goes with the adjective (the half line could be reduced to "Spetos to expoun"), it is natural to make the adjective predominate over the noun. Thus we say "a *long* row to hoe" and "a *hard* act to follow" rather than "a long *row*," "a hard *act*." If we read the phrase "a spetos sparþe to expoun" this way, we are giving *spet-* and the second syllable of *expoun* major chief status and reading *sparþe* as minor chief. Marking *sparþe* with a lowercase *c*, we can schematize the line thus:

```
      C    c       C      C       C
   A spetos sparþe to expoun in spelle, quoso myȝt
     a    a         a   /   a             x
```

In other adjective-noun sequences, we have the option, as we do in the spoken language, of emphasizing either the signified attribute or its possessor. Thus in the sentence "Gloria is a good girl," we can place primary stress on either "good" or "girl"; either reading is "correct." In deciding between minor chief and major chief status for this or that adjective in the half lines of *Gawain*, we seem sometimes to be given a clue by the alliterative pattern. It is natural, for instance, to read 'grene stele" (211) and "bryȝt grene" (220) with major emphasis on the alliterating adjective. But in "stif staf" (214) and "tryed tasselez" (219), it seems possible to signalize either the thing or the attribute; either way, an acceptable reading results. And the independence of the metrical pattern from the alliterative pattern is shown in this passage by the fact that in a dramatically expressive reading of line 224, "fyrst," which does not alliterate, requires more emphasis than "word," which does.

If it is right to read phrases like "A spetos sparþe to expoun" and "þe fyrst word þat he warp"—and to these let me add "þe bit burnyst bryȝt" (212)—as sequences in which a minor chief syllable falls between two major chief syllables, then the meter of the long line of *Gawain* has important affinities with the meters of nursery rhymes and verses chanted in action games. For the same sequence appears in "Pease porridge hot," "Ding, dong, bell," and other familiar lines. The latter differs from the slower, more emphatic sequence "Break, break, break" in Tennyson's poem, where each word is in effect a monosyllable foot and the three stresses have metrically equal status. And Tennyson's line could itself, in a different setting, be read somewhat faster, with the middle word demoted to minor chief status:

      C   c   C
    Break, break, break
      C   c   C
    An egg to bake a cake.

In nursery rhymes and game chants, such alternation is present throughout the verse; in *Gawain*, however, heavier sequences containing minor as well as major chief syllables are continually juxtaposed with—and, so to speak, reined in by—lighter sequences. It is as if "Pease porridge hot," read as we read it in the nursery rhyme, were to appear in some such context as the following: "They were civilly seated and served at once / With pease porridge hot, the plainest of fare." In fact, the second of these lines is typical in both alliterative and metrical pattern of the verse of *Gawain*.

I believe that in a sustained reading of the poem, if it is fluent and expressive, the kinds of pattern I have been arguing for will in fact emerge, more and more clearly as the cumulative swing of the meter establishes itself. One obstacle to such a reading, of course, is the alien and difficult language of the poem. But there is nothing to be gained by approaching that language with reverential timidity. Despite its unfamiliar letters and uncouth Norse words, the metrical patterns into which the poet wrought it have fewer affinities with the verse of Shakespeare and Milton than with poems we have always known, poems whose cadences are as natural to us as breathing.

NOTES

[1] The difficulties of pronouncing the language of *Gawain* will be considerably reduced if the class familiarizes itself with the values of the late Middle English long and short vowels, as explained in the introductory apparatus of any standard edition of Chaucer. As a usually reliable rule of thumb, we can assume that the vowel of a Middle English word is long if its descendant form—or a related form—in modern English has a vowel pronounced and spelled as in *mate, meat, meet, mite, moat, moot,* or *amount.* If the vowel of the modern form or related form is short, as in *mat, met, mitt, Mott,* and *mutt,* the vowel of the Middle English word was probably short also.

[2] Final *-e* is sounded in the wheels in a few words within the lines where needed to make up minimal sequences of alternating stressed and unstressed syllables, as in "Wyth rychë cote-armure" (586). It is also sounded in two rhymes, where one of the rhyming components is a phrase, as in "to þe" ("to thee") and "forsoþe" ("forsooth") (413, 415). Complete lists will be found in my *Stylistic and Metrical Study* (159-60).

Visual Approaches to *Sir Gawain* and *the Green Knight*

Donald K. Fry

Most students (and many professors) have rather odd ideas about the actual appearance of things in late fourteenth-century England. Students tend to picture events in terms of such movies as *Excalibur*, *Camelot*, and even *The Sword in the Stone*. Professors have less Walt Disneyish notions, but they tend to base their visual ideas on Howard Pyle, Arthur Rackham, the Manesse Manuscript, and the armor hall in the New York Metropolitan Museum of Art. We really do not know what the late fourteenth century looked like, nor can we ever know. We can synthesize something approximating fourteenth-century reality by putting together visual evidence from manuscript illuminations, surviving objects, and literary accounts, but such syntheses remain imaginative constructs, and nothing more.

Left to their own imaginations, students will picture the events in *Sir Gawain and the Green Knight*, yet visual materials can add precision to their ideas, deepen their appreciation of the poem, clarify certain points, and even describe the aesthetics of the period. First of all, the instructor needs to show students what castles, armor, clothing, and even the landscape looked like. Few American students have ever seen a castle outside a book, much less a wild boar. Second, students find difficult passages easier to translate and understand if they can picture the descriptions; I think particularly here of such scenes as the arming (566-669), the first sight of Bertilak's castle (763-806), and whatever the lady is (or is not) wearing for her third attempt on Gawain's chastity (1731-45). Finally, merely pointing out the obvious lack of realistic intent in manuscript illuminations conveys the extremely stylized character of the poem better than an hour's discussion of narrative techniques does.

I use a number of methods for presenting visual materials, depending on the circumstances. Most of my medieval courses begin with several lengthy slide lectures on the appearance of things, the geography, manuscripts, and medieval aesthetics. Sometimes I introduce individual literary works with a separate slide presentation. Forty slides in fifty minutes convey a great deal of information readily accessible to our visually oriented students. To illustrate individual points in class, I sometimes bring in a few pictures. To avoid the clumsy logistics of setting up a projector and screen, I use a miniature manual projector and throw the picture onto a light-colored wall or even onto the ceiling. Most camera stores sell small hand-held slide viewers, with or without internal light sources, which the students can pass around for individual viewing. In small classes, I often have students cluster around a picture in a book. I also have a large collection of pictures clipped from books or dust jackets, or even drawn to fit specific cases. I mount these pictures in "page protectors," clear vinyl folders with a sheet of black construction paper inside, available at any stationery store; for clarity, you can glue on documentation, labels, and so on. To explain Gawain's armor, I bring in a model knight constructed from a Revell plastic kit called the Silver Knight of Augsburg, found in some hobby shops. This kit does not exactly square with the text, as one might expect. If you lack a steady hand, you can probably draft some model enthusiast to make the kit for you and even to modify it to fit the text. The Metropolitan Museum sells a reproduction of a fourteenth-century chess piece of a knight in armor riding on a horse, which fits the poem well.

Most museums sell color slides of objects and manuscripts in their collections. Both the British Museum and the Bodleian Library have slide sets and will furnish lists on request. Unfortunately these commercial sets tend to be expensive and seldom suit individual requirements. Therefore, you might prefer to make your own slides with simple equipment: a single-lens reflex camera, a tripod or copystand, close-up lenses, and two photoflood lamps with reflectors. (I will furnish simple directions for making slides on request; just send me a stamped, self-addressed envelope.) For the less adept, Kodak makes a wonderful gadget called the Ektagraphic Visualmaker Camera Outfit, which automatically takes care of focus and lighting; you just slide the picture under it and poke a button. Most universities have a photographic service that can produce high-quality slides for a relatively low cost, or perhaps you could hire a local camera buff to make slides.

I like to use pictures that reconstruct medieval scenes and objects, usually found in popular books, especially storybooks for children. Selina Hastings's *Sir Gawain and the Green Knight* has brilliant illustrations by Juan Wijngaard, including a dazzling Green Knight and a particularly fetching Lady Bertilak. James Riordan's *Tales of King Arthur* features color pictures by my favorite medieval illustrator, Victor Ambrus, who gives a definitive Green Knight on pages 54, 56, and 67. Theodore Silverstein's *Sir Gawain and the Green Knight: A Comedy for Christmas* has Virgil Burnett's ink drawings; I particularly like his Green Knight and Lady Bertilak.

Turning to medieval pictures themselves, three manuscript facsimiles have especially useful plates. Longnon and Cazelles's facsimile of *The Très Riches Heures of Jean, Duke of Berry* captures the brilliant painting and color of this manuscript of about 1416. Everyone knows the famous calendar plates from this work, and several seem especially appropriate to the poem: "January," a sumptuous banquet (folio 2r); "September," a fantasy castle, though real (9v); "October," another fancy castle (10v); "December," a boar hunt (12v); "Temptation of Christ," another castle (161v). Gabriel Bise's *Medieval*

Hunting Scenes gives a selection of pictures from a fifteenth-century version of Gaston Phœbus's *Hunting Book*, with the following relevant examples: boar hunt (p. 56), stag hunt (60-61), skinning and quartering (62-63), stag hunt (64-65), stag hunt (66-67), stag hunt (70), boar hunts (74-75), fox hunt (80), boar hunt (88-89), deer hunt (94-95). Finally, Israel Gollancz reproduces the entire *Gawain* manuscript in facsimile, unfortunately printing the manuscript's illuminations in black and white. The Gawain pictures appear on folios 125-26, but they bear only general resemblance to the details of the text.

Several general books on the Middle Ages have useful pictures. Morris Bishop's *The Horizon Book of the Middle Ages* has hundreds of plates; for *Gawain*, the following may prove helpful: stag chase (51), mail and helmet (67), Jean, duke of Berry's castle at Saumur (97), aristocratic banquet (114), deer shooting (124), green men at a banquet (192).

Joan Evans's coffee-table book *The Flowering of the Middle Ages* has chapters by specialists on various aspects of medieval life. Relevant pictures include the Berry castle at Saumur, large and detailed (135); Sir Geoffrey Luttrell in full armor and trappings (142); the knight of Prato, similarly equipped (143); cutting up a doe (147); a royal banquet (148); detailed castle diagram (164); close-up of the Berry banquet (287); a beheading, unfortunately of a bishop (292). I especially recommend this volume for its pictures, descriptions, and accuracy.

Though less reliable and less colorful, H. W. Koch's *Medieval Warfare* has some good plates, especially the following: squire arming a knight (66); mail shirt, helmet, and spur (67); a formidable axe, certainly the scariest! (152); beheading a knight in armor (168).

A recent book on armor, Liliane Funcken and Fred Funcken's three-volume *The Age of Chivalry*, has a confused text but wonderful paintings of every aspect of armor. I especially recommend the following illustrations, cited by volume, page, and item number: the Black Prince in full regalia (1: 21.34); mail and helmets (1: 25); mail and helmets (1: 27); warhorse with full trappings (1: 51.1); axes, especially items 42, 46, and 50 (1: 81); castle with labels (2: 10-11; without labels, 2: 110-11); various castle details (2: 13-15); armor c. 1400 (2: 43.1); English armor thirteenth to fifteenth century (2: 51-53; esp. 51.7-11 and 53.1, a Garter knight); swords (3: 27); spurs (3: 37); gloves and sabatouns (3: 49); baldrics and scabbards (3: 75).

Finally, I offer three drawings for classroom distribution: a map, an attempt at the Green Knight (redrawn from Wijngaard's illustration in Hastings), and an armor diagram (ultimately based on Funcken and Funcken 1: 69.46). These three uncopyrighted drawings may be photocopied without permission. My thanks to Billie Keirstead for technical assistance with these illustrations.

GAWAIN'S JOURNEY

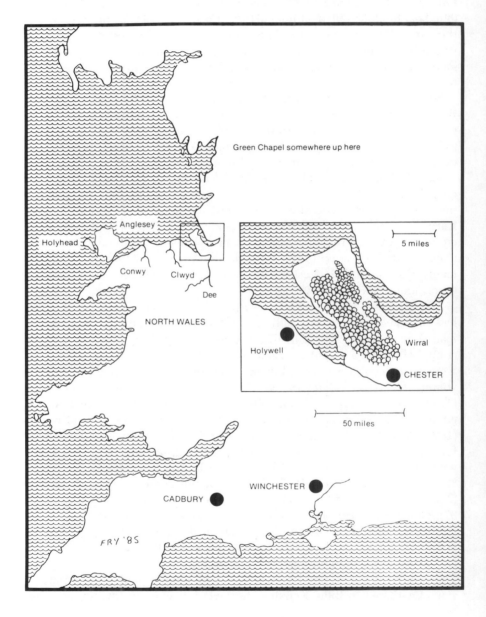

THE GREEN KNIGHT

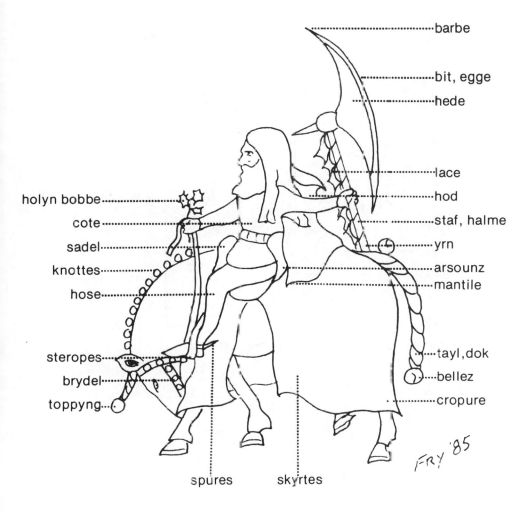

barbe

bit, egge

hede

lace

holyn bobbe

hod

cote

staf, halme

sadel

yrn

knottes

arsounz

hose

mantile

steropes

tayl,dok

brydel

bellez

toppyng

cropure

spures   skyrtes

FRY '85

GAWAIN & GRINGOLET

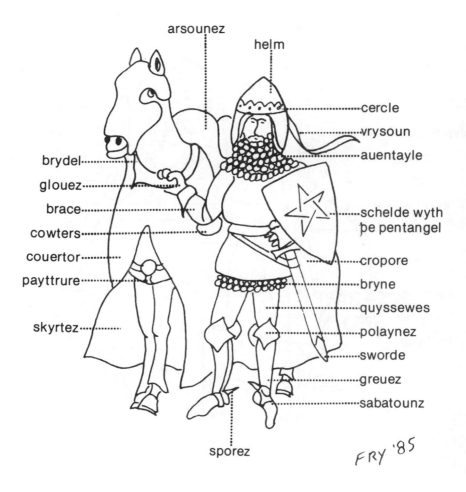

arsounez

helm

cercle

vrysoun

auentayle

brydel

glouez

brace

cowters

couertor

payttrure

skyrtez

schelde wyth
þe pentangel

cropore

bryne

quyssewes

polaynez

sworde

greuez

sabatounz

sporez

FRY '85

Researched Visual Projects

Judith Bronfman

For the past few years in my undergraduate classes at the School of Visual Arts I have assigned, in lieu of a term paper, a researched visual project. The students seem to like it, and so do I.

The School of Visual Arts is an unusual college in that all of its undergraduates are art majors, although media arts (a euphemism for advertising) and photography are our most popular majors. My students' advantages are that they have developed their visual sense more highly than the average student has and that they have all had a course in history of art that includes medieval art (indeed, a fondness for the Cimabue Madonna or the calendar pages from the *Trés riches heures* may have led them to my class). SVA is, however, usual in the disadvantages of its students: they are not particularly verbal, either in writing or speaking; they read no language other than modern English; they have little background in literature or general culture. Most of them are taking their first college literature elective Since mine are the only medieval literature classes at SVA, the students have not had a medieval class before reaching me, nor will they have medieval classes after me.

Within this framework, there are clearly limitations. For a first elective or even a first medieval course, a course devoted to one work—even one like *Sir Gawain and the Green Knight*—seems inappropriate (and I suspect it would not be approved by the humanities department). Thus I teach only survey courses: in the fall, Early Medieval Literature, and in the spring, Arthurian Literature or Late Medieval Literature. *Gawain* ends up on both spring reading lists, sharing space one spring with Chrétien de Troyes, Gottfried von Strassburg, Wolfram von Eschenbach, Thomas Malory, T. H. White, and Alfred, Lord Tennyson and sharing the other with Jean Froissart, Giovanni Boccaccio, Geoffrey Chaucer, and a group of plays (the plays are selected partly according to what is being produced in New York that year; we have recently read and seen *Everyman*, Massinger's *Roman Actor*, Jonson's *Alchemist*, and Tourneur's *Revenger's Tragedy*). This motley reading list is probably similar to the list in most unspecialized undergraduate courses.

At the beginning of the term, I outline my grade requirements: three grades, weighted equally, are given for a midterm exam, a final exam, and a researched visual project. (Because I am sensitive to the need for writing in noncomposition courses, both the midterm and the final require an essay, along with a section of short-answer questions.) The equal weight given to the visual project works in its favor; those students with weak writing skills are particularly eager to pull their grades up with a good project; the strong writers must, of course, maintain their good grades with good projects. It bodes well.

I do not give the students topics, not even a list of topics; they must come up with their own. On the first day of class, I urge them to start thinking about what interests them—are they interested in costume or architecture or travel or religion? Finding their topic within an area that already interests them is, I hope, a way to encourage a continuing interest in medieval literature, art, history, and culture.

Having decided on areas of interest, we then begin to look for a specific topic for each of the students. They may find the topic directly in the texts read, or they may find it in medieval history or culture, with only a tenuous connection to our texts. One of the best projects that I have received was a painting, roughly six feet by four feet, of Saint Roche in the wilderness, his back covered with plague sores, his faithful dog nearby. This student had found Johannes Nohl's *The Black Death* on the recommended reading list and had noted a reference to the plague saint. He then located the saint's life, which told how Saint Roche, ill with the plague, had gone into the wilderness to die. Nursed by a dog who brought him bread, however, he recovered and returned to civilization to nurse others. Using himself and his own pet dog as models, Charles came up with his painting. His report to the class was lively and fascinating to his fellow students, an excellent extension of the introduction to the *Decameron*.

Not all of my students want to create an original piece of artwork; some may find a relevant piece of art and do the background research that will explain its relevance to the course. The illustration on the cover of the Penguin translation of *Gawain* would be a good work to use: the student would be expected to have researched the picture and be able to tell us about the armor, the horse's trappings, the ladies' function, the armorial symbols, and so on. A third student, feeling even less creative, might look up military weapons and come in with photocopied illustrations that could be explained to us.

The oral presentation of the project is its main point; it is thus that I can determine the quantity and quality of the research and assign a grade to the project. I organize the students to present about six projects in a ninety-minute class. At the beginning of the class, we set up an exhibit, with some works pushpinned to the walls, others propped on chairs or set up on my desk. Each student in turn discusses a project. (No duplicate projects are allowed, so the information is new in each case.) The students are expected to be thoroughly knowledgeable about the topic, but the presentation is informal; we sit in a big circle and do a lot of admiring while each tells us about the research and answers our questions. I do not ask for a formal bibliography, nor do I let them use notes. I ask that the research be internalized, that the students simply know what they are talking about.

One recent project was given by a student who had visited the Cloisters museum and had been enthralled by the beautiful Unicorn Tapestries. She brought us some of the museum's postcards of the fifteenth-century tapestries and gave us some background on them. She discussed in fuller detail the medieval lady: what she looked like, what she wore, and how she lived. Her project was a golden-haired, grey-eyed marionette of the lady in the tapestries, dressed in a red satin gown with a golden chain girdle.

Two students collaborated to produce small glazed figures from a gory story in Froissart's *Chronicles*. This story purports to be the true version of the mysterious death of Gaston, the Comte de Foix's only legitimate heir. The comte and his wife were separated, she living with her brother the king of Navarre. Gaston visited his mother and as he was leaving Navarre, his uncle gave him a little pouch containing a powder. The powder, Gaston was told, was a love potion that, sprinkled on the comte's food, would produce love and harmony between his parents. Gaston shared a room at Foix with his illegitimate half-brother Yvain, also about fifteen years old. Yvain accidentally discovered the little pouch, and, one day after he and Gaston had quarreled over a tennis match, he told the comte about it. When the comte put a bit of the powder on a piece of bread and fed it to a greyhound, the greyhound died instantly. With some difficulty, the comte's retainers prevented him from killing Gaston on the spot. But a few days later, the comte, who had been paring his fingernails with a very small knife, visited Gaston in his prison room. In a playful moment and entirely by accident, Froissart tells us, he managed to cut a vein in Gaston's throat, and poor Gaston bled to death. Two students made figures of a marvellously dead greyhound, the comte with his tiny knife, and hapless Gaston.

One student brought in colored photocopies of knights and their weapons and gave us a discussion of how knights were trained in the fourteenth century.

Another designed a beautiful book jacket for the *Decameron*, stressing the frame of Boccaccio's collection of tales. A group of ten young people flee the plague in Florence and go to an idyllic country villa to gambol in the meadows and tell stories until the contagion has passed. The design was a black skull with large eye sockets, a colored castle (cut out from a magazine) visible in one and a field of flowers in the other.

Another project was a diorama, a three-dimensional room in a fourteenth-century castle, perhaps the one that Sir Gawain visited. The room had a stained-glass window in one wall and a window with a view in the other wall; it was furnished with wooden benches, small brass pots, and candlesticks from a dollhouse store. The student for this project explained that she had nearly finished her room when she realized that she did not know what the floor should look like. She pored over illuminated manuscript books looking at floors and came up with a checkerboard pattern worthy of a late fourteenth-century architect.

A student taking a course in stained glass made a panel using fourteenth-century designs. She brought in a book of stained glass and showed us why she had selected particular colors and design elements for her piece.

In short, the projects are fun for me and for the class. I believe that they are also completely valid and successful scholarly exercises for the students. The background knowledge that students acquire deepens their understanding of the works we are studying and will contribute to their understanding of medieval works that they may later read alone.

The real purpose of research is to uncover information that then can be applied to a problem or question or hypothesis at hand. In many undergraduate research papers, however, the research becomes an objective in itself, and many students (partially because they cannot figure out anything else to do) turn in an unfocused and often undigested summary of their reading. Others, perhaps as much from desperation as dishonesty, turn to plagiarism. In fact, when we are discussing works like *Sir Gawain and the Green Knight* or the *Canterbury Tales*, it seems unrealistic to expect an undergraduate to come up with an original hypothesis or problem related to the text; whatever topic the student chooses has almost certainly been explored in depth by one or more famous critics.

A visual project such as mine solves a major research problem by giving the student a specific focus for research; transferring the research to another medium encourages real learning. Furthermore, the project is virtually impossible to plagiarize; even if someone else did the research or the artwork, the student would have to learn the material to answer our questions and discuss the work in our informal setting. Since the student has the choice of either producing an original work or using photocopies of materials from other sources or even bringing a book to class, talent is not a prerequisite for the assignment. In other words, the assignment is adaptable for any kind of student, with or without an art background. Everybody enjoys pictures!

The Medieval Banquet

Patricia A. Moody

Almost from the inception of my college teaching, I have sponsored banquets for sophomore introductory courses, general introductions to medieval literature, graduate and undergraduate Chaucer courses, specialized courses in the *Gawain* poet, and even courses in the history of the language. At its best, the medieval banquet is an excellent device for engaging undergraduates with the poem. Preparations for the banquet allow students to learn the language, perform research on a variety of topics, and draw comparisons with other poems of the period, while improving their understanding of crucial features of the poem. The banquet itself is the culmination of a rich educational experience, a social occasion that welds together the class, and an incentive to further course work as well as to individual study.

A successful medieval banquet requires prior careful planning, thinking through, and outright selling to generate genuine class participation. Almost from the beginning of the course, as I set course requirements and the level of my expectation, I indicate that the banquet is a serious undertaking, requiring research and preparation on everyone's part but promising fun as well. (One device I have used successfully is to describe how mead is made and promise to brew a batch. Students greet me all semester long with, "How's the mead coming along?" Never mind that they are invariably disappointed with the product—the mead has served its purpose well.)

For *Sir Gawain and the Green Knight*, the banquet possibilities are immediately obvious, since the poem begins at such a (holiday) feast. I spend some class time sketching the research possibilities of the banquet, so that students will find as much information as they can about topics such as those listed below:

- The castle described in the poem—how did it compare with other castles? Where were the kitchens, where the banquet rooms? How were they furnished?
- What would banqueters have eaten at their feast? Who would have prepared the food, and how would they have prepared it?
- What would people have worn to a banquet? What was the design of their clothing, what colors (where did the dye come from), what fabrics? How functional was the clothing (and functional for what)?
- What about Arthur's Christmas *gomen*? What kinds of "gaming" took place at gatherings such as banquets? What was the nature of entertainment, who performed it, how, when where?

If the class is large enough, I permit teaming up. And of course, I provide each student or group with suggestions on looking for answers beyond the poem itself. Reports on these topics are due by midterm and constitute one-half the course grade at the midpoint.

I also invite each student in the class to choose one character from the poem to "identify" with. The student's responsibility will be to find as much information as possible about this character, first from *Gawain* itself and then from a reading list of other works that I give out. If the class is large, I give out a list of supplementary characters—those who might have been in the poem but apparently are not. Students again choose one and then must write a plausible explanation (based on reading from other works) about why that character was absent from Arthur's court that day. I reinforce the students' identities by calling them by their "poem" names and asking them to explain various points in the poem.

I set the banquet for close to the end of the course, usually during the last week of class. I generally count preparations for the banquet as a part of the final exam, as if it were a take-home question, and give an abbreviated actual exam. I believe this practice is fair, since the students also have to submit a written paper based on their "character identifications."

For the banquet, students must come in authentic costumes for the particular character they have chosen. (This prevents large numbers of students from showing up as generic peasants.) I help them by bringing to class snapshots of previous years' banquets and books on medieval costumes from the library. For those of a musical bent, I bring in recordings and instruments, such as the recorder. This kind of in-class frivolity is worth the time it takes because it primes the class for the banquet and reduces their performance anxiety. For not only must everyone come in appropriate costume, but everyone must contribute to the banquet itself, by either preparing a dish or providing an entertainment.

I meet with those students who decide they would rather cook than dance, sing, or play. After passing around copies of medieval cookbooks (Cosman, Hieatt and Butler, Sass), I talk in general terms about the cuisine (banquet fare versus peasant, methods of preparation, spices as preservatives), points to consider as we plan our menu, and which dishes previous classes have liked best. I often show them sample menus from previous banquets. In this way, I ensure success while not inhibiting the more adventurous cooks from trying something "new" or slightly more exotic. Of the three cookbooks mentioned, I have found Sass the easiest for students to use. Among the most successful dishes I would include *tartelettes, gourdes in potage, tart de Bry, blank-mang, crustade Lombarde, peeres in confyt, douce ame* (recipes for all of which are in Sass). *Fritors* (Sass) are also popular, as is *burrebred* (Cosman); the occasional bread specialist in class will triumph by coming up with rastons or a subtlety of pastry (Hieatt) or marzipan (Sass). I always make sure we have trenchers. (The recipe in Cosman's book works well.) Everyone at the banquet will eat from a trencher, but I do have pottery plates in case a given year's trenchers prove unreliable (and I suppose one could always slip a paper plate underneath the trencher).

We then decide on specific recipes and methods of preparation. I help out with spices. Students themselves generally pair up, work out details of transportation to the markets to buy ingredients, and share available kitchens and ovens. We copy our recipes, and I often ask a volunteer to print or hand-letter the menus or to arrange for their production. (A sample menu is appended.)

The most significant difficulties I have encountered with the cooking are finding the right spices or appropriate substitutes when a student departs from the tried and tested recipes (on the other hand, this difficulty creates a good occasion for research) and cooking in quantity for a class of more than ten or fifteen. (I generally solve this problem by having more than one person make the same dish, which allows for some interesting comparisons.) The students' reactions (surprised and pleased) to the distinct cuisine (they keep trying for modern equivalents—"Middle Eastern, but sweeter") make the effort expended well worth while for all concerned (including the cooks).

When I meet with the students who want to entertain, I do so individually, mostly because I've found that "performer personalities" work best one on one at this stage. From a list of possibilities, each person chooses an entertainment. I pledge them to secrecy (as I do the cooks), a strategy that builds interest, curiosity, and anticipation. The entertainments I've permitted include the following:

- the telling of a tale—often an original, but occasionally a memorized one, as often as possible in Middle English (though this project takes lots of coaching, it works well with a student who has a good ear for the language);
- an illustration—by slides, drawings, or film—of jousting (be careful—demonstrations are dangerous!);
- a demonstration of dances, which generally includes teaching the steps of at least one dance to the entire company assembled;
- a demonstration of authentic medieval peasants' games (brings out the mimes, jugglers, clowns);
- the performance of a short play with simple staging, or a scene from a play—usually from an existing one, but sometimes an original (when written by persons with some talent or by the creative writing majors [and these do not necessarily coincide], they can be quite good and lots of fun).

For those timorous or serious souls who cannot cook or generate a degree of enthusiasm for entertainments, I encourage a useful show and tell, or some sort of presentation that bears directly on the poem. I have, for example, staged critical debates about the meaning and interpretive possibilities of *Gawain*. Carefully prepared and timed, such a debate can be quite effective.

And, finally, for the last-minute emergency wailings and gnashings about botched dishes, broken recorders, or pulled leg muscles, I hold out the possibilities of furnishing the wine (regular red or white, or mulled), supplying appropriate fruit and nuts—and, of course, submitting the paper anyway. With these preparations I generally receive a good response.

Staging the banquet itself is relatively simple, or becomes so when not held in a student's apartment or my living room. I look instead for a large empty room on campus. An ideal spot on our campus is the rustic but anachronistic ski barn. Surely every campus has a room where long tables can be set up and plenty of space exists. I would not say medieval banquets cannot be successfully staged in one's home, but if the class is of any size, space is limited, and the strain on one's own kitchen (and family's patience) can be hazardous. (Small children, however, can be a welcome addition if recruited to serve as pages.)

In insisting that everyone take the banquet seriously as a course requirement, I do encounter initial grumbling. But I build the banquet into the texture of the course sufficiently that, as the banquet (whose date, time, and place I include in the syllabus) draws closer, the class generally has a high level of anticipation. With appropriate cautions—and these careful preparations—I find the medieval banquet a fine teaching tool—one well worth the effort and a little saffron.

MENU

Gourd Soup	Pork Pie
Cabbage and Almond Soup	
Lemon Whyt	
Caudele Aulmaunde	Arbolettys
Roast Suckling Pig	
Boiled Garlic	Cameline Sauce
Vegetarian Lombardy Custard	
Marchepane	Burrebrede
Pears in Confection	
Parsley Bread Trenchers	
Spiced Wine	Nuts

PARTICIPANTS IN SURVEY OF *SIR GAWAIN AND THE GREEN KNIGHT* INSTRUCTORS

The following scholars and teachers generously agreed to participate in the survey of approaches to teaching *Sir Gawain and the Green Knight* that preceded preparation of this volume. Without their invaluable assistance and support, the volume simply would not have been possible.

Mark Amsler, Univ. of Delaware; Antony W. Annunziata, State Univ. of New York Coll., Oswego; Rosemary Ascherl, Hartford State Technical Coll.; W. Bryant Bachman, Jr., Univ. of Southwestern Louisiana; Steve Barney, Univ. of California, Irvine; Larry Benson, Harvard Univ.; Gail Berkeley, Reed Coll.; Marice Bezdek, Cabrini Coll.; Robert J. Blanch, Northeastern Univ.; Morton Bloomfield, Harvard Univ.; Marie Borroff, Yale Univ.; M. Teresa Brady, Coll. of White Plains, Pace Univ.; Judith Bronfman, School of Visual Arts, New York, NY; Martin Camargo, Univ. of Missouri, Columbia; Anthony J. Cavell, Our Lady of Holy Cross Coll.; Jane Chance, Rice Univ.; Lois Allen Chapman, Thornton Community Coll.; Howell Chickering, Amherst Coll.; Richard W. Clement, Illinois State Univ.; A. J. Colaianne, Virginia Polytechnic Inst.; Terrie Curran, Providence Coll.; R. Dahood, Univ. of Arizona; Penelope B. R. Doob, Glendon Coll., York Univ.; Thomas F. Dunn, Drake Univ.; Barbara Eckstein, Univ. of New Orleans; Dan Embree, Mississippi State Univ.; Sumner Ferris, California State Coll., PA; John H. Fisher, Univ. of Tennessee, Knoxville; Elston Flohr, Bethany Coll.; Albert B. Friedman, Claremont Graduate School; Maureen Fries, State Univ. of New York Coll., Fredonia; Donald Fry, Poynter Inst. for Media Studies, St. Petersburg, FL; Michael S. Fukuchi, Atlantic Christian Coll.; John M. Fyler, Tufts Univ.; John M. Ganim, Univ. of California, Riverside; Thomas J. Gasque, Univ. of South Dakota, Vermillion; Manuel José Gomez Lara, Universidad de Sevilla; Clia Doty Goodwin, Univ. of New Hampshire; Richard H. Green, Univ. of Florida, Gainesville; Victor Yelverton Haines, Dawson Coll.; Louis B. Hall, Univ. of Colorado, Denver; Vernon Harward, Smith Coll.; Hiroshi Hasagawa, Nihon Univ.; Thomas D. Hill Cornell Univ.; Susan Hilligoss, Univ. of North Carolina, Charlotte; Julia Bolton Holloway, Univ. of Colorado, Boulder; Delmar C. Homan, Bethany Coll.; Jeffrey F.

213

Huntsman, Indiana Univ., Bloomington; Edward B. Irving, Jr., Univ. of Pennsylvania; Mark D. Johnston, Illinois State Univ.; Robert L. Kelly, Univ. of North Carolina, Greensboro; Thomas L. Kinney, Bowling Green State Univ.; Bernice W. Kliman, Nassau Community Coll.; Peggy A. Knapp, Carnegie-Mellon Univ.; Sherron E. Knopp, Williams Coll.; Virginia E. Leland, Emerita, Bowling Green State Univ.; Lauren Lepow, Univ. of Missouri, St. Louis; Bernard S. Levy, State Univ. of New York, Binghamton; Mark J. Lidman, Univ. of South Carolina, Sumter; Carl Lindahl, Univ. of Houston; Thomas R. Liszka, DePaul Univ.; Douglas McMillan, East Carolina Univ.; M. H. Means, Univ. of Dayton; Miriam Youngerman Miller, Univ. of New Orleans; Patricia A. Moody, Syracuse Univ.; Judith May Newton, Tohoku Gaknin Univ.; Ruth Olmsted, William Penn Coll.; Alexandra Hennessey Olsen, Univ. of Denver; Roger J. Owens, Whittier Coll.; Walter S. Phelan, Rollins Coll.; William F. Pollard, Maryville Coll.; Nancy Patricia Pope, Illinois Coll.; Esther C. Quinn, Hunter Coll., City Univ. of New York; Alain Renoir, Univ. of California, Berkeley; Lois Roney, Univ. of Texas, Dallas; E. C. Ronquist, Concordia Univ., Montreal; Carmen B. Schmersahl, Mt. St. Mary's Coll.; Anne Howland Schotter, Wagner Coll.; Jack Selzer, Pennsylvania State Univ.; Sally K. Slocum, Univ. of Akron; Ann M. Taylor, Salem State Coll.; Edward M. Uehling, Valparaiso Univ.; Julian N. Wasserman, Loyola Univ. in New Orleans; Victoria L. Weiss, Oglethorpe Univ.; Clem C. Williams, Jr., De Pauw Univ.; Katharina M. Wilson, Univ. of Georgia; Robert H. Wilson, Univ. of Texas, Austin; Thomas L. Wright, Auburn Univ.; Robert F. Yeager, Warren Wilson Coll.; Geraldine K. Zalazar, Indiana Univ. of Pennsylvania; Ken Zellefrow, New Mexico State Univ.

WORKS CITED

Primary Sources

Abrams, M. H., gen. ed. *The Norton Anthology of English Literature*. 4th ed. 2 vols. New York: Norton, 1979.

Adams, Richard. *Watership Down*. London: Collings; New York: Macmillan, 1972.

The Alliterative Morte Arthure. *See* Gardner, Krishna.

Anderson, George K., and William E. Buckler, eds. *The Literature of England*. 5th ed. Glenview: Scott, 1968.

Anderson, J. J., ed. *Cleanness*. New York: Barnes, 1977.

———, ed. *Patience*. New York: Barnes, 1969.

Andreas Capellanus. *The Art of Courtly Love*. Trans. John H. Parry. New York: Ungar, 1957.

Andrew, Malcolm, and Ronald Waldron, eds. *The Poems of the Pearl Manuscript*. York Medieval Texts 2nd ser. London: Arnold, 1978; Berkeley: U of California P, 1979.

Armstrong, Edward C., ed. *Le chevalier à l'épée*. Baltimore: Murphy, 1900.

Asimov, Isaac. *The Foundation Trilogy*. New York: Avon, 1974.

Augustine. *Confessions*. Trans. E. B. Pusey. New York: Dutton, 1953.

———. *On Christian Doctrine*. Trans. D. W. Robertson, Jr. Indianapolis: Bobbs, 1958.

The Awntyrs off Arthure at the Terne Wathelyne. *See* Gates, Hanna.

Banks, Theodore Howard, Jr., trans. *Sir Gawain and the Green Knight*. New York: Appleton, 1929.

Barron, W. R. J., ed. and trans. *Sir Gawain and the Green Knight*. Manchester Medieval Classics. Manchester: Manchester UP; New York: Barnes, 1974.

Barth, John. *Chimera*. New York: Random, 1972.

Beagle, Peter. *The Last Unicorn*. New York: Ballantine, 1976.

Bede. *A History of the English Church and People*. Trans. Leo Sherley-Price. Rev. R. E. Latham. Harmondsworth: Penguin, 1968.

Benson, Larry D., ed. *King Arthur's Death: The Middle English Stanzaic Morte Arthur and Alliterative Morte Arthure*. Indianapolis: Bobbs, 1974.

Berger, Thomas. *Arthur Rex: A Legendary Novel*. New York: Dell, 1978.

Bergman, Ingmar. *The Seventh Seal*. Trans. Lars Malmström and David Kushner. Modern Film Scripts. New York: Simon, 1960.

Boccaccio, Giovanni. *Filocolo*. Trans. as *Thirteen Most Pleasant and Delectable Questions of Love, . . . by H.G. . . .* Illus. Harry Carter. 1566. New York: Potter, 1974.

Boethius. *The Consolation of Philosophy*. Trans. Richard H. Green. Indianapolis: Bobbs, 1962.

Borroff, Marie, trans. *Pearl: A New Verse Translation*. New York: Norton, 1977.

———, trans. *Sir Gawain and the Green Knight: A New Verse Translation*. New York: Norton, 1967; Toronto: McLeod, 1967; London: Longman, 1968.

Bradley, Marion Zimmer. *The Mists of Avalon*. New York: Knopf, 1983.

Bradshaw, Gillian. *Hawk of May*. New York: Simon, 1980.

———. *In Winter's Shadow*. New York: Simon, 1982.

———. *Kingdom of Summer*. New York: Simon, 1981.

Brewer, Elisabeth, ed. and trans. *From Cuchulainn to Gawain: Sources and Analogues of* Sir Gawain and the Green Knight. Cambridge: Brewer; Totowa: Rowman, 1973.

Bromwich, Rachel, ed. *The Welsh Triads* [*Trioedd Ynys Prydein*]. Cardiff: U of Wales P, 1961.

Brook, G. L., and R. F. Leslie. *See* Layamon.

Buckley, Jerome H., and George B. Woods, eds. *Poetry of the Victorian Period*. 3rd ed. Chicago: Scott, 1965.

Bühler, Curt F., ed. *The Epistle of Othea; translated from the French Text of Christine de Pisan by Stephen Scrope*. Early English Text Soc. os 264. London: Oxford UP, 1970.

Burrow, J. A., ed. *Sir Gawain and the Green Knight*. 1972. New Haven: Yale UP, 1982.

Cable, James, trans. *The Death of King Arthur* [Prose Vulgate *Mort Artu*]. Baltimore: Penguin, 1971.

Canning, Victor. *The Crimson Chalice*. New York: Morrow, 1978.

Carmichael, Douglas. *Pendragon*. Hicksville: Black Water, 1978.

Carroll, Lewis. *Alice's Adventures in Wonderland*. 1865. New York: Crown, 1974.

The Castle of Perseverance. *See* Eccles.

Cawley, A. C., ed. *Pearl; Sir Gawain and the Green Knight*. Everyman's Lib. 1962. London: Dent; New York: Dutton, 1972.

Cawley,ʼA. C., and J. J. Anderson, eds. *Pearl, Cleanness, Patience, Sir Gawain and the Green Knight*. Everyman's Lib. London: Dent; New York: Dutton, 1976.

Caxton, William. *See* Ramón Lull.

Chapman, Vera. *The Green Knight*. 1975. New York: Avon, 1978.

———. *King Arthur's Daughter*. 1976. New York: Avon, 1978.

———. *The King's Damosel*. 1976. New York: Avon, 1978.

Le chevalier à l'épée. See Armstrong.

Chrétien de Troyes. *Arthurian Romances.* Trans. W. W. Comfort. 1914. London: Dent, 1970; New York: Dutton, 1975.

———. *Le chevalier au lion* [*Yvain*]. Ed. Mario Roques. Paris: Champion, 1970.

———. *Le chevalier de la charrete* [*Lancelot*]. Ed Mario Roques. Paris: Champion, 1975.

———. *Cligés.* Ed. Alexandre Micha. Paris: Champion, 1975.

———. *Le comte du graal* [*Perceval*]. Ed. Felix Lecoy. Paris: Champion, 1975.

———. *Erec et Enide.* Ed. Mario Roques. Paris: Champion, 1973.

———. *The Story of the Grail* [*Perceval*]. Trans. Robert W. Linker. Chapel Hill: U of North Carolina P, 1960.

Christian, Catherine. *The Pendragon.* New York: Knopf, 1979.

Clark, Cecily, ed. *The Peterborough Chronicle, 1070–1154.* 2nd ec. Oxford: Clarendon, 1970.

Cleanness. See J. J. Anderson, Stone, Cawley and Anderson, Gollancz.

Colin, Philipp, and Claus Wisse. *Parzifal: Eine Ergänzung der Dichtung Wolframs von Eschenbach.* Ed. Karl Schorbach. Strassburg, 1888.

Cooper, Susan. *The Dark Is Rising.* New York: Atheneum, 1973.

———. *Greenwitch.* New York: Atheneum, 1974.

———. *The Grey King.* New York, Atheneum, 1975.

———. *Over Sea, under Stone.* New York: Harcourt, 1966.

———. *Silver on the Tree.* New York: Atheneum, 1977.

Curtis, Renée L., ed. *Le roman de Tristan en prose.* 2 vols. to date; 2nd vol. incomplete. Vol. 1, Munich: Hueber, 1963; vol. 2, Leiden: Brill, 1976.

Dante Alighieri. *Inferno.* Trans. John D. Sinclair. New York: Oxford UP, 1961.

———. *Le opere.* Ed. E. Moore. Rev. Paget Toynbee. 4th ed. Oxford: Oxford UP, 1924.

Day, Mabel. *See* Gollancz, Sir Gawain

Dickins, Bruce, and R. M. Wilson, eds. *Early Middle English Texts.* 1951. New York: Norton, 1954.

Dinesen, Isak. *Anecdotes of Destiny.* New York: Random, 1958.

Dobbie, Elliott Van Kirk, ed. *The Anglo-Saxon Minor Poems.* Vol. 6 of *Anglo-Saxon Poetic Records.* 6 vols. New York: Columbia UP, 1942.

Doctorow, E. L. *The Book of Daniel.* New York: NAL-Signet, 1971.

Drake, David. *The Dragon Lord.* New York: Tor, 1979.

Dunn, Charles W., and Edward T. Byrnes, eds. *Middle English Literature.* New York: Harcourt, 1973.

Durandus, Gulielmus. *Rationale divinorum officiorum.* Venice, 1589.

Eccles, Mark, ed. *The Macro Plays.* Early English Text Soc. os 262. London: Oxford UP, 1969.

Eco, Umberto. *The Name of the Rose*. Trans. William Weaver. New York: Harcourt, 1983.

The Ellesmere Chaucer, Reproduced in Facsimile. Pref. Alix Egerton. 2 vols. Manchester: Manchester UP, 1911.

Evans, J. Gwenogvryn, and John Rhys. *The Text of* The Mabinogion *and Other Welsh Tales from the Red Book of Hergest*. Oxford, 1887.

Evans, Sebastian, trans. *Arthurian Chronicles by Wace and Layamon*. 1912. London: Dent, 1928.

———, trans. *The High History of the Holy Graal* [*Perlesvaus*]. 1907. London: Dent, [1936].

Fled Bricrend. *See* Henderson.

Ford, Patrick K., trans. The Mabinogi *and Other Welsh Tales*. Berkeley: U of California P, 1977.

Fowles, John. *The Ebony Tower*. Boston: Little, 1974.

———. *The Magus: A Revised Version*. Boston: Little, 1978.

Froissart, Jean. *Chronicles*. Trans. Geoffrey Brereton. Baltimore: Penguin, 1978.

Furnivall, F. J., ed. *Early English Meals and Manners*. Early English Text Soc. os 32. 1868. Millwood: Kraus, 1973.

Gantz, Jeffrey, trans. *Early Irish Myths and Sagas*. New York: Penguin, 1981.

———, trans. *The Mabinogion*. New York: Penguin, 1976.

Garbáty, Thomas J., ed. *Medieval English Literature*. New York: Heath, 1983.

Gardner, John, trans. *The Alliterative* Morte Arthure, The Owl and the Nightingale, *and Five Other Middle English Poems in a Modernized Version with Comments on the Poems and Notes*. Carbondale: Southern Illinois UP, 1971.

———, trans. *The Complete Works of the* Gawain-*Poet*. Chicago: U of Chicago P, 1965.

———. *Grendel*. New York: Knopf, 1971.

Gates, Robert J., ed. *The Awntyrs off Arthure at the Terne Wathelyne: A Critical Edition*. Philadelphia: U of Pennsylvania P, 1969.

Gelzer, Heinrich, ed. *Yder*. Dresden: Gesellschaft für romanische Literatur, 1913.

Geoffrey of Monmouth. *Historia regum Britanniae*. Ed. Acton Griscom. London: Longmans, 1929.

———. *Historia regum Britanniae: A Variant Version Edited from Manuscripts*. Ed. Jacob Hammer. Cambridge: Medieval Acad. of America, 1951.

———. *Histories of the Kings of Britain*. Trans. Sebastian Evans. Everyman's Lib. London: Dent; New York: Dutton, 1911.

———. *History of the Kings of Britain*. Trans. Lewis Thorpe. 1966. Baltimore: Penguin, 1968.

Godwin, Parke. *Firelord*. Garden City: Doubleday, 1980.

Goethe, Johann Wolfgang von. *Faust: Part 1*. Trans. Philip Wayne. Harmondsworth and Baltimore: Penguin, 1949.

Gollancz, Israel, ed. Pearl, Cleanness, Patience and Sir Gawain. *Reproduced in Facsimile from the Unique MS. Cotton Nero A.x. in the British Museum.* Early English Text Soc. os 162. 1923. London: Oxford UP, 1971.

———, ed. Sir Gawain and the Green Knight: *Re-edited from MS. Cotton Nero A.x. in the British Museum.* Completed by Mabel Day with notes by Mary S. Serjeantson. Early English Text Soc. os 210. 1940. London: Oxford UP, 1966.

———, ed. *Wynnere and Wastoure.* Select Early English Poems 3. Rev. Mabel Day. 1930. Cambridge: Brewer; Totowa: Rowman, 1974

Gordon, E. V., ed. *Pearl.* Oxford: Clarendon, 1953.

Green, Roger Lancelyn. *King Arthur and His Knights of the Round Table.* Illus. Lotte Reiniger. Baltimore: Penguin, 1953.

Guillaume de Lorris. *Romance of the Rose.* Trans. Charles Dahlberg. Princeton: Princeton UP, 1971.

Guillaume de Lorris and Jean de Meun. *Romance of the Rose.* Trans. Harry W. Robbins. New York: Dutton, 1962.

Hales, John W., and Frederick J. Furnivall, eds. *Bishop Percy's Folio Manuscript.* 2 vols. Vol. 2. London, 1867–68.

Hall, Joseph, ed. *Selections from Early Middle English, 1130–1250.* 2 vols. Oxford: Clarendon, 1920.

Hall, Louis B., trans. *The Knightly Tales of Sir Gawain.* Chicago: Nelson, 1976.

Hanna, Ralph, ed. *The Awntyrs off Arthure at the Terne Wathelyn.* Manchester: Manchester UP, 1974.

Hartmann von Aue. *Erec.* Ed. Albert Leitzmann and Ludwig Wolff. 5th ed. Tübingen: Niemeyer, 1972.

Haskell, Ann S., ed. *A Middle English Anthology.* Garden City: Doubleday, 1969; rpt. Detroit: Wayne State UP, 1985.

Hastings, Selina, ed. *Sir Gawain and the Green Knight.* Illus. Juan Wijngaard. New York: Lothrop, 1982.

Hellman, Robert, and Richard O'Gorman. *Fabliaux: Ribald Tales from the Old French.* New York: Crowell, 1965.

Henderson, George, ed. *Fled Bricrend.* Dublin, 1899.

Henry of Lancaster. *Livre des seintes medicines.* Ed. J. Arnould. Anglo-Norman Text Soc. 1940. New York: Johnson, 1967.

Herbert, Frank. *Chapterhouse, Dune.* New York: Putnam, 1985.

———. *Children of Dune.* New York: Berkeley, 1976.

———. *Dune.* Radnor: Chilton, 1965.

———. *Dune Messiah.* New York: Putnam, 1969.

———. *God Emperor of Dune.* New York: Putnam, 1981.

Hesse, Hermann. *Magister ludi [The Glass Bead Game].* Trans. Richard Winston and Clara Winston. New York: Bantam, 1970.

Hieatt, Constance B. *The Castle of Ladies.* New York: Crowell, 1973.

————. *The Joy of the Court*. New York: Crowell, 1971.

————. *Sir Gawain and the Green Knight*. Illus. Walter Lorraine. New York: Crowell, 1967.

Hill, Raymond T., and Thomas G. Bergin, eds. *Anthology of the Provençal Troubadours*. 2nd ed. Rev. Thomas G. Bergin. 2 vols. Yale Romantic Studies 2nd ser. 23. New Haven: Yale UP, 1973.

Homer. *The Odyssey*. Trans. Robert Fitzgerald. Garden City: Anchor-Doubleday, 1961.

The Hours of Catherine of Cleves. Ed. John Plummer. New York: Braziller, 1966.

Hugh of St. Victor. *Didascalicon: On the Study of Reading*. Trans. Jerome Taylor. New York: Columbia UP, 1961.

————. *On the Sacraments of the Christian Faith*. Trans. Roy J. Deferrari. Cambridge: Medieval Acad. of America, 1951.

Hunbaut. See Stürzinger.

Jones, Gwyn, and Thomas Jones, trans. *The Mabinogion*. Everyman's Lib. 1949. New York: Dutton, 1966.

Jones, Lowanne E., ed. and trans. *The* Cort d'Amor: *A Thirteenth Century Allegorical Art of Love*. North Carolina Studies in the Romance Langs. and Lits. 185. Chapel Hill: U of North Carolina, Dept. of Romance Langs., 1977.

Joyce, James. *Finnegans Wake*. 1939. New York: Viking, 1945.

Kafka, Franz. *The Metamorphosis*. 1916. New York: Schocken, 1968.

Kane, Gil, and John Jakes. *Excalibur!* New York: Dell, 1980.

Kermode, Frank, and John Hollander, gen. eds. *The Oxford Anthology of English Literature*. 2 vols. New York: Oxford UP, 1973.

Kinghorn, A. M., ed. *The Middle Scots Poets*. York Medieval Texts. London: Arnold, 1970.

von Kleef, Catherina. *The Hours of Catherine of Cleves*. Introd. John Plummer. New York: Metropolitan Museum of Art, 1966.

Krishna, Valerie, ed. *The Alliterative* Morte Arthure: *A Critical Edition*. New York: Franklin, 1976.

Krochalis, Jeanne, and Edward Peters, eds. *The World of* Piers Plowman. Philadelphia: U of Pennsylvania P, 1975.

Langland, William. Piers the Ploughman. Trans. J. F. Goodridge. Baltimore: Penguin, 1959.

————. *Piers Ploughman: An Edition of the C-Text*. Ed. Derek Pearsall. Berkeley: U of California P, 1979.

————. *The Vision of Piers Plowman*. Ed. A. V. C. Schmidt. New York: Dutton, 1978.

Layamon [Laȝamon, Lawman]. *Brut*. Ed. Frederic Madden. London, 1847.

————. *Brut*. Ed. G. L. Brook and R. F. Leslie. 2 vols. Vol. 1. Early English Text Soc. os 250. London: Oxford UP, 1963.

Le Guin, Ursula K. *The Dispossessed*. New York: Harper, 1974.

———. *The Farthest Shore*. New York: Atheneum, 1972.

———. *The Left Hand of Darkness*. New York: Walker; London: Macdonald, 1969.

———. *The Tombs of Atuan*. New York: Atheneum, 1971.

———. *A Wizard of Earthsea*. New York: Parnassus, 1968.

Le livre de Caradoc. *See* Roach.

Lerner, Alan Jay. *Camelot*. New York: Random, 1961.

Lewis, C. S. *Perelandra*. New York: Macmillan, 1958.

———. *That Hideous Strength*. New York: Macmillan, 1968.

Longnon, Jean, and Ramond Cazelles, eds. *The Très Riches Heures of Jean, Duke of Berry*. Trans. Victoria Benedict. New York: Braziller; London: Thames, 1969.

Loomis, Roger Sherman, and Laura Hibbard Loomis, eds. *Medieval Romances*. Modern Lib. New York: Random, 1957.

Loomis, Roger Sherman, and Rudolph Willard, eds. *Medieval English Verse and Prose in Modernized Editions*. New York: Appleton, 1948.

Løseth, Eilert, ed. *Le roman en prose de Tristan; Le roman de Palamède et la compilation de Rusticien de Pise*. Paris, 1891.

Lowell, Robert. *Imitations*. New York: Farrar, 1961.

Lull, Ramón. *The Book of the Ordre of Chyualry*. Trans. William Caxton. Ed. Alfred T. P. Byles. Early English Text Soc. os 168. 1926. Millwood: Kraus, 1971.

Luria, Maxwell, and Richard L. Hoffman, eds. *Middle English Lyrics: Authoritative Texts, Critical and Historical Backgrounds, Perspectives on Six Poems*. Norton Critical Edition. New York: Norton, 1974.

The Luttrell Psalter: Two Plates in Colour and One Hundred and Eighty-three in Monochrome from the Additional Manuscript 42130 in the British Museum. Introd. Eric George Millar. London: British Museum, 1932.

Lydgate, John. *Siege of Thebes*. 2 vols. Ed. Axel Erdmann. Early English Text Soc. extra ser. 108, 125. 1930, 1911. Millwood: Kraus, 1984, 1973.

Mabinogi, Mabinogion. *See* Evans and Rhys; Ford; Gantz; Jones and Jones.

MacDonald, George. *Phantastes and Lilith*. Introd. C. S. Lewis. Grand Rapids: Eerdmans, 1964.

Mack, Frances M., ed. *Seinte Marharete þe Meiden ant Martyr*. Early English Text Soc. os 193. 1934. London: Oxford UP, 1958.

Mack, Maynard, gen. ed. *The Norton Anthology of World Masterpieces*. 4th ed. 2 vols. New York: Norton, 1979.

Macrobius. *Commentary on the Dream of Scipio*. Trans. William Harris Stahl. New York: Columbia UP, 1952.

Madden, Frederic, ed. *Syr Gawayne and the Grene Knyȝt: A Collection of Ancient Romance-Poems*. . . . Bannatyne Club 61. 1839. New York: AMS, 1971.

Malamud, Bernard. *The Natural*. New York: Farrar, 1961.

Malory, Thomas. *Morte Darthur.* Ed. and abr. D. S. Brewer. Evanston: Northwestern UP, 1968.

Mason, Eugene, trans. *Arthurian Chronicles: Wace and Layamon.* New York: Dutton, 1976.

Matarsso, P. M., trans. *The Quest of the Holy Grail.* Baltimore: Penguin, 1969.

Mayne, William. *Earthfasts.* New York: Dutton, 1966.

McDermott, Gerald. *The Knight of the Lion.* New York: Four Winds, 1979.

Medieval Epics. [*Beowulf,* trans. William Alfred, 1963; *The Song of Roland,* trans. W. S. Merwin, 1963; *The Nibelungenlied,* trans. Helen M. Mustard, 1963; and *The Poem of the Cid,* trans. W. S. Merwin, 1959]. New York: Modern Lib., 1963.

Meiss, Millard, and Elizabeth Beatson, eds. *The Belles Heures of Jean, Duke of Berry.* New York: Braziller, 1974.

Miles gloriosus. See Pontas du Méril.

Miller, Robert P., ed. *Chaucer: Sources and Backgrounds.* New York: Oxford UP, 1972.

Miskimin, Alice, ed. *Susannah.* New Haven: Yale UP, 1969.

Missale Romanum ex decreto sacrosancti Concilii Tridentini. New York: Benzinger, 1942.

Monaco, Richard. *The Final Quest.* New York: Putnam, 1981.

———. *The Grail War.* New York, Pocket, 1979.

———. *Parsival.* New York: Pocket, 1978.

Monty Python's Flying Circus. *Monty Python and the Holy Grail.* New York: Methuen, 1977.

Moorman, Charles, ed. *The Works of the* Gawain-*Poet.* Jackson: UP of Mississippi, 1977.

Morris, William, trans. *Volsunga Saga: The Story of the Volsungs and Niblungs.* Introd. Robert W. Gutman. New York: Macmillan, 1962.

Morris and Sword Dances of England. Letchworth, Eng.: Morris Ring, n.d.

Morse, Ruth, ed. *St. Erkenwald.* Totowa: Rowman, 1975.

Munn, H. Warner. *Merlin's Godson.* New York: Ballantine, 1976.

———. *Merlin's Ring.* New York: Ballantine, 1974.

Murphy, Gerard, ed. *Early Irish Lyrics.* Oxford: Clarendon, 1962.

Myers, A. R., ed. *English Historical Documents, 1327–1485.* English Historical Documents 4. New York: Oxford UP, 1969.

Newell, William. *King Arthur and the Table Round.* 2 vols. New York: Newell, 1976.

Newman, Sharan. *The Chessboard Queen.* New York: St. Martin's, 1983.

———. *Guinevere.* New York: St. Martin's, 1981.

Nitze, William A., and T. A. Jenkins, ed. *Perlesvaus.* 2 vols. Chicago: U of Chicago P, 1937.

Norman, Diana. *A Sword for a King*. New York: St. Martin's, 198_.

O'Donoghue, Bernard, ed. and trans. *The Courtly Love Tradition*. Manchester: Manchester UP; Totowa: Barnes, 1982.

Offord, M. Y., ed. *The Parlement of the Thre Ages*. Early English Text Soc. os 246. 1959. London: Oxford UP, 1967.

Ovid. *The Art of Love*. Trans. Rolfe Humphries. Bloomington: Indiana UP, 1957.

——. The Art of Love *and Other Poems*. Trans. John Henry Mozley. Vol. 2 of *Works*. 6 vols. Loeb Classical Lib. Cambridge: Harvard UP, 1969.

The Owl and the Nightingale. *See* Gardner, Stone.

Paccagnini, Giovanni. *Pisanello*. Trans. Jane Carroll. London: Phaidon, 1973.

Paiens de Maisières. *La damoiselle à la mule* [*La mule sanz frain*]. Ed. Boreslas Orlowski. Paris: Champion; Baltimore: Forst, 1911.

The Parlement of the Thre Ages. *See* Offord.

Patience. *See* Anderson; Cawley and Anderson; Gollancz.

Pearl. *See* Borroff; Cawley; Cawley and Anderson; Gollancz; Gordon; Tolkien.

Perlesvaus. *See* S. Evans; Nitze and Jenkins.

Phoebus, Gaston. *Medieval Hunting Scenes: The Hunting Book*. Text by Gabriel Bise after Gaston Phoebus. Trans. J. Peter Tallon. Fribourg: Productions Liber, Miller Graphics, 1978.

Pierce the Ploughmans Crede. *See* Skeat.

Piers the Ploughman. *See* Langland.

de Pisan, Christine. *The Book of the City of Ladies*. Trans. Earl Jeffrey Richards. New York: Persea, 1982.

Poe, Edgar Allan. "The Masque of the Red Death." *The Complete Tales and Poems of Edgar Allan Poe*. New York: Vintage-Random, 1975. 269–73.

Ponsor, Y. R. *Gawain and the Green Knight*. New York: Macmillan, 1979.

Pontas du Méril, Edélstand, ed. *Origines latines du théâtre moderne*. 2nd ed. Leipzig, 1897.

Pope, John C., ed. *Homilies of Ælfric: A Supplementary Collection*. 2 vols. Early English Text Soc. os 259–60. London: Oxford UP, 1967–68.

——, ed. *Seven Old English Poems*. New York: Norton, 1981.

Pyle, Howard. *The Story of King Arthur and His Knights*. Illus. Howard Pyle. New York: Scribners, 1933.

——. *The Story of the Champions of the Round Table*. Magnolia: Smith, 1968.

Raffel, Burton, trans. *Sir Gawain and the Green Knight*. New York: Mentor-NAL, 1970.

Rickert, Edith, comp. *Chaucer's World*. Ed. Clair C. Olson and Martin M. Crow. New York: Columbia UP, 1948.

Ridley, M. R., trans. *The Story of* Sir Gawain *and the Green Knight in Modern English*. Rev. ed. Leicester: Ward, 1950.

Rigg, A. C., ed. *Prologue to the Tale of Beryn*. Unpublished edition.

Riordan, James. *Tales of King Arthur*. Chicago: Rand, 1982.

Roach, W. J., ed. *Continuations of the Old French* Perceval *of Chrétien de Troyes*. 4 vols. Philadelphia: U of Pennsylvania P, 1949–71.

Robertson, D. W., Jr., ed. *The Literature of Medieval England*. New York: McGraw, 1970.

Robinson, F. N., ed. *The Works of Geoffrey Chaucer*. 2nd ed. Boston: Houghton, 1957.

Rosen, Winifred. *Three Romances: Love Stories from Camelot Retold*. New York: Knopf, 1981.

Rosenberg, James L., trans. *Sir Gawain and the Green Knight*. Ed. James R. Kreuzer. New York: Holt, 1959.

St. Erkenwald. *See* Morse, Stone.

Serjeantson, Mary S. *See* Gollancz, Sir Gawain.

Serraillier, Ian. *The Challenge of the Green Knight*. Illus. Victor S. Ambrus. New York: Walck, 1967.

Seton, Anya. *Avalon*. New York: Fawcett, 1977.

Silverstein, Theodore, trans. *Sir Gawain and the Green Knight: A Comedy for Christmas*. Illus. Virgil Burnett. Chicago: U of Chicago P, 1974.

———, ed. *Sir Gawain and the Green Knight: A New Critical Edition*. Chicago: U of Chicago P, 1984.

Sir Gawain and the Green Knight. *See*:

1. Editions: Andrew and Waldron; Barron; Burrow; Cawley; Cawley and Anderson; Gollancz; Silverstein; Tolkien and Gordon; Vantuono; Waldron

2. Illustrated editions: Hastings; Silverstein

3. Facsimile: Gollancz

4. Translations: Anderson; Banks; Barron; Borroff; Gardner; Ponsor; Ridley; Rosenberg; Stone; Tolkien; Vantuono; M. Williams

Sir Orfeo. *See* Tolkien.

Skeat, Walter W., ed. *Pierce the Ploughmans Crede*. Early English Text Soc. os 30. 1867. Millwood: Kraus, 1973.

Sommer, H. O., ed. *The Vulgate Version of the Arthurian Romances*. 8 vols. Washington: Carnegie Inst., 1908–16.

Sophocles. *Sophocles I*. Ed. David Grene and Richmond Lattimore. Chicago: U of Chicago P, 1954.

Spencer, Hazelton, gen. ed. *British Literature*. 3rd ed. Lexington: Heath, 1974.

Spenser, Edmund. *Poetical Works*. Ed. J. C. Smith and E. de Selincourt. 1912. London: Oxford UP, 1965.

Steinbeck, John. *The Acts of King Arthur and His Noble Knights*. Ed. Chase Horton. New York: Ballantine, 1976.

Stewart, Mary. *The Crystal Cave*. New York: Morrow, 1970.

———. *The Hollow Hills*. New York: Morrow, 1973.

————. *The Last Enchantment.* New York: Morrow, 1979.

————. *The Wicked Day.* New York: Morrow, 1983.

Stone, Brian, trans. *Medieval English Verse.* Baltimore: Penguin, 1964.

————, trans. The Owl and the Nightingale, Cleanness, *and* St. Erkenwald. Baltimore: Penguin, 1971.

————, trans. *Sir Gawain and the Green Knight.* 1959. Rev. ed. Baltimore: Penguin, 1974.

Stürzinger, Jakob, ed. *Hunbaut.* Dresden: Gesellschaft für romanische Literatur, 1914.

Susannah. See Miskimin.

Sutcliff, Rosemary. *The Sword and the Circle: King Arthur and the Knights of the Round Table.* New York: Dutton, 1981.

————. *Sword at Sunset.* New York: Coward, 1963.

Szarmach, Paul, ed. *Vercelli Homilies ix–xxiii.* Toronto: Centre for Medieval Studies, U of Toronto P, 1981.

Tennyson, Alfred, Lord. *Idylls of the King.* 1885. Ed. George Barker. New York: NAL, 1961.

————. *Idylls of the King.* 1885. New York: Airmont, 1968.

Thomas, Marcel, ed. *The Grandes Heures of Jean, Duke of Berry* Trans. Victoria Benedict and Benita Eisler. New York: Braziller, 1971.

Tolkien, J. R. R. ed. *The English Text of the Ancrene Riwle: Ancrene Wisse.* Early English Text Soc. os 249. London: Oxford UP, 1962.

————. *The Hobbit: or, There and Back Again.* 1937. New York: Ballantine, 1965.

————. *The Letters of J. R. R. Tolkien.* Ed. Humphrey Carpenter London: Allen; Boston: Houghton, 1977.

————. *The Lord of the Rings.* 3 vols. Rev. ed. 1965. New York: Ballantine, 1966.

————, trans. Sir Gawain and the Green Knight, Pearl *and* Sir Orfeo. London: Allen; Boston: Houghton, 1975.

————. Smith of Wootton Major *and* Farmer Giles of Ham. 1969. New York: Ballantine, 1975.

————. *The Tolkien Reader.* 1966. New York: Ballantine, 1975.

————. *Unfinished Tales.* Ed. Christopher Tolkien. London: Allen; Boston: Houghton, 1980.

Tolkien, J. R. R., and E. V. Gordon, eds. *Sir Gawain and the Green Knight.* 2nd ed. Rev. Norman Davis. 1967. New York: Oxford UP, 1968.

Trapp, J. B., ed. *Medieval English Literature.* New York: Oxford UP, 1973.

Les très riches heures du duc de Berry. Paris: Nomis, n.d. *See also* Longnon and Cazelles; Meiss and Beatson; Thomas.

von dem Türlin, Heinrich. *Diu Crône.* Ed. Gottleb Heinrich Friedrich Scholl. 1852. Amsterdam: Rodopi, 1966.

Turton, Godfrey Edmund. *The Emperor Arthur.* Garden City: Doubleday, 1967.

Twain, Mark. *A Connecticut Yankee in King Arthur's Court*. 1889. Baltimore: Penguin, 1972.

Vantuono, William, ed. *The* Pearl *Poems: An Omnibus Edition*. 2 vols. New York: Garland, 1984.

Vinaver, Eugène, ed. *Malory: Works*. 2nd ed. Oxford: Oxford UP, 1971.

Volsunga Saga. See Morris.

Vonnegut, Kurt. *The Sirens of Titan*. New York: Delacorte, 1971.

———. *Slaughterhouse-Five; or, The Children's Crusade, A Duty-Dance with Death*. New York: Dell, 1969.

Voragine, Jacobus de. *The Golden Legend*. Trans. Granger Ryan and Helmut Ripperger. New York: Longmans, 1941.

Vulgate Version of the Arthurian Romances. See H. O. Sommer.

Wace. *Le roman de Brut*. Ed. Le Roux de Lincy. Rouen, 1836–38.

Waldron, R. A., ed. *Sir Gawain and the Green Knight*. York Medieval Texts. London: Arnold; Evanston: Northwestern UP, 1970.

White, T. H. *The Book of Merlyn: The Unpublished Conclusion to* The Once and Future King. Austin: U of Texas P, 1977.

———. *The Once and Future King*. 1958. New York: Berkeley, 1966.

Whitelock, Dorothy, ed. *English Historical Documents, c. 500–1042*. Vol. 1 of *English Historical Documents*. 11 vols. to date. London: Eyre; New York: Oxford UP, 1955– .

Wilhelm, James J., and Laila Zamuelis Gross, eds. *The Romance of Arthur: An Anthology*. New York: Garland, 1984.

Williams, Charles. *The Region of the Summer Stars*. London: Oxford UP, 1950.

———. *Taliessen through Logres*. London: Oxford UP, 1938.

———. *War in Heaven*. Grand Rapids: Eerdmans, 1965.

Williams, G. J., and E. J. Jones. *Gramadegau'r Penceirddiaid*. Caerdydd: Gwasg Prifyscol Cymru, 1934.

Williams, Margaret, trans. *The* Pearl-*Poet: His Complete Works*. New York: Random, 1967.

Winters, Yvor. "Sir Gawaine and the Green Knight." *Quest for Reality*. Ed. Yvor Winters and Kenneth Fields. Chicago: Swallow, 1969. 158.

Wynnere and Wastoure. See Gollancz.

Yder. See Gelzer.

von Zatzikhoven, Ulrich. *Lanzelet: A Romance of Lancelot*. Trans. K. C. T. Webster. New York: Columbia UP, 1951.

———. *Lanzelet: Eine Erzählung*. Ed. K. A. Hahn. 1845. Berlin: de Gruyter, 1965.

Zupitza, Julius. *Beowulf: Autotypes of the Unique Cotton MS Vitellius A.xv in the British Museum, with a Transliteration and Notes*. Early English Text Soc. os 245. 1959. London: Oxford UP, 1981.

Secondary Sources

Ackerman, Robert W. *Backgrounds to Medieval English Literature*. New York: Random, 1966.

———. "Gawain's Shield: Penitential Doctrine in *Gawain and the Green Knight*." *Anglia* 76 (1958): 254–65.

———, comp. *An Index of Arthurian Names in Middle English*. 1952. New York: AMS, 1967.

———. "Middle English Literature to 1400." *The Medieval Literature of Western Europe: A Review of Research, Mainly 1930–1960*. John H. Fiske, gen. ed. New York: New York UP, for the MLA; London: U of London P, 1966. 75–123.

Alcock, Leslie. *Arthur's Britain*. London: Lane, 1971.

Allen, Judson B. *The Ethical Poetic of the Later Middle Ages*. Toronto: U of Toronto P, 1982.

———. *The Friar as Critic: Literary Attitudes in the Later Middle Ages*. Nashville: Vanderbilt UP, 1971.

Allmand, C. T., ed. *Society at War*. New York: Barnes, 1973.

Amsler, Mark E. "Literary Theory and the Genres of Middle English Literature." *Genre* 13 (1980): 389–96.

Anderson, George K. *Old and Middle English Literature from the Beginnings to 1485*. 1950. New York: Collier, 1962.

Andrew, Malcolm, comp. *The Gawain-Poet: An Annotated Bibliography, 1839–1977*. New York: Garland, 1979.

Ashdown, Charles Henry. *European Arms and Armour*. New York: Brussel, 1967.

Ashe, Geoffrey, et al. *The Quest for Arthur's Britain*. London: Pall Mall, 1968.

Auerbach, Erich. "Figura." Trans. Ralph Manheim. 1944. *Scenes from the Drama of European Literature* 11–76.

———. *Mimesis: The Representation of Reality in Western Literature*. Trans. Willard Trask. 1946. Garden City: Anchor-Doublday, 1957.

———. *Scenes from the Drama of European Literature*. 1959. Theory and History of Literature 9. Minneapolis: U of Minnesota P, 1984.

Bachman, W. Bryant, Jr. "*Sir Gawain and the Green Knight*: The Green and the Gold Once More." *Texas Studies in Literature and Language* 23–24 (1981): 495–516.

Baker, Derek, ed. *The Later Middle Ages (1212–1485)*. London: Hutchinson, 1968.

Baker, J. H. *An Introduction to English Legal History*. 2nd ed. London: Butterworths, 1979.

Bakhtin, Mikhail. *Rabelais and His World*. Trans. Hélène Iswolsky. Cambridge: MIT Press, 1968.

Baldwin, Charles Sears. *Medieval Rhetoric and Poetic (to 1400) Interpreted from Representative Works*. 1928. Gloucester: Smith, 1959.

Barber, Richard W., ed. *Arthurian Literature II*. Cambridge: Brewer; Totowa: Rowman, n.d.

———. *Arthur of Albion: An Introduction to the Arthurian Literature and Legends of England*. London: Barrie; New York: Barnes, 1961.

———. *The Knight and Chivalry*. 2nd ed. 1975. New York: Harper, 1982.

———. *The Reign of Chivalry*. New York: St. Martin's, 1980.

Barraclough, Geoffrey. *Social Life in Early England*. Historical Assn. Essays. New York: Barnes, 1960.

Barron, W. R. J. *Trawthe and Treason: The Sin of Gawain Reconsidered*. Manchester: Manchester UP, 1980.

Baugh, Albert C., ed. *A Literary History of England*. 2nd ed. New York: Appleton, 1967.

Baugh, Albert C., and Thomas Cable. *A History of the English Language*. 3rd ed. Englewood Cliffs: Prentice, 1978.

Beale, Walter H., comp. *Old and Middle English Poetry to 1500: A Guide to Information Sources*. Detroit: Gale, 1976.

Beer, Gillian. *The Romance*. Critical Idiom 10. London: Methuen, 1970.

Bennett, Michael J. *Community, Class and Careerism: Cheshire and Lancashire Society in the Age of* Sir Gawain and the Green Knight. Cambridge Studies in Medieval Life and Thought 3rd ser. 18. Cambridge: Cambridge UP, 1983.

Benson, Larry D. "The Alliterative *Morte Arthure* and Medieval Tragedy." *Tennessee Studies in Literature* 11 (1966): 75–87.

———. *Art and Tradition in* Sir Gawain and the Green Knight. New Brunswick: Rutgers UP, 1965.

———. "The Authorship of *St. Erkenwald*." *Journal of English and Germanic Philology* 64 (1965): 393–405.

Benson, Larry D., and John Leyerle, eds. *Chivalric Literature: Essays on Relations between Literature and Life in the Later Middle Ages*. Spec. issue of *Studies in Medieval Culture* 14 (1980).

Bercovitch, Sacvan. "Romance and Anti-Romance in *Sir Gawain and the Green Knight*." *Philological Quarterly* 44 (1965): 30–37.

Berne, Eric. *Games People Play: The Psychology of Human Relationships*. New York: Grove, 1964.

Berry, Francis. "*Sir Gawayne and the Grene Knight*." Ford, *Age of Chaucer* 146–56.

Bestul, Thomas H. *Satire and Allegory in* Wynnere and Wastoure. Lincoln: U of Nebraska P, 1974.

Bethurum, Dorothy, ed. *Critical Approaches to Medieval Literature*. New York: Columbia UP, 1960.

Bise, Gabriel. *See* Phoebus.

Bishop, Morris. *The Horizon Book of the Middle Ages*. New York: American Heritage, 1968.

Blake, Norman. *The English Language in Medieval Literature*. London: Dent; Totowa: Rowman, 1977.

Blanch, Robert J. "The Game of Invoking Saints in *Sir Gawain and the Green Knight*." *American Benedictine Review* 31 (1980): 237–62.

———. "Games Poets Play: The Ambiguous Use of Color Symbolism in *Sir Gawain and the Green Knight*." *Nottingham Mediaeval Studies* 20 (1976): 64–85.

———. "Imagery of Binding in Fitts One and Two of *Sir Gawair and the Green Knight*." *Studia Neophilologica* 54 (1982): 53–60.

———. "The Legal Framework of 'A twelmonyth and a day' in *Sir Gawain and the Green Knight*." *Neuphilologische Mitteilungen* 84 (1983): 347–52.

———, comp. Sir Gawain and the Green Knight: *A Reference Guide* Troy: Whitson, 1984.

———, ed. Sir Gawain and Pearl: *Critical Essays*. Bloomington: Indiana UP, 1966.

Blanch, Robert J., and Julian N. Wasserman. "Medieval Contracts and Covenants: The Legal Coloring of *Sir Gawain and the Green Knight*," *Neophilologus* 68 (1984): 598–610.

Bloch, Marc. *Feudal Society*. Trans. L. A. Manyon. Chicago: U of Chicago P, 1961.

Bloomfield, Morton W. "The Problem of the Hero in the Later Medieval Period." Burns and Reagan 27–48.

———. *The Seven Deadly Sins: An Introduction to the History of a Religious Concept, with Special Reference to Medieval English Literature*. Studies in Lang. and Lit. 1952. East Lansing: Michigan State UP, 1967.

———. "*Sir Gawain and the Green Knight*: An Appraisal." *PMLA* 76 (1961): 7–19. Rpt. in Howard and Zacher 24–55.

———. "Symbolism in Medieval Literature." *Modern Philology* 56 (1958): 73–81.

Boase, Roger. *The Origin and Meaning of Courtly Love: A Critical Study of European Scholarship*. Manchester: Manchester UP; Totowa: Rowman, 1977.

Bogdanow, Fanni. "The Character of Gauvain in the Thirteenth Century Prose Romances." *Medium Aevum* 27 (1958): 154–61.

Boitani, Piero. *English Medieval Narrative in the Thirteenth and Fourteenth Centuries*. Trans. Joan Krakouer Hall. Cambridge: Cambridge UP, 1982.

Bornstein, Diane. *Mirrors of Courtesy*. Hamden: Archon, 1975.

Borroff, Marie. Sir Gawain and the Green Knight: *A Stylistic and Metrical Study*. New Haven: Yale UP, 1962.

Brandt, William. *The Shape of Medieval History: Studies in Modes of Perception*. New Haven: Yale UP, 1966.

Braswell, Mary Flowers. *The Medieval Sinner: Characterization and Confession in the Literature of the English Middle Ages*. Rutherford: Fairleigh Dickinson UP, 1983.

Braunfels, Wolfgang. *The Monasteries of Western Europe: The Architecture of the Orders.* 3rd ed. Princeton: Princeton UP, 1973.

Brengle, Richard L., ed. *Arthur King of Britain: History, Chronicle, Romance, and Criticism.* Englewood Cliffs: Prentice, 1964.

Brewer, Derek S. *Chaucer and His World.* New York: Dodd, 1978.

———. *Chaucer in His Time.* London: Nelson, 1963.

———. "Courtesy and the *Gawain*-Poet." Lawlor 54–85.

———. *Symbolic Stories: Traditional Narratives of the Family Drama in English Literature.* Cambridge: Brewer, 1980.

Brewster, H. Pomeroy. *Saints and Festivals of the Christian Church.* New York: Stokes, 1904.

Brooke, Christopher. *The Structure of Medieval Society.* New York: McGraw, 1971.

Bruce, James Douglas. *The Evolution of Arthurian Romance: From the Beginnings Down to the Year 1300.* 2nd ed. 2 vols. Supp. Alfons Hilka. 1928. Gloucester: Smith, 1958.

Burns, Norman T., and Christopher J. Reagan, eds. *Concepts of the Hero in the Middle Ages and the Renaissance.* Albany: State U of New York P, 1975.

Burrow, J[ohn] A[nthony]. *Medieval Writers and Their Work: Middle English Literature and Its Background, 1100–1500.* Oxford: Oxford UP, 1982.

———. *A Reading of* Sir Gawain and the Green Knight. London: Routledge, 1965.

———. *Ricardian Poetry: Chaucer, Gower, Langland, and the* Gawain *Poet.* London: Routledge; New Haven: Yale UP, 1971.

———. "The Two Confession Scenes in *Sir Gawain and the Green Knight.*" *Modern Philology* 57 (1959): 73–79. Rpt. in Blanch, Sir Gawain *and* Pearl 123–34.

Busby, Keith. *Gauvain in Old French Literature.* Amsterdam: Rodopi, 1980.

———. "Gauvain in the Prose *Tristan.*" *Tristania* 2 (1976): 13–28.

The Cambridge Medieval History. 2nd ed. 8 vols. Cambridge: Cambridge UP, 1924.

Campbell, Joseph. *The Hero with a Thousand Faces.* 2nd ed. Princeton: Princeton UP, 1968.

Carney, James. *Studies in Irish Literature and History.* Dublin: Dublin Inst. for Advanced Studies, 1955.

Carpenter, Humphrey. *J. R. R. Tolkien: A Biography.* Boston: Houghton, 1977.

Chambers, Edmund K. *Arthur of Britain.* 1927. New York: Barnes, 1964.

Chance, Jane. *See* Jane Chance Nitzsche.

Chapman, Coolidge Otis, comp. *An Index of Names in* Pearl, Purity, Patience, *and* Gawain. 1951. London: Greenwood, 1980.

Charles-Edwards, T. M. "The Date of the Four Branches of the *Mabinogi.*" *Transactions of the Honourable Society of Cymmrodorion* 1970: 263–98.

Colaianne, Anthony J. Piers Plowman: *An Annotated Bibliography of Editions and Criticism, 1550–1977.* New York: Garland, 1978.

Colish, Marcia L. *The Mirror of Language: A Study in the Medieval Theory of Knowledge.* New Haven: Yale UP, 1968.

Cook, Robert G. "The Play-Element in *Sir Gawain and the Green Knight.*" *Tulane Studies in English* 13 (1963): 5–31.

Cooke, Thomas D., ed. *The Present State of Scholarship in Fourteenth Century Literature.* Columbia: U of Missouri P, 1983.

Cosman, Madeleine Pelner. *Fabulous Feasts: Medieval Cookery and Ceremony.* New York: Braziller, 1976.

Coulton, G. G. *Medieval Panorama: The English Scene from Conquest to Reformation.* 1949. New York: Norton, 1974.

Culler, Jonathan. *On Deconstruction.* Ithaca: Cornell UP, 1982.

Curtius, Ernst Robert. *European Literature and the Latin Middle Ages.* Trans. Willard R. Trask. Bollingen Series 36. 1948 New York: Harper, 1953.

Daiches, David. *A Critical History of English Literature.* 2nd ed. New York: Ronald, 1970.

Danker, Frederick E. "Teaching Medieval Literature: Texts, Recordings, and Techniques." *College English* 32 (1970): 340–57.

Davenport, W. A. *The Art of the* Gawain *Poet.* London: Athlone; Atlantic Highlands: Humanities, 1978.

Davis, William Stearns. *Life on a Medieval Barony.* 1923. New York: Harper, 1951.

Delort, Robert. *Life in the Middle Ages.* Trans. Robert Allen. Lausanne: Edita Lausanne, 1973.

Denis-Boulet, Noële M. *The Christian Calendar.* Trans. P. Hepburne-Scott. New York: Hawthorn, 1960.

de Rougemont, Denis. *Love in the Western World.* Trans. Montgomery Belgion. Rev. ed. New York: Pantheon, 1956.

Dodd, William George. *Courtly Love in Chaucer and Gower.* Harvard Studies in English 1. 1913. Gloucester: Smith, 1959.

Donahue, Charles. "Patristic Exegesis in the Criticism of Medieval Literature: Summation." Bethurum 61–82.

Donaldson, E. Talbot. "Patristic Exegesis in the Criticism of Medieval Literature: The Opposition." Bethurum 1–26.

———. *Speaking of Chaucer.* New York: Norton, 1970.

Doob, Penelope B. R. "The Labyrinth in Medieval Culture: Exploration of an Image." *Revue de l'Université d'Ottawa* 52 (1982): 207–18.

Dove, Mary. "Gawain and the *Blasme des Femmes* Tradition." *Medium Aevum* 41 (1972): 20–26.

Dronke, Peter. *Medieval Latin and the Rise of European Love-Lyric.* 2 vols. Oxford: Clarendon, 1965–66.

———. *The Medieval Lyric.* 2nd ed. New York: Cambridge UP, 1977.

Du Boulay, F. R. H. *An Age of Ambition: English Society in the Late Middle Ages.* London: Nelson, 1970.

Duby, Georges. *The Chivalric Society.* London: Arnold, 1978.

Eagan, Joseph F. "The Import of Color Symbolism in *Sir Gawain and the Green Knight.*" *Saint Louis University Studies* ser. A 1 (1949): 12–86.

Eagleton, Terry. *Marxism and Literary Criticism.* London: Methuen, 1976.

Elliott, Ralph W. V. "Landscape and Rhetoric in Middle English Alliterative Poetry." *Melbourne Critical Review* 4 (1961): 65–76.

Evans, Joan, ed. *The Flowering of the Middle Ages.* New York: McGraw, 1966.

Everett, Dorothy. "The Alliterative Revival." *Essays on Middle English Literature.* Oxford History of English Literature 1.2. Ed. Patricia Kean. Oxford: Clarendon, 1955. 68–96. Rpt. in Fox 13–23.

Ferrante, Joan M. "*Cortes' Amor* in Medieval Texts." *Speculum* 55 (1980): 686–95.

Ferrante, Joan M., and George D. Economou, eds. *In Pursuit of Perfection: Courtly Love in Medieval Literature.* Port Washington: Kennikat, 1975.

Fichte, Joerg O. "The Middle English Arthurian Verse Romance: Suggestions for the Development of a Literary Typology." *Deutsche Vierteljahrsschrift für Literaturwissenschaft und Geistesgeschichte* 55 (1981): 567–90.

Finlayson, John. "Definitions of Middle English Romance." *Chaucer Review* 15 (1980): 44–62, 168–81.

———. "The Expectations of Romance in *Sir Gawain and the Green Knight.*" *Genre* 12 (1979): 1–24.

———. "Formulaic Technique in *Morte Arthure.*" *Anglia* 81 (1963): 372–93.

———. "Rhetorical *Descriptio* of Place in the Alliterative *Morte Arthure.*" *Modern Philology* 61 (1963): 1–11.

Finucane, Ronald C. *Miracles and Pilgrims: Popular Beliefs in Medieval England.* Totowa: Rowman, 1977.

Fish, Stanley. *Self-Consuming Artifacts: The Experience of Seventeenth Century Literature.* Berkeley: U of California P, 1972.

Fletcher, Robert Huntington. *The Arthurian Material in the Chronicles, Especially Those of Great Britain and France.* Burt Franklin Bibliographical Series 10. 1906. New York: Franklin, 1958.

Folda, Jaroslav. *Crusader Manuscript Illuminations at St. Jean d'Acre, 1275–1291.* Princeton: Princeton UP, 1976.

Ford, Boris, ed. *The Age of Chaucer.* 1954. Baltimore: Penguin, 1969.

———, ed. *Medieval Literature, Part One: Chaucer and the Alliterative Tradition.* 1982. Vol. 1 of *The New Pelican Guide to English Literature.* Ed. Ford. 7 vols. to date. Harmondsworth: Penguin, 1982–

Fox, Denton, ed. *Twentieth Century Interpretations of* Sir Gawain and the Green Knight: *A Collection of Critical Essays.* Englewood Cliffs: Prentice, 1968.

Frappier, Jean. "Le personnage de Gauvain dans la première continuation de *Perceval.*" *Romance Philology* 11 (1957–58): 331–44.

Freeman, Margaret B. *The Unicorn Tapestries*. New York: Metropolitan Museum of Art, 1976.

Freud, Sigmund. *The Interpretation of Dreams*. Trans. James Strachey. 1900. New York: Avon, 1965.

Friedman, Albert B. "Folklore and Medieval Literature: A Look at Mythological Considerations." *Southern Folklore Quarterly* 43 (1979): 135–48.

———. "Morgan le Fay in *Sir Gawain and the Green Knight*." Blanch, Sir Gawain and Pearl 135–58.

Friedman, Albert B., and Richard H. Osberg. "Gawain's Girdle as Traditional Symbol." *Journal of American Folklore* 90 (1977): 301–15.

Fries, Maureen. "The Characterization of Women in the Alliterative Tradition." Levy and Szarmach 24–45.

Frye, Northrop. *Anatomy of Criticism: Four Essays*. 1957. New York: Atheneum, 1966.

Funcken, Liliane, and Fred Funcken. *The Age of Chivalry*. 3 vols. Englewood Cliffs: Prentice, 1983.

Gallacher, Patrick J. *Love, the Word, and Mercury: A Reading of John Gower's Confessio Amantis*. Albuquerque: U of New Mexico P, 1975.

Ganim, John M. *Style and Consciousness in Middle English Narrative*. Princeton: Princeton UP, 1983.

Geertz, Clifford. "Deep Play: Notes on the Balinese Cockfight." *Myth, Symbol, and Culture*. Ed. Geertz. New York: Norton, 1971. 1–37.

Gerould, Gordon Hall. "King Arthur and Politics." *Speculum* 2 (1927): 33–54.

Gies, Joseph, and Frances Gies. *Life in a Medieval Castle*. New York: Crowell, 1974.

Gilman, Stephen. *The Art of* La Celestina. Madison: U of Wisconsin P, 1956.

Gilson, Etienne. *The Spirit of Mediaeval Philosophy*. Trans. A. H. C. Downes. New York: Scribner's, 1940.

Gimpel, Jean. *The Medieval Machine: The Industrial Revolution of the Middle Ages*. 1976. New York: Penguin, 1977.

Gist, Margaret Adlum. *Love and War in the Middle English Romances*. Philadelphia: U of Pennsylvania P, 1947.

Glassie, Henry. *All Silver and No Brass: An Irish Christmas Mumming*. Bloomington: Indiana UP, 1976.

Göller, Karl Heinz, ed. *The Alliterative Morte Arthure: A Reassessment of the Poem*. Cambridge: Brewer, 1981.

Goldhurst, William. "The Green and the Gold: The Major Theme of *Gawain and the Green Knight*." *College English* 20 (1958): 61–65.

Goldin, Frederick. *Lyrics of the Troubadours and Trouvères: An Anthology and a History*. Garden City: Anchor-Doubleday, 1973.

Gradon, Pamela. *Form and Style in Early English Literature*. London: Methuen, 1971.

Graves, Robert. *The White Goddess: A Historical Grammar of Poetic Myth*. New York: Creative Age, 1948.

Green, Dennis H. *Irony in the Medieval Romance*. Cambridge: Cambridge UP, 1979.

Green, Richard Firth. *Poets and Princepleasers: Literature and the English Court in the Late Middle Ages*. Toronto: U of Toronto P, 1980.

Green, Richard Hamilton. "Gawain's Shield and the Quest for Perfection." *ELH* 29 (1962): 121–39. Rpt. in *Middle English Survey: Critical Essays*. Ed. Edward Vasta. Notre Dame: U of Notre Dame P, 1965. 71–92. Also rpt. in Blanch, Sir Gawain *and* Pearl 176–94.

Haines, Victor Yelverton. "Allusions to the *Felix culpa* in the Prologue of *Sir Gawain and the Green Knight*." *Revue de l'Université d'Ottawa* 44 (1974): 158–77.

———. *The Fortunate Fall of Sir Gawain: The Typology of* Sir Gawain and the Green Knight. Washington: UP of America, 1982.

Hammer, Jacob. "Geoffrey of Monmouth's Use of the Bible in the *Historia regum Britanniae*." *Bulletin of the John Rylands University Library of Manchester* 30 (1946–47): 293–311.

Hamp, Eric P. "*Mabinogi*." *Transactions of the Honourable Society of Cymmrodorion* 1975–76: 243–49.

Hampson, R. T. *Medii aevi kalendarium*. 2 vols. London, 1841.

Hanna, Ralph, III. "Unlocking What's Locked: Gawain's Green Girdle." *Viator* 14 (1983): 290–302.

Hanning, Robert. "Sir Gawain and the Red Herring: The Perils of Interpretations." *Acts of Interpretation.: The Text in Its Contexts, 700–1600*. Ed. Mary Carruthers and Elizabeth Kirk. Norman: Pilgrim, 1983. 5–23.

Harris, Adelaide Evans. *The Heroine of the Middle English Romance*. 1928. Danby: Folcroft, 1969.

Hartley, Dorothy. *Lost Country Life*. New York: Pantheon, 1979.

Hawkes, Terence. *Structuralism and Semiotics*. London: Methuen, 1977.

Heninger, S. K., Jr. "The Tudor Myth of Troy-novant." *Southern Atlantic Quarterly* 61 (1961–62): 378–87.

Henisch, Bridget Ann. *Food and Feast in Medieval Society*. University Park: Pennsylvania State UP, 1976.

Henry, Derrick. *The Listener's Guide to Medieval and Renaissance Music*. New York: Facts on File, 1983.

Hieatt, A. Kent. "*Sir Gawain*: Pentangle, *Luf-Lace*, Numerical Structure." *Papers on Language and Literature* 4 (1968): 339–59. Rpt., rev., in *Silent Poetry: Essays in Numerological Analysis*. Ed. Alastair Fowler. London: Routledge, 1970. 116–40.

Hieatt, Constance B., and Sharon Butler. *Pleyn Delit: Medieval Cookery for Modern Cooks*. Toronto: U of Toronto P, 1976.

Hofstätter, Hans H. *Art of the Late Middle Ages*. New York: Abrams, 1968.

Holland, Norman. *The Dynamics of Literary Response*. New York: Norton, 1975.

Holloway, Julia Bolton. "The Asse to the Harpe: Boethian Music in Chaucer." *Boethius and the Liberal Arts*. Ed. Michael Masi. Berne: Lang, 1981. 175–86.

Hopper, Vincent F. *Medieval Number Symbolism: Its Sources, Meanings, and Influences on Thought and Expression*. Columbia U Studies in English and Comparative Lit. 132. New York: Columbia UP, 1938.

Horn, Walter William, and Ernest Born. *The Plan of St. Gall: A Study of the Architecture and Economy of, and Life in a Paradigmatic Carolingian Monastery*. 3 vols. Trans. Charles W. Jones. Berkeley: U of California P, 1979.

Howard, Donald R. "*Sir Gawain and the Green Knight*." Severs, *Recent* 29–54.

———. "Structure and Symmetry in *Sir Gawain*." Howard and Zacher 159–73. Fox 44–56. Blanch, Sir Gawain and Pearl 195–208.

———. *The Three Temptations: Medieval Man in Search of the World*. Princeton: Princeton UP, 1966.

Howard, Donald R., and Christian K. Zacher, eds. *Critical Studies of* Sir Gawain and the Green Knight. Notre Dame: U of Notre Dame P, 1968.

Hughes, Derek W. "The Problem of Reality in *Sir Gawain and the Green Knight*." *University of Toronto Quarterly* 40 (1971): 217–35.

Huizinga, Johan. *Homo Ludens: A Study of the Play Element in Culture*. Trans. R. F. C. Hull. 1950. Boston: Beacon, 1962.

———. *The Waning of the Middle Ages: A Study of the Forms of Life, Thought, and Art in France and the Netherlands in the Fourteenth and Fifteenth Centuries*. 1924. Garden City: Anchor-Doubleday, 1954.

Hulbert, James. "A Hypothesis concerning the Alliterative Revival." *Modern Philology* 27 (1931): 405–22.

Huntsman, Jeffrey F. "Celts and Saxons: Creolization and Syntactic Change in Historical Linguistics." *Error Analysis and Interlanguage*. Special issue of *Lektos* 1976: 79–82.

Hussey, Maurice. *Chaucer's World: A Pictorial Companion*. Cambridge: Cambridge UP, 1967.

Jackson, W. T. H. *The Literature of the Middle Ages*. New York: Columbia UP, 1960.

Jacobs, Nicolas. "Alliterative Storms: A Topos in Middle English." *Speculum* 47 (1972): 695–719.

Jameson, Fredric. "Magical Narratives: On the Dialectical Use of Genre Criticism." *The Political Unconscious: Narrative as Social and Symbolic Act*. Ithaca: Cornell UP, 1981. 103–50.

———. *Marxism and Form*. Princeton: Princeton UP, 1971.

———. "Metacommentary." *PMLA* 86 (1971): 9–18. Rpt., rev., and exp. in *Marxism and Form* 306–416.

Johnson, Lynn Staley. *The Voice of the Gawain-Poet*. Madison: U of Wisconsin P, 1984.

Joll, James. *Gramsci*. London: Fontana, 1977.

Jones, Charles. *An Introduction to Middle English*. New York: Holt, 1972.

Jones, Terry. *Chaucer's Knight: The Portrait of a Medieval Mercenary*. London: Weidenfeld; Baton Rouge: Louisiana State UP, 1980.

Jordan, Richard. *Handbook of Middle English Grammar: Phonology*. Trans. and rev. Eugene Joseph Crook. The Hague: Mouton, 1974.

Jung, Carl G. "On the Psychology of the Trickster-Figure." *The Archetypes and the Collective Unconscious*. Vol. 9, pt. 1, of *Collected Works*. 2nd ed. Bollingen Series 20. Trans. R. F. C. Hull. Princeton: Princeton UP, 1969. 255-72. New York: Pantheon, 1959.

Kane, George. *Middle English Literature: A Critical Study of the Romances, the Religious Lyrics, Piers Plowman*. 1951. London: Methuen; New York: Barnes, 1970.

Kaske, Robert E. "Gawain's Green Chapel and the Cave at Wetton Mill." *Medieval Literature and Folklore Studies: Essays in Honor of Francis Lee Utley*. Ed. Jerome Mandel and Bruce A. Rosenberg. New Brunswick: Rutgers UP, 1970. 111-21.

———. "Patristic Exegesis in the Criticism of Medieval Literature: The Defense." Bethurum 27-60.

———. "*Sir Gawain and the Green Knight*." *Proceedings of the Southeastern Institute of Medieval and Renaissance Studies* 10 (1979): 24-44.

Keegan, John. *The Face of Battle*. New York: Vintage, 1977.

Keen, Maurice Hugh. *Chivalry*. New Haven: Yale UP, 1984.

———. *England in the Later Middle Ages: A Political History*. London: Methuen, 1973.

Keenan, Joan. "Feasts and Fasts in *Sir Gawain and the Green Knight*." *American Notes and Queries* 17 (1978): 34-35.

Kelly, Douglas. *Medieval Imagination, Rhetoric and the Poetry of Courtly Love*. Madison: U of Wisconsin P, 1978.

Kelly, Francis M., and Randolph Schwabe. *A Short History of Costume and Armour, Chiefly in England, 1066-1800*. 1931. New York: Arco, 1972.

Kelly, Henry Ansgar. *Love and Marriage in the Age of Chaucer*. Ithaca: Cornell UP, 1975.

Ker, William P. *Epic and Romance: Essays on Medieval Literature*. 2nd ed. 1908. New York: Dover, 1957.

———. *Medieval English Literature*. 1912. London: Oxford UP, 1969.

Kermode, Frank. *The Sense of an Ending: Studies in the Theory of Fiction*. New York: Oxford UP, 1967.

Kernan, Anne. "Theme and Structure in *The Parlement of the Thre Ages*." *Neuphilologische Mitteilungen* 75 (1974): 253-78.

Kindrick, Robert L. "Gawain's Ethics: Shame and Guilt in *Sir Gawain and the Green Knight*." *Annuale medievale* 20 (1980): 5-32.

Kittredge, George Lyman. *A Study of* Sir Gawain and the Green Knight. 1916. Gloucester: Smith, 1960.

Knapp, Peggy A. "Gawain's Quest: Social Conflict and Symbolic Mediation." *Clio* 6 (1977): 289–306.

Knight, William Francis Jackson. *Cumaean Gates- A Reference of the Sixth Aeneid to the Initiation Pattern.* Oxford: Blackwell, 1936.

Knowles, David. *The Evolution of Medieval Thought.* New York: Random, 1964.

———. *The Monastic Order in England.* Cambridge: Cambridge UP, 1949.

Koch, Hannsjoachim W. *Medieval Warfare.* London: Bison, 1978.

Köhler, Erich. *Ideal und Wirklichkeit in der höfischen Epik: Studier zur Form der frühen Artus- und Graldichtung.* 2nd ed. Tübingen: Niemeyer, 1970.

Kottler, Barnet, and Alan M. Markman, comps. *Concordance to Five Middle English Poems:* Cleanness, St. Erkenwald, Sir Gawain and the Green Knight, Patience, Pearl. Pittsburgh: U of Pittsburgh P, 1966.

Kuhn, Hugo. *"Erec." Dichtung und Welt im Mittelalter.* 1959. Stuttgart: Metzler, 1969. 133–50.

Kurath, Hans, Sherman M. Kuhn, et al., eds. *Middle English Dictionary.* Ann Arbor: U of Michigan P, 1952– .

Labarge, Margaret Wade. *A Baronial Household of the Thirteenth Century.* New York: Barnes, 1965.

Laing, Ronald Davis. *Knots.* New York: Vintage, 1972.

Lampe, David. "The Satiric Strategy of *Peres the Ploughmans Crede.*" Levy and Szarmach 69–80.

Lawlor, John, ed. *Patterns of Love and Courtesy: Essays in Memory of C. S. Lewis.* London: Arnold; Evanston: Northwestern UP, 1966.

Lawrence, R. F. "The Formulaic Theory and Its Application to English Alliterative Poetry." *Essays on Style and Language: Linguistic and Critical Approaches to Literary Style.* Ed. Roger Fowler. London: Routledge, 1966. 166–83.

Lawton, David E., ed. *Middle English Alliterative Poetry and Its Literary Background: Seven Essays.* Cambridge Brewer, 1982.

Leach, Edmund. *Claude Lévi-Strauss.* New York: Viking, 1970.

Leff, Gordon. *The Dissolution of the Medieval Outlook: An Essay on the Intellectual and Spiritual Change in the Fourteenth Century.* New York: Harper, 1976.

———. *Medieval Thought: St. Augustine to Ockham.* Baltimore Penguin, 1958.

Lehmann, Ruth P. M. "Color Usage in Irish." *Studies in Language, Literature, and Culture of the Middle Ages and Later.* Ed. E. B. Atwood and Archibald A. Hill. Austin: U of Texas P, 1969. 73–79.

Leonard, Frances McNeely. *Laughter in the Courts of Love: Comedy in Allegory from Chaucer to Spenser.* Norman: Pilgrim, 1981.

Lévi-Strauss, Claude. "The Structural Study of Myth." *Structural Anthropology.* New York: Anchor-Doubleday, 1963. 206–31.

Levy, Bernard S. "Gawain's Spiritual Journey: *Imitatio Christi* in *Sir Gawain and the Green Knight*." *Annuale mediaevale* 6 (1965): 65–106.

Levy, Bernard S., and Paul E. Szarmach, eds. *The Alliterative Tradition in the Fourteenth Century.* Kent: Kent State UP, 1981.

Lewis, C. S. *The Allegory of Love: A Study in Medieval Tradition.* 1936. New York: Oxford UP, 1958.

———. "The Anthropological Approach." Howard and Zacher 59–71.

———. *The Discarded Image: An Introduction to Medieval and Renaissance Literature.* Cambridge: Cambridge UP, 1964.

———. "On Science Fiction." *Of Other Worlds: Essays and Stories.* Ed. Walter Hooper. New York: Harcourt, 1967. 59–73.

Leyerle, John. "The Game and Play of Hero." Burns and Reagan 49–82.

———. "The Major Themes of Chivalric Literature." Benson and Leyerle 131–46.

Longo, Joseph A. "*Sir Gawain and the Green Knight*: The Christian Quest for Perfection." *Nottingham Medieval Studies* 11 (1967): 57–85.

Loomis, Laura Hibbard. "*Gawain and the Green Knight*." Roger Sherman Loomis, *Arthurian Literature* 528–40. Rpt. in Howard and Zacher 3–23.

Loomis, Roger Sherman, ed. *Arthurian Literature in the Middle Ages: A Collaborative History.* 1959. Oxford: Oxford UP, 1974.

———. *Arthurian Tradition and Chrétien de Troyes.* New York: Columbia UP, 1949.

———. *Celtic Myth and Arthurian Romance.* Rev. ed. 1927. New York: Haskell, 1967.

———. *The Development of Arthurian Romance.* London: Hutchinson U Lib., 1963.

———. *A Mirror of Chaucer's World.* Princeton: Princeton UP, 1965.

———. "The Oral Diffusion of the Arthurian Legend." Roger S. Loomis, *Arthurian Literature* 52–63.

———. *Studies in Medieval Literature.* New York: Franklin, 1970.

———. *Wales and the Arthurian Legend.* Cardiff: U of Wales P, 1956.

Macaulay, David. *Castle.* Boston: Houghton, 1977.

MacRae, Suzanne H. "The End Is the Beginning: *Sir Gawain and the Green Knight*." *Avalon to Camelot* 1.2 (1983): 26.

Mâle, Emile. *The Gothic Image: Religious Art in France of the Thirteenth Century.* Trans. Dora Nussey. 1913. New York: Harper, 1958.

———. *Religious Art in France: The Twelfth Century.* Trans. Marthiel Mathews. 1949. Princeton: Princeton UP, 1978.

Mann, James. *Monumental Brasses.* London: Penguin, 1957.

Mann, Jill. *Chaucer and Medieval Estates Satire.* Cambridge: Cambridge UP, 1973.

Manning, Stephen. "A Psychological Interpretation of *Sir Gawain and the Green Knight*." Howard and Zacher 279–94.

Markman, Alan M. "The Meaning of *Sir Gawain and the Green Knight*." Blanch, Sir Gawain *and* Pearl 159–75.

Mathew, Gervase. *The Court of Richard II*. New York: Norton, 1968.

——. "Ideals of Knighthood in Late-Fourteenth-Century England." Fox 68–72.

Matonis, A. T. E. "An Investigation of Celtic Influences on MS Harley 2253." *Modern Philology* 70 (1972): 91–108.

Matonis, Ann. "*Gawain and the Green Knight*: Flux and the *Fayntyse of the Flesche*." *Journal of Narrative Technique* 1 (1971): 43–48.

Matthews, William, comp. *Old and Middle English Literature*. New York: Golden-tree Bibliographies–Davidson, 1968.

——. *The Tragedy of Arthur: A Study of the Alliterative Morte Arthure*. Berkeley: U of California P, 1960.

Matthews, William H. *Mazes and Labyrinths: A General Account of Their History and Development*. London: Longmans, 1922.

Mazzotta, Giuseppe. "Dante's Literary Typology." *Modern Language Notes* 87 (1972): 1–19.

McKisack, May. *The Fourteenth Century, 1307–1399*. Vol. 5 of *Oxford History of England*. 16 vols. Oxford: Clarendon, 1959.

Medcalf, Stephen. *The Later Middle Ages*. Context of English Literature. London: Methuen, 1981.

Mehl, Dieter. *The Middle English Romances of the Thirteenth and Fourteenth Centuries*. London: Routledge, 1968.

Micha, Alexandre. "Miscellaneous French Romances in Verse." In Roger Sherman Loomis, *Arthurian Literature* 348–57.

Mills, David. "An Analysis of the Temptation Scenes in *Sir Gawain and the Green Knight*." *Journal of English and Germanic Philology* 67 (1968): 612–30.

Mitchell, Sabrina. *Medieval Manuscript Painting*. New York: Viking, 1965.

Moller, Herbert. "The Social Causation of the Courtly Love Complex." *Comparative Studies in Society and History* 1 (1958–59): 137–63.

Moore, John C. *Love in Twelfth Century France*. Philadelphia: U of Pennsylvania P, 1972.

Moorman, Charles. *A Knyght There Was: The Evolution of the Knight in Literature*. Lexington: U of Kentucky P, 1967.

——. "Myth and Medieval Literature: *Sir Gawain and the Green Knight*." *Mediaeval Studies* 18 (1956): 158–72. Rpt. in Blanch, Sir Gawain and Pearl 209–35.

——. *The Pearl-Poet*. Twayne English Authors Series 64. New York: Twayne, 1968.

Moorman, Charles, and Ruth Moorman, comps. *An Arthurian Dictionary*. Jackson: UP of Mississippi, 1978.

Mossé, Fernand. *A Handbook of Middle English*. Trans. James A. Walker. Baltimore: Johns Hopkins UP, 1952.

Murphy, Gerard. *Early Irish Metrics*. Dublin: Royal Irish Acad., 1961.

Murray, James A. H., et al., eds. *Oxford English Dictionary*. 13 vols. Oxford: Clarendon, 1933. Compact ed., 2 vols., 1971.

Muscatine, Charles. *Poetry and Crisis in the Age of Chaucer*. Notre Dame: U of Notre Dame P, 1972.

Myers, Alec R. *England in the Late Middle Ages (1307–1536)*. Rev. ed. Pelican History of England 4. Baltimore: Penguin, 1966.

———. *London in the Age of Chaucer*. Norman: U of Oklahoma P, 1972.

Neaman, Judith S. "Sir Gawain's Covenant: Troth and *Timor Mortis*." *Philological Quarterly* 55 (1976): 30–42.

Newman, Francis X., ed. *The Meaning of Courtly Love*. Papers of the First Annual Conference of the Center for Medieval and Early Renaissance Studies. Albany: State U of New York P, 1968.

Nickel, Helmut. "The Arming of Gawain." *Avalon to Camelot* 1.2 (1983): 16–19.

Nitze, William Albert. "The Character of Gauvain in the Romances of Chrétien de Troyes." *Modern Philology* 50 (1952–53): 219–25.

Nitzsche, Jane Chance. *Tolkien's Art: A "Mythology for England."* London: Macmillan; New York: St. Martin's, 1979.

Nohl, Johannes. *The Black Death: A Chronicle of the Plague, Compiled from Contemporary Sources*. Trans. C. H. Clarke. London: Allen, 1926; New York: Harper, 1927.

Oakden, James Parker. *Alliterative Poetry in Middle English*. Vol. 1: *The Dialectal and Metrical Survey*; vol. 2: *A Survey of the Traditions*. Pubs. of the U of Manchester 205, 236; English ser. 18, 22. Manchester: Manchester UP, 1930, 1935. Rpt. in 1 vol. Hamden: Archon, 1968.

Olson, Glending. *Literature as Recreation in the Later Middle Ages*. Ithaca: Cornell UP, 1982.

O'Rahilly, Thomas F. *Early Irish History and Mythology*. Dublin: Dublin Inst. for Advanced Studies, 1964.

Origo, Iris. *The Merchant of Prato, Francisco di Marco Datini*. New York: Knopf, 1957.

Pace, George B. "Gawain and Michaelmas." *Traditio* 25 (1969): 404–11.

Painter, Sidney. *French Chivalry: Chivalric Ideas and Practices in Medieval France*. Baltimore: Johns Hopkins UP, 1940.

Panofsky, Erwin. *Early Netherlandish Painting: Its Origins and Character*. Vol. 1 New York: Harper, 1971. 2 vols.

———. *Gothic Architecture and Scholasticism*. 1957. New York: NAL, 1976.

———. *Studies in Iconology: Humanistic Themes in the Art of the Renaissance*. 1939. New York: Harper, 1967.

Parry, John J. "The Chronology of Geoffrey of Monmouth's *Historia*, Bks. I and II." *Speculum* 4 (1929): 316–22.

Parry, John J., and Margaret Schlauch. *Arthurian Bibliography*. 2 vols. New York: MLA, 1922–35.

Partridge, A. C. *A Companion to Old and Middle English Studies*. London: Deutsch; Totowa: Barnes, 1982.

Paton, Lucy Allen. *Studies in the Fairy Mythology of Arthurian Romance*. 1903. 2nd ed., enl. Ed. Roger Sherman Loomis. New York: Franklin, 1960.

Pearsall, Derek. "The Development of Middle English Romance." *Medieval Studies* 27 (1965): 91–116.

———. *Old and Middle English Poetry*. Routledge History of English Poetry 1. London: Henley; Boston: Routledge, 1977.

———. "The Origins of the Alliterative Revival." Levy and Szarmach 1–24.

Pearsall, Derek, and Elizabeth Salter. *Landscapes and Seasons of the Medieval World*. London: Elek; Toronto: U of Toronto P, 1973.

Peters, Edward. *Europe in the Middle Ages*. Englewood Cliffs: Prentice, 1983.

Pickering, Frederick. *Literature and Art in the Middle Ages*. Miami: U of Miami P, 1970.

Pickford, Cedric Edward. *L'évolution du roman arthurien en prose vers la fin du Moyen Age*. Paris: Nizet, 1959.

Pickford, Cedric Edward, and R. W. Last, comps. *The Arthurian Bibliography*. Vol. 1: *Author Listing*. Arthurian Studies 3. Cambridge: Brewer, 1981.

Pirenne, Henri. *Economic and Social History of Medieval Europe*. 1936. New York: Harcourt, n.d.

Poole, Austin L., ed. *Medieval England*. New ed. 2 vols. Oxford: Clarendon, 1958.

Postan, M. M. *Medieval Economy and Society: An Economic History of Britain in the Middle Ages*. Baltimore: Penguin, 1972.

Power, Eileen. *Medieval People*. 10th ed. New York: Barnes, 1963.

———. *Medieval Women*. Ed. M. M. Postan. Cambridge: Cambridge UP, 1975.

Pyles, Thomas, and John Algeo. *Origins and Development of the English Language*. 3rd ed. New York: Harcourt, 1982.

Rahner, Hugo. *Man at Play*. Trans. Brian Battershaw and Edward Quinn. New York: Herder, 1972.

Rees, Alwyn, and Brinley Rees. *Celtic Heritage: Ancient Tradition in Ireland and Wales*. New York: Grove, 1961.

Rees, William. "Survivals of Ancient Celtic Custom in Medieval England." *Angles and Britons: The O'Donnell Lectures*. Cardiff: U of Wales P, 1963. 148–68.

Reiss, Edmund, Lillian Horner Reiss, and Beverly Taylor. *Arthurian Legend and Literature: An Annotated Bibliography*. 2 vols. New York: Garland, 1984.

Renoir, Alain. "Descriptive Technique in *Sir Gawain and the Green Knight*." *Orbis litterarum* 13 (1958): 126–32.

Richards, Melville. "The Population of the Welsh Border." *Transactions of the Honourable Society of Cymmrodorion* [no vol.] (1970): 77–100.

Robertson, D. W., Jr. *Chaucer's London*. New York: Wiley, 1968.

———. *A Preface to Chaucer: Studies in Medieval Perspectives*. Princeton: Princeton UP, 1962.

Rowland, Beryl. "The Three Ages of *The Parlement of the Three Ages*." *Chaucer Review* 9 (1975): 342–52.

————. *Companion to Chaucer Studies*. Rev. ed. New York: Oxford UP, 1979.

Rowling, Marjorie. *Everyday Life in Medieval Times*. London: Batsford; New York: Putnam, 1968.

Runciman, Steven. *A History of the Crusades*. 3 vols. Cambridge: Cambridge UP, 1951–54.

Ryding, William W. *Structure in Medieval Narrative*. The Hague: Mouton, 1971.

Salter, Elizabeth. "Alliterative Modes and Affiliations in the Fourteenth Century." *Neuphilologische Mitteilungen* 79 (1978): 25–35.

————. "The Alliterative Revival, Parts I and II." *Modern Philology* 64 (1966–67): 146–50, 233–37.

————. *Fourteenth-Century English Poetry: Contexts and Readings*. Oxford: Clarendon, 1983.

————. "The Timeliness of *Wynnere and Wastoure*." *Medium aevum* 47 (1978): 40–65.

Sapora, Robert William, Jr. *A Theory of Middle English Alliterative Meter with Critical Applications*. *Speculum* Anniversary Monographs 1. Cambridge: Medieval Acad. of America, 1977.

Sass, Lorna J. *To the King's Taste: Richard II's Book of Feasts and Recipes*. New York: Metropolitan Museum of Art, 1975; London: Murray, 1976.

Savage, Henry L[yttleton]. "The Feast of Fools in *Sir Gawain and the Green Knight*." *Journal of English and Germanic Philology* 51 (1952): 537–44.

————. *The* Gawain-*Poet: Studies in His Personality and Background*. Chapel Hill: U of North Carolina P, 1956.

————. "The Significance of the Hunting Scenes in *Sir Gawain and the Green Knight*." *Journal of English and Germanic Philology* 27 (1928): 1–15.

Scholes, Robert. *Semiotics and Interpretation*. New Haven: Yale UP, 1982.

Schultz, James A. *The Shape of the Round Table: Structures of Middle High German Arthurian Romance*. Toronto: U of Toronto P, 1983.

Severs, J[onathan] Burke, ed. *Recent Middle English Scholarship and Criticism: Survey and Desiderata*. Pittsburgh: Duquesne UP; Louvain: Nauweloerts, 1971.

Severs, J[onathan] Burke, and Albert E. Hartung. *A Manual of the Writings in Middle English, 1050–1500*. 6 vols. to date. New Haven: Connecticut Acad. of Arts and Sciences, 1967– .

Sharkey, John. *Celtic Mysteries: The Ancient Religion*. London: Thames, 1975.

Shepherd, Geoffrey. "The Nature of Alliterative Poetry in Late Medieval England." *Proceedings of the British Academy* 56 (1970): 57–76.

Shoaf, R. A. *The Poem as Green Girdle: Commercium in Sir Gawain and the Green Knight*. Gainesville: U of Florida P, 1984.

Sims, James H. "Gawayne's Fortunate Fall in *Sir Gawayne and the Grene Knight*." *Orbis litterarum* 30 (1975): 28–39.

Smith, Nathaniel B., and Joseph T. Snow. *The Expansion and Transformations of Courtly Literature*. Athens: U of Georgia P, 1980.

Southern, R. W. *The Making of the Middle Ages* New Haven Yale UP, 1953.

Spearing, A. C. "The Awntyrs off Arthure." *The Alliterative Tradition in the Four-teenth Century.* Levy and Szarmach 183–202.

———. *Criticism and Medieval Poetry.* 2nd ed. New York: Barnes, 1972.

———. *The* Gawain-*Poet: A Critical Study.* Cambridge: Cambridge UP, 1970.

———. *Medieval Dream Poetry.* Cambridge: Cambridge UP, 1976.

Speirs, John. *Medieval English Literature: The Non-Chaucerian Tradition.* London: Faber, 1957.

———. "Sir Gawain and the Green Knight." Fox 79–94.

Staley, Vernon. *The Liturgical Year: An Explanation of the Origin, History and Significance of the Festival Days and Fasting Days of the English Church.* London: Mowbray, 1907.

Stevens, John. *Medieval Romance: Themes and Approaches.* London: Hutchinson U Lib., 1973.

Stevens, Martin. "Laughter and Game in *Sir Gawain and the Green Knight.*" *Speculum* 47 (1972): 65–78.

Stiller, Nikki. *Eve's Orphans: Mothers and Daughters in Medieval English Litera-ture.* Westport: Greenwood, 1980.

Stouck, Mary-Ann. "*Mournynge* and *Myrthe* in the Alliterative *St. Erkenwald.*" *Chaucer Review* 10 (1976): 243–54.

Strayer, Joseph R., ed. *Dictionary of the Middle Ages.* 4 vols to date. New York: Scribner's, 1982– .

Strohm, Paul. "The Origin and Meaning of Middle English *Romaunce.*" *Genre* 10 (1977): 1–28.

———. "*Storie, Spelle, Geste, Romaunce, Tragedie* Generic Distinctions in the Middle English Troy Narratives." *Speculum* 46 (1971): 348–59.

Suleiman, Susan R., and Inge Crosman, eds. *The Reader in the Text: Essays on Audience and Interpretation.* Princeton: Princeton UP, 1980.

Tamplin, Ronald. "The Saints in *Sir Gawain and the Green Knight.*" *Speculum* 44 (1969): 403–20.

Tatlock, J. S. P. "Certain Contemporaneous Matters in Geoffrey of Monmouth." *Speculum* 6 (1931): 206–24.

Taylor, Henry D. *The Medieval Mind: A History of the Development of Thought and Emotion in the Middle Ages.* 4th ed. 2 vols. Cambridge: Harvard UP, 1962.

Thiébaux, Marcelle. *The Stag of Love: The Chase in Medieval Literature.* Ithaca: Cornell UP, 1974.

Thompson, James W. *Economic and Social History of the Middle Ages* 2 vols. 1928. New York: Ungar, 1959.

Tolkien, J. R. R. "*Beowulf:* The Monsters and the Critics." *Proceedings of the British Academy* 22 (1936): 245–95. Rpt. in *An Anthology of* Beowulf *Criticism.* Ed. Lewis E. Nicholson. Notre Dame: U of Notre Dame P, 1963. 51–103. Also rpt. in Tolkien, *"The Monsters and the Critics" and Other Essays* 5–48.

————. "The Monsters and the Critics" and Other Essays. Ed. Christopher Tolkien. Boston: Houghton, 1984.

————. "Sir Gawain and the Green Knight." "The Monsters" 72–108.

Tompkins, Jane P., ed. Reader-Response Criticism: From Formalism to Post-Structuralism. Baltimore: Johns Hopkins UP, 1980.

Topsfield, L. T. Troubadours and Love. London: Cambridge UP, 1975.

Trevelyan, G. M. England in the Age of Wycliffe. 3rd ed. 1900. New York: AMS, 1975.

————. English Social History: A Survey of Six Centuries, Chaucer to Queen Victoria. 3rd ed. 1946. New York: Barnes, 1961.

Tuchman, Barbara W. A Distant Mirror: The Calamitous Fourteenth Century. New York: Knopf, 1978.

Turville-Petre, Thorlac. The Alliterative Revival. Cambridge: Brewer; Totowa: Rowman, 1977.

Tuve, Rosemond. Allegorical Imagery: Some Medieval Books and Their Posterity. Princeton: Princeton UP, 1966.

Utley, Francis Lee. The Crooked Rib: An Analytical Index to the Argument about Women in English and Scots Literature to the End of the Year 1568. 1944. New York: Octagon, 1970.

————. "Folklore, Myth and Ritual." Bethurum 83–109.

Vantuono, William. "John de Mascy of Sale and the Pearl Poems." Manuscripta 25 (1981): 77–88.

Vickery, John B., ed. Myth and Literature: Contemporary Theory and Practice. Lincoln: U of Nebraska P, 1966.

Vinaver, Eugène. The Rise of Romance. New York: Oxford UP, 1971.

Waldron, Ronald A. "Oral-Formulaic Technique and Middle English Alliterative Poetry." Speculum 32 (1957): 792–804.

Wasserman, Loretta. "Honor and Shame in Sir Gawain and the Green Knight." Benson and Leyerle 77–90.

Watkins, Calvert. "Indo-European Metrics and Archaic Irish Verse." Celtica 6 (1963): 194–249.

Weston, Jessie L. From Ritual to Romance. 1920. Garden City: Anchor-Doubleday, 1957.

White, Lynn, Jr. Medieval Technology and Social Change. 1962. New York: Oxford UP, 1966.

Whiting, B. J. "Gawain: His Reputation, His Courtesy, and His Appearance in Chaucer's Squire's Tale." Die neueren Sprachen 9 (1947): 189–239. Rpt. in Fox 73–78.

Whitmore, Mary E. Medieval English Domestic Life and Amusements in the Works of Chaucer. 1937. New York: Cooper Square, 1972.

Wildman, Mary, comp. "Twentieth-Century Arthurian Literature: An Annotated Bibliography." Barber, Arthurian Literature II 127–62.

Wilhelm, James J. *Seven Troubadours: The Creators of Modern Verse.* University Park: Pennsylvania State UP, 1970.

Williams, Gwyn. *An Introduction to Welsh Poetry.* London: Faber, 1953.

Wilson, Edward. *The Gawain-Poet.* Medieval and Renaissance Authors Series. Leiden: Brill, 1976.

Wimsatt, James I. *Allegory and Mirror: Tradition and Structure in Middle English Literature.* New York: Pegasus, 1970.

Wise, Terence. *Medieval Warfare.* London: Osprey; New York: Hastings, 1976.

Wittig, Susan. *Stylistic Narrative Structures in the Middle English Romances.* Austin: U of Texas P, 1978.

Wrenn, C. L. "Saxons and Celts in South-west Britain." *Transactions of the Honourable Society of Cymmrodorion* [no vol.] (1959): 38–75.

Zesmer, David M. *Guide to English Literature: From Beowulf through Chaucer and Medieval Drama.* College Outline Series 53. New York: Barnes, 1961.

Ziegler, Philip. *The Black Death.* London: Collins, 1969.

Audiovisual Materials

Recordings

The Ars Nova. Cond. Alejandro Planchart. Capella Cordina. Music of the Middle Ages 9. Music Heritage Society, MHS 899, 1969.

Bessinger, Jess B., Jr., and Marie Borroff. *Dialogues from* Sir Gawain and the Green Knight *and the* Pearl *(in Middle English).* Caedmon, TC 1192 (cassette, SWC 1192), 1965.

Bornstein, Diane. *A History of the English Language: Discourse with Illustrative Passages.* Caedmon, TC 3008, 1973.

Carols and Motets for the Nativity of Medieval and Tudor England. Dir. René Clemencic. Deller Consort, Musica Antiqua Wien. Bach Guild, BGS 5066, 1963.

Dufay, Guillaume. *Messensätze, Motetten und Hymnen.* Cond. Konrad Ruhland. Capella Antiqua München. Telefunken, SAWT 9439-B, 1960, 1969.

Dunn, Charles. *Early English Poetry.* Folkways, FL 9851, 1958.

In a Medieval Garden, Instrumental and Vocal Music of the Middle Ages and Renaissance. Stanley Buetens Lute Ensemble. Nonesuch, H 71120, 1966.

Instruments of the Middle Ages and Renaissance. Musica Reservata of London. 3 records. Vanguard, VSD71219-20, 1977.

A Medieval Christmas. Cond. Joel Cohen. Boston Camerata. Nonesuch, H-71315, 1975.

Medieval English Lyrics. Ed. and dir. Frank L. Harrison and Eric J. Dobson, in assn. with the British Council. Argo, ZRG 5443, 1965.

Medieval Roots. Conds. Noah Greenberg and Joan Reeves White. New York Pro Musica et al. Decca, D1 79438, 1971.

The Medieval Sound. Peerless, ORYX, EXP 46, 1974.

Music from the Court of Burgundy. Cond. Roger Blanchard. Club français du disque. Nonesuch, H 71058, 1965.

"Music of the Early Middle Ages." Pt. 1 of *History of European Music.* 3 records. Dir. Denis W. Stephens. Orpheus, OR 349–51, 1970.

Music of the Hundred Years War [Musik aus dem Hundertjährigen Krieg]. Cond. John Beckett. Musica Reservata. Philips, 839 753 LY, 1969.

Music of the Late Middle Ages and Renaissance. Cond. Laurence Solomon. Festival Consort. Musical Heritage Society, MHS 1141, 1972.

Music of the Middle Ages. Cond. Robert Haass. Collegium Musicum, Krefeld. Lyrichord, LLST 785, 1960.

Of Glad Tidings: [A Celebration of Christmas Music across the Years]. Purcell Consort. 3 records. Argo, ZRG 526, 590, and 5446, 1976.

The Pleasure of the Royal Courts. Early Music Consort of London. Nonesuch, H-71326, 1976.

Seraphim Guide to Renaissance Music. Dir. Kees Otter. Syntagma Musicus of Amsterdam. Seraphim, SIC-6052, 1969.

Films, Filmstrips, and Videotapes

Bergman, Ingmar, dir. *Det Sjunde Inseglet [The Seventh Seal].* Svensk Filmindustri, 1956. 105 min.

Boorman, John, dir. *Excalibur.* Orion-Warner Bros., 1981. 140 min.

Bresson, Robert, dir. *Lancelot du Lac.* Mara, 1974. 85 min.

Ceremony and Allegory of the Hunt in Late Medieval Europe. Writ. Robin Healey. Acad. Consultant Colin Chase. Toronto: U of Toronto Videotape Collection, 1984.

Clark, Kenneth, writ. and narr. *Civilisation.* Dir. Michael Gill and Peter Montagnon. 12 programs. BBC, 1969. (Relevant programs include "The Great Thaw" and "Romance and Reality.")

The Fifteen Joys of Marriage. Writ. Roberta Frank and Carolyn Eisen. Toronto: U of Toronto Videotape Collection, 1972.

Garnett, Tay, dir. *The Black Knight.* Columbia, 1954.

———, dir. *A Connecticut Yankee in King Arthur's Court.* Paramount, 1949.

Gilliam, Terry, and Terry Jones, dirs. *Monty Python and the Holy Grail.* Python–Cinema 5, 1975.

King Arthur: From Romance to Archaeology. Writ. James Carley. Toronto: U of Toronto Videotape Collection, 1975.

Logan, Joshua, dir. *Camelot*. Warner Bros.–Seven Arts 1967. 179 min.

The Luttrell Psalter. New York: American Lib. Color Slide Cc., 1970. 5 slides.

The Making of a Manuscript. Writ. A. C. Rigg. Toronto: U of Toronto Videotape Collection, 1974.

Reitherman, Wolfgang, dir. *The Sword in the Stone*. Disney, 1963. 75 min.

Rohmer, Eric, dir. *Perceval*. Gaumont–New York, 1975.

Thorpe, Richard, dir. *Knights of the Round Table*. MGM, 1954.

To Syngen and to Playe: Music and Instruments in Chaucer's Day. Writ. David Klousner. Toronto: U of Toronto Videotape Collection, 1973.

Wilde, Cornel, dir. *Sword of Lancelot*. Universal, 1963 116 min.

Index